the learning brain

lessons for education

Sarah-Jayne Blakemore and
Uta Frith

Blackwell
Publishing

BLACKWELL PUBLISHING
350 Main Street, Malden, MA 02148-5020, USA
9600 Garsington Road, Oxford OX4 2DQ, UK
550 Swanston Street, Carlton, Victoria 3053, Australia

First published 2005 by Blackwell Publishing Ltd

1   2005

Library of Congress Cataloging-in-Publication Data

Blakemore, Sarah-Jayne.
    The learning brain : lessons for education / Sarah-Jayne Blakemore and Uta Frith.—
1st ed.
        p.   cm.
    Includes bibliographical references and index.
    ISBN-13: 978-1-4051-0622-1 (hard cover : alk. paper)
    ISBN-10: 1-4051-0622-0 (hard cover : alk. paper)
    ISBN-13: 978-1-4051-2401-0 (pbk. : alk. paper)
    ISBN-10: 1-4051-2401-6 (pbk. : alk. paper)
1. Learning.   2. Education.   3. Neuropsychology.   I. Frith, Uta.   II. Title.
QP408.B58   2005
153.1'5—dc22

                                                                              2004024910

A catalogue record for this title is available from the British Library.

Set in 10/12½ pt Dante
by SNP Best-set Typesetter Ltd, Hong Kong
Printed and bound in the United Kingdom
by TJ International Ltd, Padstow, Cornwall

The publisher's policy is to use permanent paper from mills that operate a sustainable
forestry policy, and which has been manufactured from pulp processed using acid-free
and elementary chlorine-free practices. Furthermore, the publisher ensures that the
text paper and cover board used have met acceptable environmental accreditation
standards.

For further information on
Blackwell Publishing, visit our website:
www.blackwellpublishing.com

contents

acknowledgements

We could not have written this book without the help of many friends and colleagues who provided us with information, talked to us about their work, and provided us with graphs and other visual aids. For this we are deeply grateful. We would also like to thank our colleagues at the Institute of Cognitive Neuroscience and Wellcome Department of Imaging Neuroscience for checking facts and reading sections of the manuscript, in particular, Jon Simons, Sam Gilbert, Lauren Stewart, Suparna Choudhury, and Antonia Hamilton. We are very grateful to the following people for reading and reviewing drafts of our book: Paul Howard-Jones, Andrée Blakemore, Chris Frith, Colin Blakemore, and James Kilner. We have benefited immensely from the comments on earlier versions of the book by Christopher Ball, Christopher Brookes, Janet Hatcher, Maggie Snowling, and Sam Hood. Erin Hope Thompson helped a great deal with the index. We are also grateful to the Wellcome Trust, the MRC, and the Royal Society for funding our research.

Chapter 1

introduction

Evolution and education, like nature and nurture, have often been put into opposition. Here, our aim is to bring them together. The brain has evolved to educate and to be educated, often instinctively and effortlessly. The brain is the machine that allows all forms of learning to take place—from baby squirrels learning how to crack nuts, birds learning to fly, children learning to ride a bike and memorizing times tables, to adults learning a new language or mastering how to program a video recorder. Of course, the brain is also our natural mechanism that places limits on learning. It determines what can be learned, how much, and how fast.

Knowledge of how the brain learns could, and will, have a great impact on education. Understanding the brain mechanisms that underlie learning and memory, and the effects of genetics, the environment, emotion, and age on learning could transform educational strategies and enable us to design programs that optimize learning for people of all ages and of all needs. Only by understanding how the brain acquires and lays down information and skills will we be able to reach the limits of its capacity to learn.

Neuroscientific research has already shed a great deal of light on how the brain learns. Recent advances in technology have provided an amazing tool for neuroscientists to discover more about how the brain functions. Techniques such as brain imaging, which measures activity in the brain as people perform a certain task, have significantly pushed forward our knowledge of the human brain and mind. Brain scientists can now offer some understanding of how the brain learns new information and deals with it throughout life.

In the past few years, interactions between educators and brain scientists have begun to take place. One of the authors spent three months in the spring of 2000 working at the Parliamentary Office of Science and Technology (POST), on secondment from her PhD in Neuroscience at University College London. The remit of POST is to provide the British Houses of Commons and Lords with timely briefing material on topical scientific issues.

At the time, the Early Years Education subcommittee was holding an inquiry into the appropriate care and education of children between birth and six years. The subcommittee had been bombarded with letters, reports, and manifestos from early years charities, schools, psychologists, and educators, many of whom cited research on brain development as grounds for changing early years education in the UK. Some of the arguments put forward contradicted each other. On the one hand, some argued that formal education should not start until six or seven years old because the brain is not ready to learn until this age. On the other hand, others argued that it was clear from research on brain development that children should be "hothoused"—taught as much as possible as early as possible. What were the Members of Parliament on the subcommittee to make of the conflicting evidence?

Both authors were engaged in these kinds of debates when, in June 2000, we compiled a report for the Economic and Social Research Council (ESRC) to indicate whether insights from neuroscience could inform the research agenda in education. The first thing we did was to organize a multidisciplinary workshop on brain research and education at the beginning of September 2000. Given the very short notice and the fact that the workshop was being held on a Saturday at the end of the summer, we predicted that it would be a very small meeting. Advertising the meeting locally, and only to people we thought might have a specific interest in the subject, we nevertheless received over 140 emails from people interested in participating—scientists and educators in equal proportions. It was an exciting and fascinating day. The only criticism of the workshop was that one day was not enough. In our discussions with teachers and education researchers, it became clear, to our surprise, that there is almost no literature on the links between brain science and education.

Yet scientists now know a considerable amount about learning—how brain cells develop before and after birth; how babies learn to see, hear, talk, and walk; how infants acquire a sense of morality and social understanding; and how the adult brain is able to continue learning and growing. What amazed us was, despite this growing body of knowledge and its relevance to education policy, how few links exist between brain research and education policy and practice.

One of the major contributions neuroscience is capable of making is illuminating the nature of learning itself. Despite major advances in our understanding of the brain and learning, neuroscientific research has not yet found significant application in the theory or practice of education.

Why is this? It might, in part, be due to difficulties of translating knowledge of how learning takes place in the brain into information of value to people concerned with education. We know one brain scientist who, after giving a talk about the brain to a group of educators, was told that "there is no point in showing teachers pictures of brain images—they just aren't interested in that."

We do not believe this to be true of all teachers, but we have to admit that there is currently very little material about the relevance of brain research to education that is readily accessible to the nonspecialist. In writing this book our aim was to reduce the gap that unfortunately separates brain science and education science.

Misconceptions about neuroscience

There are many obstacles to interdisciplinary understanding, not least the confusion caused by claims and counterclaims in brain research. One finding about the brain can be contradicted just months later by another scientist's research. But disagreements, findings and counterfindings, are part and parcel of normal scientific progress and integral to the evolution of our understanding about the brain.

Misconceptions about neuroscience—what neuroscientists are interested in, and how far neuroscience can extend in terms of its application to education— are only too easy to foster. Take, for instance, the popular idea about how few brain cells (is it 5 percent? 10 percent?) we actually use. There is no evidence for this whatsoever! Let's consider the percentage of the brain used just to tap one finger. As you can see in the brain image shown in Figure 1.1, a large proportion of the brain is activated when a finger is tapped. Tap your finger at the same time as reading this, and as well as maintaining your balance, breathing, and body temperature, almost *all* of your brain will be active. But don't worry—the brain has a fantastic capacity to reorganize itself, and although you use all of your brain at some point, you can always learn more.

But what about Mrs. W., who has massive brain damage and apparently lives a perfectly normal life? Does such a case demonstrate that the brain plays an insignificant role in controlling behavior—that we can effectively do with-out it? The contradictions in this example are less real than apparent. This brain-damaged person reveals remarkable but counterintuitive facts about the brain.

First, the case demonstrates the resilience of the brain: just a tiny proportion of cells left intact in an otherwise damaged region of the brain can be sufficient to perform a task. These cells can start the process of repair. Neuroscience is studying how this is possible.

Secondly, the case demonstrates not only the possibility for compensation but also its limits. Mrs. W. may well not have undergone extensive psychological assessments. So, superficially, she may seem to behave normally, but this might be because she has learned strategies to compensate for any difficulties caused by her condition. Indeed, she might well show abnormalities when tested on appropriately sensitive tasks. Before her brain damage she was right-handed. Now she would be unable even to pick up a pen with her right hand. She has

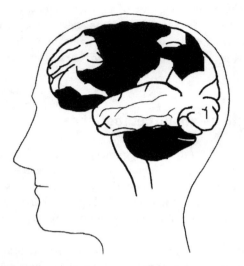

Figure 1.1   We use a lot of the brain a lot of the time. This figure shows that a large proportion of the brain is activated during the simple act of tapping one finger. Activations are shown in black.

learned to compensate almost perfectly with her left hand, using only her left hand to pour tea, pick up objects, write, and so on. This is just one example of the need for rigorous science when drawing conclusions about how much we depend on a properly working brain.

What about genetics?

The expansion in genetics research over the past few decades has revealed how important genes are in creating the individual. It is likely that genes play a significant role in learning and learning disabilities, and this is the kind of question beginning to be investigated by research groups worldwide. Thinking about the educational implications of genetics research will be a hugely important task for the future. The jump from gene to behavior is much greater than the jump from brain to behavior. We believe this jump can be made more easily once we have understood the links between brain and behavior.

A word about nature and nurture interaction

Genetic programming is not enough for normal brain development to occur. Environmental stimulation is needed as well. It is a scientific fact that sensory

Figure 1.2 Research into the genetics of learning is beginning. Can we imagine a day when it will be possible to select genes for teaching and learning?

areas of the brain can develop only when the environment contains a variety of sensory stimuli—visual stimuli, textures, and sounds. We will discuss this in more detail in the next chapter. It is plausible that the same is true for all areas of the brain, not just the sensory areas, and for all mental functions. From well before birth, the brain is shaped by environmental influences, not just by genetic programs. Take an acorn seed, which cannot grow without the right conditions of light, water, and nourishment, even though it contains all the necessary genetic material to become a mighty oak. It is meaningless to debate which is more important, nature or nurture, since both are needed to produce a living plant. Similarly, both nature and nurture are needed for normal development of the brain.

Here is another example that shows how nature and nurture go together. Many people like to lie in the sun to achieve a desirable tan. Melanin is responsible for this, and the more you have, the deeper your tan. To modern eyes, at least in the West, this looks healthy and beautiful. Imagine a Northern European woman with very pale skin, an African woman with very dark skin, and a Mediterranean woman with what is often called olive skin. No matter how much the Northern woman lies in the sun, her skin will only burn and will not turn dark. No matter how much the African woman avoids the sun, her skin will not turn pale. But in the case of the olive-skinned woman, we can see pronounced differences in skin color that are directly correlated with the amount of exposure to the sun. In this case, environmental effects (sun exposure) are the most striking observation; in the case of the other women, genetic effects (melanin production) are the most striking. When one type of effect is highlighted in some examples, say nature, this does not mean that the other effect, nurture, is thereby diminished.

Disorders of the developing brain

It may be possible to ignore the brain when talking about normal child development, but the brain cannot be ignored when discussing developmental disorders. Throughout this book when we talk about developmental disorders, we mean disorders that are caused by some subtle genetic programming fault that has an effect on brain development. Examples are autism, attention deficit/hyperactivity disorder (ADHD), and dyslexia. These disorders may have subtle origins in the brain but can have far-reaching consequences for cognitive development. They can come in mild to severe form and they usually persist for life. They are very different from temporary difficulties of, say, attention or language, which can occur from time to time during development for all sorts of reasons.

Diagnosing a developmental disorder and distinguishing it from a temporary difficulty is sometimes difficult. It depends not just on a few incidental observations, but can be arrived at only after systematic assessment of a child's developmental history. Because there are as yet no biological markers for most developmental disorders, the diagnosis depends on reports and analysis of behavior. This is not a trivial matter and the assessment tools used are constantly being improved.

What happens once a diagnosis is obtained? A chance conversation with a youth worker revealed the following anxiety. One of the young people he supervised had been diagnosed with dyslexia. He felt that this had given the student a passport to be lazy and not to bother with written work. As he saw it, the young man in question could now use the excuse of having a neurological disorder whenever somebody demanded an effort of learning.

In another conversation with a 30-year-old woman, she told us about her great relief when she was at last diagnosed with dyslexia, only after her son, who was experiencing the same difficulties that she had experienced as a child, had been seen by a specialist. She got in touch with other people who had similar problems and who had feared until then that they were just too stupid to learn. She now reports that both she and her son have made vast improvements in reading since their diagnoses. They each obtained remedial teaching that they would not have received without the diagnosis.

Between the double dangers of using a diagnosis as an excuse for opting out of learning and, conversely, of having low self-esteem due to lack of explanation for a learning problem, there are many other shades of experience. The value of diagnosis depends on the attitude of individuals and their willingness and motivation to overcome their difficulties. These issues surrounding developmental disorders will be discussed in Chapters 4–7.

A common vocabulary

If brain research is ever to inform education, then what is needed most urgently is a common vocabulary between brain scientists and educators. We have included a short Glossary of terms at the end of this book. In this book, we use the word *learning* to encompass all kinds of learning. When we refer to *neuroscience*, we include all kinds of study of the brain. That is, we include the study of molecules and cells in the brain although we concentrate mainly on cognitive and neuropsychology studies. By *cognition* we mean anything that refers to the "mental domain," which includes thinking, memory, attention, learning, mental attitudes, and, importantly, emotions. When we refer to *cognition* or *mind*, we do not mean to separate them from the *brain*. We believe that the brain and mind have to be explained together.

Brain science sheds counterintuitive light on learning

It might be hazardous to suggest that educational research itself does not or could not provide the best approach to many educational issues from its own resources and sound scientific thinking. As well as asking how neuroscience can inform education, it might often be useful to think about how brain science challenges commonsense views about teaching and learning.

The brain can work "behind your back"

One topic that comes to mind, and which will be discussed later in this book, is learning without awareness.

Did you know that the brain can acquire information even when you are not paying attention to it and don't notice it? This tendency of the brain to do things "behind one's back" is pervasive and is likely to have repercussions on theories

Figure 1.3   Scientists are notorious for using jargon, which can only be understood by other scientists in the particular field. This is a real obstacle when different disciplines attempt to interact and understand each other. In this book, we try not to use too much scientific jargon. Where it is impossible to avoid using a specialist term, we define it in the Glossary.

of teaching. We will discuss this ability of the brain to process information *implicitly* in Chapter 10.

The aging brain can learn

Until relatively recently, it was widely believed that the adult brain is incapable of change. There used to be a strong assumption amongst brain scientists that after the first few years of life the brain is equipped with all the cells it will ever have, and that adulthood represents a downward spiral of loss of brain cells and deterioration in learning, memory, and performance generally. But research is beginning to show that this view of the brain is too pessimistic: the adult brain is flexible, it can grow new cells and make new connections, at least in some regions such as the hippocampus. Although laying down new information becomes less efficient with age, there is no age limit for learning.

The brain's *plasticity*—its capacity to adapt continually to changing circumstances—depends critically on how much it is used. Research on plasticity suggests that the brain is well set up for lifelong learning and adaptation to the environment, and that educational rehabilitation in adulthood is possible and well worth investment. On the other hand, the research also suggests that there is no biological necessity to rush and start formal teaching earlier and earlier. Rather, late starts might be reconsidered as perfectly in time with natural brain and cognitive development. Of course, the aging brain becomes less malleable and, as everyone getting older experiences, learning new things takes longer.

What about cognitive psychology?

Interdisciplinary dialogue needs a mediator to prevent one or other discipline dominating. When it comes to dialogue between brain science and education, cognitive psychology is tailor-made for this role. We believe that brain science can influence research on teaching and learning most readily through cognitive psychology.

However, although we believe that psychology is an important mediator of brain science, and has its own implications for education, we strongly feel that now is the time to explore the implications of brain science itself for education. From time to time in this book we necessarily refer to cognitive psychology experiments, since, in the words of John Bruer, the most outspoken critic of a premature application of brain research to education, it is cognitive psychology that "bridges the gap" between neuroscience and education.

Nevertheless, the aim of this book is to explore the world of the brain. So we try to focus on the results of brain research but make links to cognitive psychology research.

We are very aware that this book is not an exhaustive review of all the brain science that is relevant to learning—we simply cannot cover everything. In each chapter, we pick out and focus on a few seminal studies that we believe demonstrate the vigor of the field. You will see that we have written several pages about certain experiments, while other equally important studies are only briefly mentioned, or not even mentioned at all. This is just because we have had to be selective, and we think it is more interesting for the reader to hear about recent experiments that have not yet been widely reported. Naturally, we often dwell on studies that have been performed in our lab or by close colleagues.

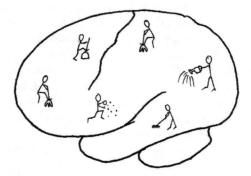

Figure 1.4   Teachers are a bit like gardeners when it comes to learning. Just like gardeners, teachers can sow seeds in a learner's mind, and can nourish and sustain good ideas and important facts, and weed out misunderstandings and mistakes. Here, the front of the brain is on the left.

Landscaping the brain

Individual brains, like individual bodies, are different from each other, but there is almost nothing that you cannot improve or change. When we look at the world around us there are many examples of how culture has enhanced nature, or improved on nature. A few examples that come to mind are glasses that improve eyesight, nutrition for growth, and orthodontists for crooked teeth. The brain is just the same. While orthodontists can improve your teeth, teachers can improve your brain.

Education may be considered a kind of "landscaping" of the brain and educators are, in a sense, like gardeners. Of course, gardeners cannot grow roses without the right soil and roots in the first place, but a good gardener can do wonders with what is already there. Just as with gardening, there are many different ideas of what constitutes the most admirable, and there are distinct cultural differences and fashions over time. Nevertheless, individual gardens involve making the best of what is there and it is possible to make astonishing new and influential designs. As we shall see throughout this book, this analogy can illustrate what we mean by shaping the brain through teaching and learning.

How does the brain work?

The brain is one of the most complex systems in the universe, and although we are starting to learn a great deal about it, we are still a long way from understanding exactly how it all works. This remains a puzzle that thousands of

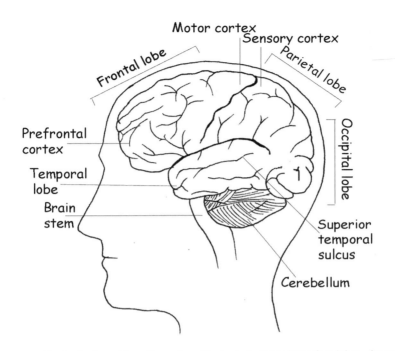

Figure 1.5   The brain viewed from its surface. The brain is divided into four lobes: the temporal, frontal, parietal, and occipital lobes. The brain's outermost surface is known as the cortex.

scientists all round the world are trying to figure out. But we do know some facts about the brain (see Figure 1.5).

The adult brain weighs about 3 pounds (1.4 kg) and contains about 100 billion brain cells (or *neurons*—see Figure 1.6). This is a gigantic number of cells. Neurons have both short and long fibers that contact the bodies of other neurons, and there are about one million billion connections between cells in the brain. 100 billion cells is such a large number, it is hard to imagine. One million is 1,000 times 1,000, the population of a very large town, for example. One billion is 1,000 times one million. The number of connections in the human brain is much bigger than the whole earth's population, which is about 6 billion.

In discussing relevant functions such as "experiencing fear," "learning words," "doing sums," or "imagining movement," we are never talking about individual nerve cells. Instead, it is regions of brain tissue containing millions of neurons that are responsible for cognitive functions like these.

So how do neurons do these things? Like all other cells in the body, neurons act like tiny batteries. There is a difference in voltage (nearly one-tenth of a volt) between the inside and the outside of the cell, with the inside being more

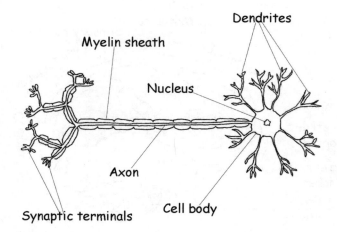

Dendrites

Myelin sheath

Nucleus

Axon

Synaptic terminals   Cell body

Figure 1.6   A neuron comprises a cell body, an axon, and dendrites. The axon of most neurons is covered in a sheath of myelin, which speeds up transmission of impulses down the axon. The synaptic terminals on the dendrites are the contact points with other neurons.

negative. When a neuron is activated it fires an impulse, called an *action potential*. Here, sodium ions rush in through pores in its membrane, briefly reversing the voltage across the membrane. This causes the release of chemicals (*neurotransmitters*) from the axon terminal of one neuron. These chemicals cross the synaptic gap and are received by receptor sites on another neuron's *dendrites*. This is illustrated in Figure 1.8. This is the "language" of the brain, the action potentials causing the brain's "activity."

Almost all sensory information crosses from one side of the body to the opposite side of the brain. So a touch to your left arm is processed by the right side of your brain, and the sight of objects on the right side of you are sent to the left visual cortex to be processed. This is true for all the senses except smell; it is also true for movement—your right *motor cortex* controls movement of your left arm. There are structures in the brain that are not crossed in this way, such as the cerebellum, which, for some reason that we do not yet fully understand, controls movement on the *same* side of the body.

How do we study the brain?

Here we give only a very brief taste of the kinds of techniques used to study the brain. If you want to know about these in more detail, you could have a look at

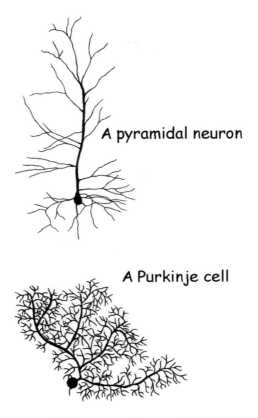

A pyramidal neuron

A Purkinje cell

Figure 1.7 There are several different types of neurons in the brain, including pyramidal neurons and Purkinje cells. Pyramidal neurons, which appear pyramid-shaped under a microscope, are found in the cortex. Purkinje cells, named after the Czech scientist who first discovered them, are only found in the cerebellum.

the Appendix at the back of this book, in which we explore in detail the different techniques that are currently used in brain research.

There are now several tools that can be used to study the brain. *Electrophysiology* studies involve recording from single neurons in the brains of animals while the animal is performing a certain task. This technique gives a direct measure of neuronal activity. Recording neuronal activity in humans is difficult, and studies recording from neurons of the human brain (for example, during open skull surgery) are extremely rare. But such studies are astounding in the wealth of detail they reveal about memories and actions that can be accessed by a mere "touch" of a particular tiny part of the brain's surface.

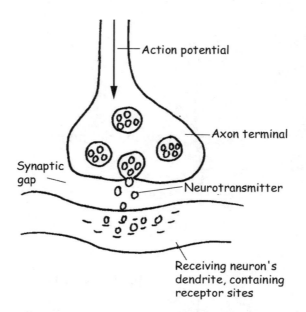

Figure 1.8   Action potentials are the language of the brain. When a neuron is activated it fires an impulse—an *action potential*. This briefly reverses the voltage across the cell membrane, which in turn causes the release of chemicals (*neurotransmitters*) from the axon terminal of one neuron. These chemicals cross the synaptic gap and are received by receptor sites on another neuron's *dendrites*.

Fortunately, there are several noninvasive ways of evaluating electrical brain activity in humans and these relate to the behavior of thousands or millions of neurons that are linked together in particular brain regions. *Electroencephalography* (*EEG*) and *magnetoencephalography* (*MEG*) measure electrical and magnetic activity (respectively) arising from the brain. Recordings are made with electrodes placed on the skull.

Blood flow is an indicator of brain activity and can be measured using brain-imaging techniques. Blood flows to regions of the brain in which neuronal activity is highest and that require a replenishment of oxygen and glucose. *Positron emission tomography* (*PET*) and *functional magnetic resonance imaging* (*fMRI*) detect changes in blood flow. Recordings are made in special brain scanners.

Neuropsychological studies investigate the behavioral consequences of brain damage, and thus give an indication of what functions a particular brain region normally subserves. There is now also a way to study the effects of a temporary disruption of the brain using a technique called *transcranial magnetic stimulation* (*TMS*).

The story told in this book

The aim of this book is to demonstrate by examples how research on the brain and learning could influence the way we think about teaching. All the time while discussing brain research on learning at different ages, we attempt to point out implications, often speculative, for education where there are any. We are not trained as teachers, and we do not do educational research, so it would be presumptuous of us to make concrete suggestions about teaching. But we would imagine that readers with qualifications in and experience of teaching might be able to come up with their own ideas based on the research we discuss. On the other hand, much of the research is not yet ready for implications to be drawn, and where we believe this is the case, we say so.

We go on a neuroscientific journey through childhood, teenage years, and adulthood. If you are only interested in adult learning, feel free to start at Chapter 9—you will not need to have read the early chapters to understand the later chapters. The Glossary and Appendix will hopefully help with any jargon we inevitably use.

The book starts by giving an overview of research on brain development and considering whether such research can directly inform educational practice or policy. Many spurious beliefs about brain development still pervade educational dogma. We hear all the time about *critical periods* in learning. A friend of ours told us that she believed that the best thing for her young child would be "hot-housing" by listening to classical music and recordings of grammar and vocabulary in several different languages, and by being shown flash cards with numbers and letters on. She wanted to make sure her child learned everything possible during his critical period, and was worried that after four years it might be "too late" for her child to learn as much as he could.

But are there really critical periods for learning in early childhood? Is it ever too late to learn? Do enriched early childhood environments improve brain development? Or are normal environments rich enough? Is hothousing a good thing or could it harm a baby's development? How do children learn about the world and other people? Does this knowledge arise from formal instruction? Or does it develop better without any explicit teaching, through play, exploration, everyday talk, and social interaction with peers and siblings? In Chapter 2, we attempt to tackle controversial questions such as these by evaluating the scientific evidence of how the brain develops.

Many people think of education as learning to read, write, and do arithmetic. We know someone who claimed that their six-month-old baby could count after being taught using flashcards. Can this really be true? Surely, skills such as arithmetic thrive through formal instruction? Or do babies have subtle mathematical abilities? What develops before instruction even begins? Would children develop mathematical understanding through everyday behaviors such as sharing?

Many of our Japanese friends cannot hear the difference between R and L sounds. Why is this? How can infants learn grammatical rules without explicitly being taught them? In many countries children are starting school earlier and earlier and being taught to read and write before the age of five. But brain science has shown that fine finger coordination does not usually develop until at least five years and is slower to develop in boys than in girls—so is five too early to teach children to write? Some children have profound difficulties with writing, and often this is due to problems in motor coordination called *dyspraxia.* The development of reading, writing, and arithmetic will be discussed in Chapter 3.

Chapter 4 describes the brain processes involved in mathematics. Why is it that certain types of math depend on spatial calculations and others depend on language? We explore how different parts of the brain are involved with different aspects of math. We address the subtle brain abnormalities that can lead to developmental *dyscalculia* and innumeracy.

Do you think of yourself as left-brained or right-brained? Should this influence the way people are educated? Or is this all a load of hyped-up nonsense?

Surely we know that women are worse at math and have poorer spatial abilities than men? Or is it really that simple?

In Chapter 4 we tackle these two controversial issues: the left brain/right brain theory, and gender differences in the brain.

Brain research has started to reveal the brain systems involved in literacy and Chapter 5 explores these. This research has shown that the effect of literacy on the brain also affects spoken language processing. Are there sensitive periods for learning language? What about learning more than one language early and late? How do deaf people's brains process sign language?

In Chapter 6, we discuss what brain research has told us about learning to read and *dyslexia*. Is learning to read music the same as learning to read words? Is it possible to show changes in the brain after training dyslexic people to read?

In Chapter 7, we look at developmental disorders that affect social and emotional experience, in particular autism, conduct disorder, and attention deficit disorders. Theories of these developmental disorders and their basis in the brain have implications for remedial teaching.

Research is revealing that the brain undergoes a second wave of brain development during adolescence. Adolescence is a time characterized by change—hormonally, physically, and mentally. In the last few years, a number of pioneering projects have been initiated that evaluate the development of brain processes during the secondary school years. These studies have shown that the brain is still developing during adolescence, and this will be the subject of Chapter 8.

In the remaining chapters, we look at how the adult brain learns. As hinted at above, recent research on the brain has revealed the exciting finding that, contrary to what was previously believed, the adult brain is able to change in size. Did you know that in London taxi drivers, whose spatial memories have to be exceptional, the part of the brain that stores spatial memories is much bigger than usual? And, remarkably, its size depends on the numbers of years the person has been driving taxis around London. How does exercise boost both learning and brain function? In Chapter 9, we look at research that shows that the adult brain can change, in size and activity, and these changes generally occur as a result of usage. This research demonstrates that learning happens all through life.

Perhaps the most important implication from neuroscience for education is that it may be possible to identify and modify the neural structures that under-lie different learning and memory processes that simply happen without having to pay attention. How can we learn without awareness? Is there a difference between remembering names and dates, and remembering events in one's life? One of the major contributions of neuroscience is illuminating the nature of learning itself, and this is the subject of Chapter 10.

Is imitation a good thing or does it stifle creativity? Can you learn a new skill just by thinking about it? How can learning be enhanced? Neuroscientists are beginning to understand the brain mechanisms underlying different methods of learning, and these will be the focus of Chapter 11.

Based on findings from neuroscience, we can imagine a day when we will be able to use all sorts of radical new ways to improve learning and memory. In the final chapter, Chapter 12, we speculate about how various diverse lines of research are currently shedding light on how context, which includes bio-logical as well as social factors, affects learning. How does your brain lay down memories while you sleep? Does your diet affect how efficient you are at learn-ing? Why are negative emotional events better remembered than nonemotional events? Should learning be rewarded and nonlearning be punished? Can a time be envisaged in which you could pop a pill to improve learning for an exam?

Finally, if you are really interested in the brain and the tools used to study brain function, consult the Appendix at the back of the book. We also give sug-gestions for further reading and a Glossary of terms.

the developing brain

What changes in the brain during development?

An adult human brain contains about 100 billion brain cells (*neurons*); at birth the brain has a remarkably similar number of neurons to that in the adult brain. Almost all the neurons in the brain are generated well before birth—mainly in the first three months of pregnancy. The generation of neurons is called *neurogenesis*. This is a complex process beginning with the division of *stem cells*, the providers of all new cells in the brain. This division gives rise to other stem cells, or neurons, or support cells called *glia*. To mature and survive, the neurons must migrate away from the stem cells. After migration, only about half survive, while the rest die. Many more brains cells are generated than are needed. Only cells that form active connections with other neurons survive.

A human baby is born with almost all the brain cells it will ever have except for the cerebellum and hippocampus, where there is a large increase in cells after birth. During development the brain undergoes several waves of reorganization. It is not the neurons themselves that change, but the "wiring" between them. The wiring is the intricate network of connections between cells (the *dendrites* and the *synapses*, see Figure 2.1). Short fibers connect neurons that are close to each other and long fibers can connect neurons that are very far apart.

During the first year of life, the human brain changes in particularly dramatic ways. Shortly after birth, the number of connections between brain cells starts to increase rapidly, so much so that the number of connections in a baby's brain greatly exceeds adult levels. Many of these excess connections have to be cut back, and this cutting back, or *pruning*, is just as important a part of development as is the initial growth of connections.

Over the past 50 years, a great amount has been discovered about how the brain develops in young animals, and much of this knowledge will apply to the human brain too, although direct observations of the developing human brain are still few. Nevertheless, research on the development of the brain during the first few years of life has already begun to play a role in education policy debates.

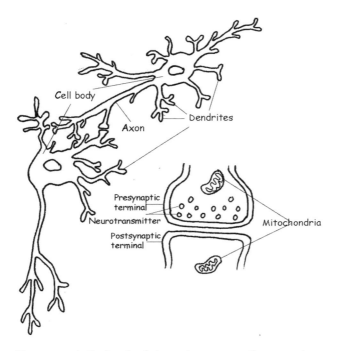

Figure 2.1   The *synapse* is the junction between two neurons. One neuron's axon connects with a second neuron's dendritic terminals. When a nerve impulse (*action potential*) occurs in the first neuron, *neurotransmitters* are released from the axonal terminal of the first neuron and are received by the receptors of the dendritic spines of the second neuron.

Is three years too late? The early years education debate

In April 1996, the White House convened a conference on early child development in which Hillary Clinton cited research on brain development. Clinton claimed that "we know much more now than we did even a few years ago about how the human brain develops and what children need from their environments to develop character, empathy, and intelligence." She cited research demonstrating that the environment affects brain development early in life as evidence for the importance of certain types of environmental stimulation in the first three years of a child's life. Clinton claimed that "experiences [between birth and three years] can determine whether children will grow up to be peaceful or violent citizens, focused or undisciplined workers, attentive or detached parents. . . ." She appealed to doctors in the USA to encourage parents to read to their young children, and she called for a greater investment in children under three.

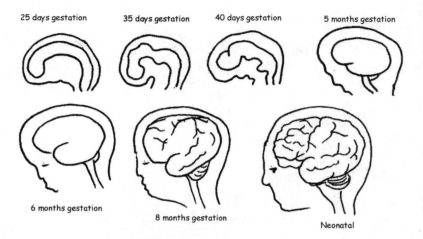

25 days gestation   35 days gestation   40 days gestation   5 months gestation

6 months gestation

8 months gestation

Neonatal

Figure 2.2   Almost all the neurons in the brain are generated well before birth—mainly in the first three months of pregnancy. After birth, the brain changes dramatically, mainly in terms of the number of *synapses*.

Some childcare centers in the USA have begun to structure their curricula around the idea of enriching the experience of young children. The school day for two- and three-year-olds at certain American infant centers is now crammed with sensory stimulation. According to one such center based in Oregon, each activity is "designed to stimulate a key area of the children's brains." Several educational groups in the USA have gone further still, suggesting that children should begin the study of languages, advanced mathematics, logic, and music as early as possible, and that the baby's environment should be enriched for optimal brain development.

In Britain, the early years education debate has also begun to focus on brain development. In 2000, the House of Commons Subcommittee for Early Years Education was asked to examine several aspects of early years education, that is, the education and care of children between the age of birth and six years. These included the appropriate content of early years education, how nursery education should be taught, how nursery teaching and learning should be assessed, and at what age formal schooling should start.

These are controversial issues because primary schools in the UK admit children at the beginning of the year in which they become five. This is earlier than in many other European countries, where children do not start formal education until the age of six or seven. In these countries, from the age of three until they enter school, children normally go to kindergarten in which the development of the emotional, social, and general cognitive skills is encouraged, mainly through play.

Figure 2.3   Some people favor hothousing their child, using flashcards, videos and other audiovisual materials to teach academic skills such as reading, logic, and mathematics.

In 1999, the British government introduced the Early Learning Goals for the education of children aged three to the end of their first school year. This outlined expectations for nursery age children to develop social, physical, and intellectual skills. The introduction of the Early Learning Goals provoked strong reaction. Several high-profile reports in the British media argued that the introduction of strict goals is too much for nursery-age children.

Conversely, other groups argued that the Early Learning Goals did not go far enough. Following the arguments described above, which emerged in the 1990s in the USA, these groups proposed that the critical age for learning is between birth and three years and that children should be hothoused in the first few years of life in order for optimal learning to take place. Hothousing means teaching infants academic skills such as reading, logic, and mathematics, using flashcards, videos, and other audiovisual materials.

Does brain research provide an answer?

On both sides of the Atlantic, arguments for an early start in education have frequently been grounded in three major findings in developmental neurobiology, based on animal research. First, in infancy there are dramatic increases in the number of connections between brain cells. Second, there are *critical periods* when experience shapes the development of the brain. Third, *enriched environ-*

ments cause more connections to form in the brain than impoverished environments.

In reality, the neurobiological picture of brain development is more complex. In this chapter we describe some of the studies that established the above three findings, and subsequent studies that have clarified and expanded on the earlier research findings. It is important to know about the research because this explains why there are as yet no simple conclusions. Many neuroscientists question whether we know enough about the developing brain to link that understanding directly to instruction and educational practice.

The first argument: Brain connections in infancy

From early in postnatal development, the brain begins to form new connections (synapses, see Figure 2.1), so that the *synaptic density* (the number of synapses per unit volume of brain tissue) increases enormously. The growth of dendrites on nerve cells and the sprouting of synapses along them can be compared with the vigorous growth of young plants in spring. In the brain this process, called *synaptogenesis*, lasts for some time: for different lengths of time depending on the species of animal. It is followed by a period of *synaptic pruning* in which frequently used connections are strengthened and infrequently used connections are eliminated. Again, this can be likened to the pruning that is necessary after the often rampant growth of plants in the garden. If it were not carried out, the plants might well choke.

The first demonstration of synaptogenesis was in 1975, when it was found that in the visual system the number of synapses per neuron first increases rapidly and then gradually decreases to mature levels. This research was carried out in cats. Further research carried out in monkeys demonstrated that synaptic densities reach maximal levels two to four months after birth, after which time pruning begins. Synaptic densities gradually decline to adult levels at around three years of age, about the time monkeys reach sexual maturity. This process, which occurs over a period of years, reduces the overall synaptic density to adult levels.

Early on in development there is also a first wave of dramatic proliferation and growth of nerve fibers and long-range connections between nerve cells. In addition to this, the long stems (the axons, see Figure 1.6) of each nerve cell start to become coated with a layer of *myelin*, which acts as an insulator, speeding up movement of electrical impulses down the neuron. This is a key process in brain development because it massively accelerates the speed of signals traveling between neurons. However, although all these processes happen in early development, perhaps the most studied aspect of development is the number of synapses.

So, as soon as a baby is born, its brain connections start growing and changing. Which connections survive and grow, and which fade away and die, is determined partly by the genes the baby inherits from its parents and partly by the baby's early experiences. Should babies therefore be exposed to as many learning experiences as possible during their early years?

Not necessarily. The assumption is that the time course of synaptogenesis and pruning is the same for humans as it is for monkeys, where indeed it takes place during the first three years. However, given that the development of monkeys is much quicker than that of humans and their span of childhood much shorter, the period of rapid growth in brain development in humans is likely to be considerably longer than in monkeys. At three years monkeys are sexually mature, so this age might well be equivalent to about 12 or 13 years in human beings.

Development in the human brain

All the research discussed so far has involved animal brains. What about the development of the human brain? Unfortunately, there is not much research on the development of the human brain, because this research relies mainly on post-mortem brains. Most of the data on human brain development come from the human *visual cortex*, a large area at the back of the brain that makes sense of the visual stimuli that enter the eyes (see Figure 2.4). In this area, there is a rapid increase in the number of synaptic connections at around two or three months of age, which reaches a peak at eight to 10 months. After that there is a steady decline in synaptic density until it stabilizes at around age 10 years and remains at this level throughout adult life (see Figure 2.5).

In the human *frontal cortex* (shown in Figure 2.4)—the brain area responsible for planning actions, selecting and inhibiting responses, controlling emotions, and decision-making—synaptogenesis occurs later and the pruning process takes much longer than in the visual cortex. In this area, neuronal development continues throughout adolescence—synaptic densities start to decline throughout adolescence and do not reach adult levels until at least age 18 (see Figure 2.5 and Chapter 8).

Do you remember the myelin sheaths that cover the axons of each neuron and speed up the signals that travel along nerve fibers (shown in Figure 1.6)? This process of adding myelin to axons continues for decades in some brain areas, in particular in the frontal lobes. This process continues well into the teens and twenties, as we shall discover in Chapter 8.

Development in the first year of life

Psychological studies have been carried out with human infants to examine the skills and behavior that develop at the same time as synaptogenesis. When con-

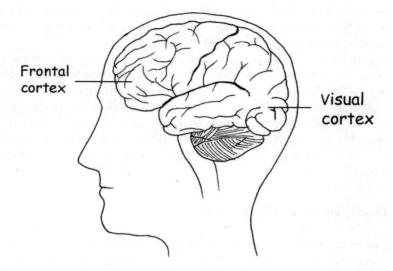

Figure 2.4 Most of the research on brain development comes from studies on the development of the visual cortex in animals. Much less is known about how the frontal cortex develops. The frontal cortex is the part of the brain in humans that is responsible for planning actions, selecting and inhibiting responses, controlling emotions, and decision making.

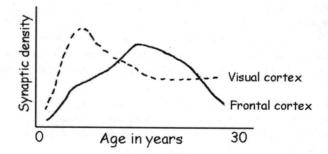

Figure 2.5 Synaptogenesis, the proliferation of synapses, occurs in the first few months of life, after which time synapses are pruned back so that synaptic densities gradually decline. In the human visual cortex synaptic densities gradually decline to adult levels long before adult synaptic densities are reached in the human frontal cortex. Source: adapted from Huttenlocher & Dabholkar. *Journal of Comparative Neurology* 1997; 387(2): 167–78. Copyright © 1997 by John Wiley. Reprinted by permission of John Wiley & Sons, Inc.

nections start to proliferate in the visual cortex, at around two months of age, human infants start to lose some of their innate, infantile reflexes. At age three months, infants can reach for an object while visually fixating on it. At four to five months, infants' visual capacities increase—they can detect and distinguish objects by their color, edges, and whether the objects are moving or not. At eight months, infants first show the ability to perform visual memory tasks, such as delayed-response tasks. In these tasks, an object is hidden from the infant's view and, after a certain time delay, the infant is allowed to reach for the object. Children's memory for hidden objects improves markedly between eight and 12 months.

Although the emergence of these capacities coincides with reorganization in the visual cortex, they may not necessarily be *caused* by these changes. Increases in synaptic density occur at the same time as the initial emergence of some skills and capacities, but these continue to improve after synaptic densities are cut back through pruning. Thus synaptogenesis may be linked with the initial emergence of some abilities, but it cannot account for their continued refinement.

The second argument: Critical periods in brain development

Researchers have known for the past 30 years that an animal requires certain kinds of environmental stimulation at specific times—a *critical period*—during its development for the brain's sensory and motor systems to develop normally.

critical period

To investigate the way neurons are able to adapt their function according to demand, in the 1960s Torsten Wiesel and David Hubel at Harvard University carried out some groundbreaking research, for which they were later awarded the Nobel prize. They asked what would happen in the brain of a newborn animal (in this case the animals in question were cats) if one eye were temporarily covered, thus preventing the animal from seeing.

After about three months, the eye was uncovered and the researchers studied the connections between the two eyes and the brain. The effects were startling. Early visual deprivation led to a severe deterioration of neuronal connections in the visual areas of the brain of the covered eye. Furthermore, it led to virtual blindness in this eye. This is because the brain had received no stimulation from the deprived eye and it had wired itself to receive information only from the other, open, eye. Even months after the eye had been uncovered the cats remained blind in the initially deprived eye. By comparison, in fully grown cats, the same or longer periods of complete visual deprivation had no such effects on the visual system nor on the cat's ability to use the deprived eye to guide its behavior when the eye was subsequently uncovered.

This research has been replicated many times and it is accepted that certain sensory experiences must occur by a certain age for the corresponding sensory areas of the brain to develop optimally. The irreversible consequences of early visual deprivation are often cited as evidence for the importance of early childhood education. The research findings have been used to suggest that certain learning experiences must occur by a certain age or the brain will never develop properly and it will be impossible for the child ever to acquire those skills or abilities.

The story does not end there, however. Subsequent research by Hubel, Wiesel, and other researchers has suggested that some recovery of function is possible, depending on the specific period of deprivation and the circumstances following deprivation. The shorter the period of deprivation, the more recovery of function is possible. This is enhanced if the animal is trained to use the initially deprived eye after it is uncovered. Although certain sensory stimulation should be experienced before a certain age for optimal brain development, if it is unavailable, remedial stimulation and training at a later age can bring about a certain level of recovery of the corresponding brain area.

Sensitive, not critical, periods

Most neuroscientists now believe that critical periods are not rigid and inflexible. Rather, most interpret them as *sensitive periods* comprising subtle changes in the brain's ability to be shaped and changed by experiences that occur over a lifetime. For some functions to develop normally, the animal must receive appropriate sensory input from the environment at a particular stage during development. However, appropriate input need not be in any way sophisticated. Instead it tends to be basic and general, and is readily available in normal environments. The presence of patterned and colored visual stimuli, sounds, and objects to touch and manipulate, for example, is ample stimulation for the developing sensory cortices of the human brain. What is particularly important in the case of human infants is interaction with other human beings, including language and communication.

Sensory skills at birth in human babies

Human babies are born with certain sensory capacities, for example basic vision and hearing, which are refined and developed throughout childhood. The brain's visual system is partly constructed at birth, but continues to develop throughout the first few years of life.

At birth, babies can distinguish between different visual forms—newborn babies get bored and look away when they have been shown the same visual stimulus for some time, and only look again if a new visual stimulus is presented. Babies are born with a very basic, but impressive, capacity to recognize faces. At birth, the brain seems to be equipped with some information of what a face should look like. Newborn babies prefer to look at drawings of whole faces than drawings of faces whose features have been "scrambled." Within a few days of birth babies learn to recognize their mother's face—they will look at a picture of their mother's face longer than at a picture of a stranger's face.

This remarkable early ability to recognize faces is probably controlled by different brain pathways than those involving later, more sophisticated, face recognition. John Morton and Mark Johnson from the University of London have proposed that the early recognition of faces might have evolved because it produces an automatic attachment (or "imprinting") of newborn babies onto the people they see most often.

This early face recognition probably relies on *subcortical* (meaning below the *cerebral cortex*) structures such as the *superior colliculus*. Subcortical structures are part of a pathway in the brain that allows us to make movements extremely quickly and automatically on the basis of what we see. These abilities are shared with many other animals. They develop very early because they are immensely important. Just as chicks "imprint" on their mother and follow her automatically wherever she goes, so it is useful for newborn babies to imprint onto the face they see most. Only from about two or three months do cortical brain regions in the *temporal* and *occipital lobes* start to take over a baby's face recognition ability.

The brain's hearing (*auditory*) system is also partially developed at birth. Newborn babies can distinguish sounds and are sensitive to the rhythm, intonation, and sound components of speech. Research on premature babies has demonstrated that babies are responsive to speech sounds in the last trimester of fetal life. At this premature age they can discriminate between male and female voices. Two-day-old full-term babies can distinguish between their own language and a foreign language. Three-day-old babies recognize their mother's voice—they prefer to listen to their mother's voice than to a stranger's voice. These exceptionally early abilities probably benefited from hearing the muted but still audible sounds in the womb.

Sensitive periods and fine-tuning in babies' brains

An intriguing study on early face recognition abilities was carried out by Olivier Pascalis from the University of Sheffield and Michelle de Haan from the University of London. This study demonstrated that, between six and nine months of age, babies' abilities to perceive individual differences in faces become *fine-tuned*.

Figure 2.6 It is difficult for us to tell the difference between faces from different species, such as monkeys. Young babies are able to tell the difference between different monkey faces, an ability they lose after about six months.

Babies under the age of six months are very good at discriminating between all sorts of faces—they can even tell the difference between monkey faces, which to adults look very similar and are hard to tell apart. However, after six months, this ability deteriorates until gradually babies become quite poor at discriminating between monkey faces, but remain good at discriminating human faces. This is useful, for in a baby's world there are very few monkey faces but lots of different human faces. It is much more important to be able to distinguish between things that are common in our environment than between things that we hardly ever come across.

During this same time period, babies' abilities to perceive tiny differences in the speech patterns of their own language are fine-tuned as well. Fine-tuning comes at a cost. In both modalities, seeing and hearing, it means a certain degree of loss: babies gradually lose the ability to discriminate between faces that are not of their own species and between sounds that are not of their own language. This cost is well worth it because it results in the brain's amazing speed and accuracy when it comes to recognizing other people around you and what they say. What scientists do not yet know is whether fine-tuning only occurs during a narrow window.

What happens if fine-tuning cannot occur between six and nine months? This would be the case if the child were unable to see or hear. Will children deprived of sensory input during this time not achieve the same efficiency?

What happens when learning cannot occur during sensitive periods?

Occasionally babies are born with cataracts, which give rise to blindness. But in some cases an operation can be performed to restore vision. These cases can provide insight into the importance of visual stimulation in early life, and this was realized by Daphne Maurer in Canada, who conducted a series of unique studies on babies who had had cataracts removed. There was a very practical question to be answered. Should the operation be done as early as possible, or should it be carried out at a later time when there is less medical risk to the baby? In her initial studies Maurer found that even when the operation was carried out at nine months, and there were therefore nine months of visual deprivation, sight developed quickly. In some cases, as little as one hour of visual stimulation resulted in a large gain in visual acuity.

However, did the lack of fine-tuning, which would normally occur in the first nine months but could not have occurred in these cases, cause any problems? Sadly, it seems so. The lack of early experience had subtle but permanent consequences. These were only seen when particular aspects of visual perception were studied later at the age of nine years. The children who had been operated on experienced subtle difficulties that showed that their perception of faces was not quite normal. They could distinguish between different faces but failed to distinguish faces that differed only in the arrangements of their features, an easy task for children who had no visual deprivation. This was true even for those children whose cataracts had been removed early and whose visual deprivation had been relatively short, that is, between two and six months.

So this research suggests that, although it is possible to develop sensory capacities even after the sensitive period, skills that are acquired after the sensitive period are subtly different, and perhaps rely on different strategies and brain pathways than if they had been acquired during the sensitive period.

Do sensitive periods limit the capacity to learn?

The research discussed in this chapter indicates that the brain undergoes fast development shortly after birth and throughout early childhood and has sensitive periods for learning. Preferences for important stimuli, such as faces, are set early, so that very fine-tuned discriminations are possible for stimuli that occur most frequently in the immediate environment. At the same time, the ability to discriminate between stimuli that occur very rarely seems to diminish. Why is this?

Think of an adaptable washing machine that can wash, in principle, with all sorts of water, all sorts of detergents and all sorts of textiles and colors. Naturally, setting all the controls for all eventualities of water and detergent quality and quantity is quite an elaborate affair. Imagine that the machine gets used to a particular range of conditions after a certain number of washes. Now the machine has available certain "preferences" and can reduce the possible number of settings. This is a loss of the initial almost limitless flexibility, but it is also a gain in efficiency. There will be fewer sources of error and faster programming. We

Figure 2.7 The natural fine-tuning of perceptual abilities is a bit like a clever washing machine, which learns to adapt to certain preferred and most frequently used washes. While this makes it ultimately less flexible, it is more efficient and less error-prone. In terms of the brain, the sharpening of some distinctions and the loss of others is useful for the necessary fast processing of important stimuli.

believe the owners of the machine will be pleased with this progress and will call it learning. What happens if they move elsewhere, somewhere with much harder water, for example? Being such a clever machine, it will learn again. But perhaps it is a little stupid after all, because the engineers have decided that the machine must be reset to start all over again, so that all previous learning will be erased. This is where it differs from the brain. In the brain, previous learning might well come in useful.

Self-closing windows

Sensitive periods have often been likened to a window for learning, which slams shut after a certain critical period in development. Windows for fast learning exist, but experience itself closes these windows. This is useful. At first a broad range of all sorts of faces and voices can be distinguished, but later on some of these distinctions become less relevant and are "lost." They may not be irrecoverable and later relearning is possible if necessary. The sharpening of some distinctions and the loss of others is useful for the necessary fast processing of important stimuli. There is no point in expecting everything and anything to happen—this would lead to stimulation overload, slow you down, and make errors very likely. Instead, the important stimuli need to be identified, and quickly.

Does the image of the closing window seem a little sad? It should not. There is no getting away from the fact that we have a limited capacity for new learning and so we need to husband resources. New learning means opening and setting neural connections for important events and closing others that are no longer important and would only be distracting and confusing.

Beyond sensory development

So far, we have been talking only about the development of sensory skills. This is simply because the development of sensory skills is the only aspect of brain development that has been studied in detail. Little is known about whether certain experiences are required for the development of nonsensory skills and the corresponding brain areas. Whether sensitive periods exist for culturally transmitted knowledge systems, such as those responsible for reading and arithmetic, is not known. There is evidence that several sensitive periods exist for language development. In contrast, learning new words and increasing your vocabulary continues throughout life, and nobody has yet found that there is a sensitive period for vocabulary learning. Brain research on language development will be discussed in Chapters 3, 5, and 6.

The research on sensitive periods is fascinating and has revealed a great deal about how the brain develops. One day, no doubt, research findings will illuminate what relevance sensitive periods have for skills and capacities that depend on formal education. Currently, the one main implication of the research findings on sensitive periods is that it is important that we identify and, if possible, treat children's sensory problems, such as visual and hearing difficulties, so that even belatedly they can regain normal function. The findings suggest that early sensory deprivation can have lasting consequences, possibly very subtle ones, undetectable in everyday life. They also suggest that even after sensory deprivation, recovery and learning can still occur. Such late learning may be different from the type of learning that occurs naturally during sensitive periods.

Most of what is known about brain development corresponds to the emergence of visual, movement, and memory functions, which are acquired in almost any environment throughout the world at approximately the same age. They are learned naturally, given adequate stimulation. This learning occurs well before children enter formal education. For the most part, it is formal education that implants skills such as reading, writing, and numeracy. However, how synaptogenesis relates to the acquisition of such skills and to later educational learning is as yet unknown. Very likely, while teachers teach, connections are formed in the brains of the learners: dendrites branch out from the nerve cells and millions of synapses sprout alongside them. This invisible process is the basis for retaining new information and for sorting it so that it can be retrieved later at will.

The third argument: Brain development requires an enriched environment

A fundamental characteristic of brain development is that environmental experiences are as important as genetic programs. For several decades, Bill Greenough and his colleagues at the University of Illinois have carried out neurobiological research that has revealed how the environment affects the brain's synapses during development. This research is often cited as evidence for the importance of enriched early childhood environments.

Greenough's studies, involving rats, demonstrated the existence of a general adaptive process that updates the organization of the brain on the basis of the animal's experience. Early studies showed that laboratory rats raised in an enriched environment, with wheels to spin in, ladders to climb on, and other rats to play with, had up to 25 percent more synapses per neuron in brain areas involved in sensory perception than "deprived" rats, raised alone in a lab cage with no playmates or toys.

Furthermore, the rats raised in complex environments performed learning tasks better and were quicker to navigate around mazes than were deprived rats. Enriched early environments, then, seem to create cleverer rats. In addition to neural consequences, experience also affects other aspects of brain cellular structure. The amount of physical activity and exercise a baby rat does determines the long-term state of the blood supply to its brain.

The take-home message from these experiments is that, for rats at least, environments that are rich in sensory stimulation, provide challenges and adventure, contain other rats, and encourage physical exercise, produce brains with more neuronal connections and stronger blood supplies, and cleverer rats. By contrast, environments that lack stimulation, adventure, other rats, and the possibility of physical exercise stifle brain development and produce more stupid rats.

Do these results mean that a baby's environment should be specially manipulated to make it richer than it is normally? There is no suggestion from the experi-

Figure 2.8 In Bill Greenough's studies, rats were raised in an enriched environment, with wheels to spin, ladders to climb on, and other rats to play with.

Figure 2.9 Enriched early environments seem to create cleverer rats. Rats raised in complex environments performed learning tasks better and were quicker to navigate around mazes than were deprived rats.

ments on rats that "the richer the environment the better." In these experiments, the enriched environment in the laboratory was actually more like the normal environment of a rat in the wild. Sewers are far from boring! The rat's most popular natural environment often comprises complicated and lengthy maze-like settings full of objects, tunnels, smells, sounds, and many other rats and animals.

So, rather than showing that extra stimulation leads to an increase in synaptic connections, it might be more accurate to say that a "normal" environment leads to more synaptic connections than a deprived environment. It is unlikely that children brought up in any "normal" child-oriented environment could be deprived of sensory input. The research does, however, suggest that there is a threshold of environmental richness below which a deprived environment could harm a baby's brain.

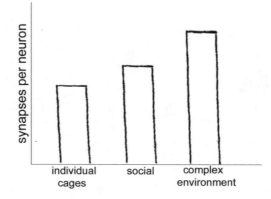

Figure 2.10   Compared with rats raised alone in a lab cage with no playmates or toys ("individual cages") and rats raised in a cage with one or more companions ("social cages"), rats who lived in enriched cages with toys, playmates, and exercise wheels ("complex environment") had up to 25 percent more synapses per neuron in brain areas involved in sensory perception. Source: adapted from Grossman, et al. *Progress in Brain Research*. 2002; 138: 91–108. Copyright © 2002 by Elsevier Science. By permission of the authors and Elsevier Science.

Enriched environments and lifelong learning

Greenough's groundbreaking studies showed that the environment does not just affect the developing rat's brain. Experience can also shape the *adult* rat brain. In subsequent studies, Greenough and his colleagues showed that the brains of adult rats also form new synapses in response to new experiences and toys. In rats at least, therefore, the effects of complex environments on the brain endure throughout life. Overall, the research does not support the argument for a selective educational focus specifically on children's earliest years.

The pernicious effects of environmental deprivation

Sadly, opportunities are still arising in modern times for us to observe the physical and mental effects of neglect upon the development of babies. Some years ago, the orphanages of Ceaucescu's regime in Romania were opened and the horror of the fate of abandoned babies became known. Many people in Western countries adopted babies from these orphanages who had lived there under appalling conditions from six weeks to up to two or three years. In the UK the progress of these babies was monitored and compared with the progress of other adopted children. This large-scale study is being carried out by Michael Rutter and colleagues at the University of London.

These studies clearly demonstrated that babies cannot be neglected without being harmed. The babies who had been reared in severely deprived conditions, with poor nutrition, ill-health, and little sensory or social stimulation, were more likely to have delayed development of skills such as walking and talking, and impaired social, emotional, and cognitive development. Rutter and his team of researchers found a close association between the duration of deprivation and the severity of the child's intellectual retardation. A small but significant proportion of the Romanian adoptees showed autistic-like patterns of behavior, such as indiscriminate approaches to strangers, clinging behavior, and narrow obsessive interests.

However, the recovery of intellectual capacities and improvement of autistic-like behaviors of the severely deprived children in these studies was remarkable. Most babies made a full recovery—certainly, their sensory capacities, walking and talking, and social and emotional skills improved. So although it is clearly damaging to deprive a baby, and the length of deprivation relates to the extent of adverse effects, this research does suggest that even very deprived babies can recover to a large extent if given remedial stimulation and care. If anything, these studies strongly suggest that it is never too late for remedial care.

Back to the early education debate

What does the research discussed in this chapter suggest as regards this hot debate? The debate has, after all, been strongly influenced by findings from brain research. This is a cautionary tale. For research findings to be established as replicable facts and as facts that apply to developing human beings, much more work has still to be done. Answers from neuroscience research that can be applied to education will have to be patiently scrutinized before they are translated into practice. If this takes years, this is nothing compared to the centuries of ignorance when the relevant questions could not be studied at all.

We believe that the research we have discussed in this chapter does not support the argument for a *selective* educational focus only on children's earliest years. Rather, learning opportunities need to be available at all ages. To put it simply, deprived environments are never good for your brain. Deprivation is certainly bad for the brain; on the other hand, enrichment may not necessarily be good for the brain. There is no evidence that hothousing is beneficial to brain development. This is not to say that hothousing is necessarily damaging—it might be, but the necessary studies have not yet been carried out.

We are reminded here of our use of vitamins in our daily diet. It is important that a certain minimum level is exceeded. Yet we sometimes hear warnings of not adding vitamins to our diet when it is not necessary. It is conceivable that there is another threshold above which vitamins could be harmful. Similarly, it is conceivable that the developing brain can be overstimulated. What is not known is what the effects of such an overdose might be.

What of the need to take advantage of sensitive periods of learning? The research tells us that sensitive periods exist at least for vision, and also encourages us in the optimistic belief that missed opportunities can to some extent be reversed.

The early education debate has not been in vain. It is good that early experiences are being discussed and it may well be that their overwhelming importance will be strongly supported by brain research in the future.

Chapter 3

words and numbers in early childhood

We still know very little about human brain development during the first 10 years of life. By contrast, cognitive psychology has provided a wealth of detail on the *cognitive* development of children. This knowledge has not yet been related in systematic ways to brain development. One reason for this is that the necessary technology is only slowly becoming available. What is needed are ways of looking at the developing brain directly: first, to see what happens to the anatomical structure, and second, to look at the development of brain function during childhood. Recent technological advances, such as the refinement of brain-imaging devices, mean that we are now able to carry out this kind of research, and an exciting new domain is starting to evolve. Here, we mainly summarize work by cognitive psychologists, which, we believe, will in the future be matched by brain studies.

The changes in behavior from the ages of two years to six and then again from six to ten are staggering. One example is language. Language and its components—sounds (or *phonemes*), vocabulary, and grammar—are mastered in early childhood using powerful learning mechanisms that help children to learn simply by listening to and interacting with adults and other children. By the age of two, most children are beginning to learn to speak. At the age of six, knowledge of the whole sound system of the child's native language (*phonology*), its grammar, and a great deal of the meaning that language encodes, is more or less complete. A conversation with a six year old can be just as linguistically sophisticated as with a 16 year old, even though the topics might well be different. In many countries, between the ages of roughly six and ten, written language is acquired through schooling and this marks another milestone in the development of the brain.

Learning to talk

Is language *innate*? This is an old question, which can only be answered simultaneously "yes" and "no." No, in that there are many different languages, some more complex than others, and each can only be learned by listening to it and speaking it. Artificial languages that are governed by different rules are much harder to learn. In this way, learning one's own specific language is clearly not innate. On the other hand, there are various abstract rules that seem to be inherent in every spoken language. In this way, the ability to learn a natural language is innate. There is further evidence for an inbuilt preference for human speech over and above other sounds. Human babies orient toward speech automatically and almost all babies, as long as they are brought up in an environment where language is spoken, learn to speak naturally and effortlessly. Granted, some children learn more slowly than others, and children who do not get sufficient experience, as well as those who have certain brain disorders, will have great difficulties in learning to talk. But in what way is the still developing brain in babies equipped to acquire their native language?

There is evidence that learning the sounds of one's own language begins *in utero*—newborn babies can distinguish between sentences spoken in their parents' native language and sentences in another language, presumably on the basis of prenatal experience with maternal speech. At only a few days old, babies listening to the sound "a" open their mouth in a way that corresponds to this sound, and listening to "e" makes them open their mouth in a different way. It is as if they are programmed to imitate sounds they hear, even before they have knowledge of what their own mouth looks like.

A pioneering experiment, carried out by a French research team lead by Stanislas Dehaene and Ghislaine Dehaene-Lambertz in Paris, scanned the brains of babies as young as three months while they were asleep and listening to speech. Remarkably, the same brain regions were active in these three-month-old babies as in adults when they hear speech in their native language. These brain regions are those specialized for language. This experiment suggests that brain organization does not have to wait years for experience to be accumulated—the processing mechanisms are working already. Babies' brains seem to be geared up to learn and understand language at a very young age.

Categorizing sounds

Learning one's own language initially requires categorizing the sounds that make up language. These sounds are often called *phonemes*. Newborn babies are able to distinguish between all speech sounds. In fact, young babies are more sensitive than adults to the sounds that distinguish one word from another. This is akin to the finding that young babies are also more sensitive than adults to faces of different species, which we mentioned in Chapter 2. Just as facial discrimination is determined by the faces present in a baby's natural environment, so sound discrimination is determined by the sounds in a baby's environment in the first

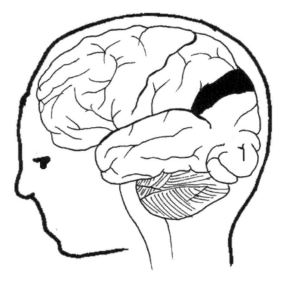

Figure 3.1 The left angular gyrus, a language area, is activated when two- to three-month-old infants are presented with words. At this very young age the brain already seems to be geared up to process language. Source: adapted from figure 2C in Dehaene-Lambertz et al. *Science* 2002; 298: 2013–5. Copyright © 2002 by AAAS. Adapted by permission of the authors and AAAS.

12 months of life. By the end of their first year babies lose the ability to distinguish between sounds to which they are not exposed. This is an example of a *sensitive period*.

It is well known that Japanese people cannot distinguish between R and L sounds. However, research in the 1980s by Patricia Kuhl at the University of Washington in Seattle revealed that Japanese *babies* can detect the difference between R and L, but only before about 10 months. The Japanese language does not contain distinct R and L sounds, so Japanese babies are not exposed to these sounds and eventually lose the ability to distinguish between them. By one year, they can no longer detect the difference between R and L. In contrast, babies brought up in the USA become even better at hearing this distinction because they are exposed to these distinct sounds in their language. If Japanese babies were continuously exposed to English as well as Japanese during this time they would also learn the L–R difference.

There are many sounds from different languages that American and British people cannot distinguish. Janet Werker and Renée Desjardins and their colleagues in Canada carried out an ingenious experiment in which they presented young babies, children, and adults with two different sounds (like "da" and "ba") and trained them to indicate when they heard a difference between the sounds. None of the babies, children, or adults had any problem detecting the difference between "da" and "ba." However, something different happened when the researchers then presented the same participants with two very similar sounds common in the Hindi language. The children and adults simply could not detect any difference between the two sounds. The Canadian researchers themselves found the two sounds impossible to distinguish. But babies under 12 months were able to detect the difference. Further studies have demonstrated that the cut-off occurs somewhere between 8 and 12 months: before this age babies brought up in North America can detect the difference between certain sounds from the Hindi language, an ability that, after 8–12 months, is lost.

Learning sounds after the sensitive period

This research reminds us of the "closing window" we discussed in Chapter 2. Is the window closed to such an extent that Japanese adults can no longer learn the difference between L and R? Not so. With effort, learning can happen, although this is not equally successful in all people. Remarkably, measurement of electrical activity in the brain of adult speakers when listening to sounds in a language other than their own reveals sensitivity to physical differences in foreign sounds, even when the person is quite unaware of these differences. This result, which was found by Annette Karmiloff-Smith and colleagues at the University of London, suggests that what the brain loses is not the ability to "hear" subtle differences, but the ability to treat them as significant. As we argued in Chapter 2, this loss is also a gain as it allows the fast and efficient organization of the most commonly encountered, and hence the most relevant, speech sounds.

[margin note: Social interaction with other people]

For new learning to occur after the sensitive period, social interaction with other people seems to be key. A recent study by Patricia Kuhl once again confirmed that infants older than nine months are able to learn new speech sounds to which they have not previously been exposed, after the sensitive period for sound categorization. However, this new study showed that later learning occurred only if the new sounds came from a real person who interacted with the babies. No learning occurred at this age if the same sounds were presented on a tape recorder or video.

Second language learning

Many children in the world grow up learning two or more languages. Yet in Western countries it has been common for children to learn just one language, and this is particularly the case with dominant languages, such as English, French, Spanish, and German. In countries where these languages are spoken, learning a second language is often not attempted until the teens. Of course, it has always been seen as a mark of education to have some knowledge of another language. The value of this additional language is not only seen in practical terms (you might go on vacation to a country where it's spoken) but also in terms of its intrinsic cultural worth.

Because of the current dominance of English throughout the world as the international means of communication, millions of people now learn English as a second language. The necessity to be bilingual, or even multilingual, creates new opportunities and it is fair to ask what the consequences might be if native English speakers miss out on the pressure to become bilingual. What does the need to be bilingual mean for the developing brain?

A possible scenario for a child learning more than one language is as follows. The mother and her relatives only speak French. The father and his relatives only speak English. They all mutually understand each other but they only ever use their mother tongue to speak. One child we know, who grew up in such a family, used one language for speaking and both languages for listening. When he went to school he was most surprised that the other children did not understand him when he talked to them in English while they spoke French!

Another child we know was brought up in a family of diplomats who were always abroad. He learned his native language and spoke it in the home, but also learned to speak the language that was used in the country where they lived. When the family returned to their country of origin, the child was astonished to hear the language of the home spoken in the street by strangers! He thought that every family had their own private language spoken only at home.

Thinking about language (and meaning)

Many children learn to be bilingual from an early age and appear to cope admirably. Babies brought up in two-language households are slightly slower to develop language than babies brought up speaking one language. However, there are clear advantages of having been exposed to both languages from birth. Such children normally have better pronunciation and grasp of syntax in both languages than children who begin learning a second language at a later age. Moreover, they come early to reflect on language, which is normally quite a late achievement. They are aware that quite different spoken words can refer to the same object: "dog" can mean the same as "chien." Perhaps this is an advantage, but we don't know how, and we can be sure that monolingual children will catch up.

The impetus for the ability to think about language and meaning—for example, that the same sound can have two different meanings (e.g., bank, as in river bank and money bank)—becomes very strong after learning to read. The fact that language is visible in print makes a huge difference to the ability to think and reason about it as an object of interest.

Is the following sentence correct: "Dirt makes me clean"? Well, it is grammatically correct, but semantically it is nonsense. Young children before school age find this subtle distinction hard to make. They refuse to admit a sentence such as this can be "correct." Meaning trumps syntax to such an extent that syntax is invisible and is difficult to think about in its own right. The same goes for word sound. Which word is bigger: "cat" or "caterpillar?" Meaning trumps again and the young child is likely to answer "cat."

True bilingualism, in the sense that neither language has preferential status, does not exist. Many people who are not bilingual find this surprising. Even if exposed to two languages equally from birth, one language is always chosen as the "mother tongue." Brain-imaging studies have demonstrated that, whatever the language, the mother tongue is processed in universally similar regions, mainly in the left hemisphere. On the other hand, the brain areas used for a second language partially overlap, but also occupy additional regions, which differ somewhat from person to person.

Many children these days learn a second language at school. It is often argued that because of children's flexible brains they have a much larger capacity for learning than adults. Indeed, bilingual studies show that grammar and accent are mastered better when learned at a young age. However, this may not be true for semantics and vocabulary, which may be learned at any age.

A foreign accent

Why do nonnative speakers retain a recognizable accent in their adopted language even if they have been speaking it for years, longer than they spoke their native language? What is it about one's mother tongue that leaves such an indelible mark? We have already seen that sound categorization sets in early and results in closing windows. From then on you do not learn again from scratch, as it were. Instead, you use your native sound structure as a base and adapt it for another language rather than build up a completely new structure. Thus, a second language learned after age five or so will almost always be marked by an accent.

It is intriguing to find large individual differences in foreign accent. Some people have hardly any accent, even if they learned their second language after the age of 10, but others improve only slightly—if at all—after years and years of practice. So far, no one has discovered why. A foreign accent, just like your particular dialect within your native language, and just like your physical appearance, is a marker of your identity. Perhaps such markers have played an important evolutionary role in recognizing family members and more distant relatives.

Speaking before speech

Well before babies are able to utter any recognizable words, they start to babble. From about seven months, babies produce all sorts of sounds, such as "bababa" and "dadada," and noises, such as clicks and gurgles. Not all of these will later be part of their native speech. But babbling often includes sounds that make up the language in the babies' environment. It seems plausible that this is a useful mechanism to learn how to produce the sounds of one's language. On the other hand, even children who hardly babble at all still learn to speak. Thus learning to speak may go on without any external signs of practice.

Deaf children babble with their hands

Babbling was originally thought to be determined by the development of the vocal tract anatomy and the brain mechanisms underlying the control of verbal speech—and therefore specific to spoken language production. However, this theory is clearly insufficient because deaf children appear to babble with their hands. Laura-Ann Petitto and colleagues at McGill University in Toronto made videos of 10–14-month-old deaf babies (with deaf parents) and hearing babies (with hearing parents) in their natural environment. The researchers then analyzed the videos and found that the deaf babies seem to do a similar thing to hearing babies' babbling, but with their hands. They produce hand movements that are a subset of the hand movements that comprise the sign language produced by their deaf parents. A study published in 2004 by the same group found that even hearing babies with deaf parents babble with their hands. This suggests that babbling is an inherent part of language learning, no matter what the language is. Babbling is a clear sign that babies are discovering how to the map the perceived structure of language (heard or seen) on to the means for producing this structure.

Fast-mapping

When babies are about one year old they start to move from sounds to words. In a process called *fast-mapping*, babies begin to map words to objects on the basis of words they hear other people use. From about 18 months to two years, when most infants have established a core of around 20–50 single words, the speed at which they learn new words accelerates. By the time they are five, most children have a vocabulary of 2,000 words or more, and this pace of learning new words continues in the primary years of school. The ability to acquire new vocabulary continues throughout our lifetimes. According to Paul Bloom at Yale University, there are no dramatic changes in the speed of acquisition of new words. Adults also pick up new words at a fast rate.

Learning grammar

As children's vocabulary increases, they begin to join words together in sequences and to establish a basic understanding of grammar. Children develop grammatical rules (e.g., plurals, verb tenses) without explicitly being taught them. At age two, children may correctly say "mice" and "went," and then, later, occasionally you may hear them say, "mouses" and "goed." This suggests that, on some occasions, infants copy words they hear adults speak, whereas on others they use the rules about language that they have unconsciously extracted. Sometimes, they may overextend the use of these rules because many languages are not governed by only one set of rules.

Noam Chomsky from MIT in Boston famously suggested that human infants are naturally equipped with a language-learning device. Steven Pinker, who propagated this theory, conducted some compelling experiments. If three- to five-year-old children are asked for a word for a "monster that eats mice," 90 percent of them come out with "mice-eater." But when the same children are asked for a word for a monster that eats rats, only 2 percent respond "rats-eater." So young children seem to have an idea of how to form compound words with regular and irregular plurals. It is remarkable that young children can extrapolate the grammatical rules simply from hearing regular and irregular plurals produced by their parents, without being explicitly taught anything. Pinker interprets this impressive ability as a consequence of the inherent organization of children's grammatical system that develops as soon as babies are exposed to language.

Children differ in their ability to learn and use grammar, and some children cannot learn grammar because of a subtle brain abnormality. They have a specific language impairment, or SLI. Heather van der Lely at the University of London found that these children lack the apparently innate ability to unpack and generate normal sentences. They can learn to speak and to understand sentences, but slowly, and many have subtle problems even as adults. In other areas of learning, SLI children can be very fast and very able.

Some languages have more complex grammatical rules than others and take longer to learn. This is true for sound structure as well as grammar and word formation. It is not enough to have a genetic program for learning language; children learn their particular language through listening to adults and other children using words to communicate with them, and imitating what they hear.

Adults, especially in the early years, play an essential role in language development, without making any real effort to do so, for example, by using language

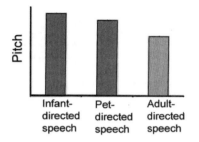

Figure 3.2   Mothers tend to speak in a high-pitched way to pets and babies. However, talking to pets does not include the elongated vowel sounds that mothers tend to use with babies. Source: adapted from figure 1B from Burnham et al. *Science* 2002; 296: 1435. Copyright © 2002 by AAAS. By permission of the authors and AAAS.

that is easy for babies to learn. *Motherese*, or *parentese*, is a term used to refer to the way in which adults often talk to babies—using high-pitched and long, exaggerated, vowel sounds. Motherese occurs in all cultures and is advantageous because the short and simple sentences and long vowels help children learn the sounds and structure of their language. This behavior on the part of adults seems almost unintentional—it is as if adults are programmed to behave in a way that aids the development of children.

A charming study recently showed that mothers talk differently to their babies compared to their pets. Women talked very affectionately to both their babies and their pets, using higher pitch than when talking to adults. However, they use lengthened vowels in this affectionate speech only for their babies. The lengthening of vowels can act as a teaching device because it can direct the child's attention to particular features of speech that they will later have to produce. Clearly pets do not learn to speak a language so do not require those lengthened vowels.

How the brain learns grammar

Grammar and semantic (vocabulary) processing appear to rely on different neural systems within the brain. This can be shown by comparing the brain regions that are activated when one reads words like "cat," "house," or "car," which provide semantic information, with the regions that are activated when reading words like "up," "of," or "from," which provide grammatical information. Research with electroencephalogram (EEG; see Appendix) by Helen Neville in Portland, Oregon has shown that semantic processing activates both the right and the left hemispheres of the brain, whereas grammatical processing usually recruits the left hemisphere only.

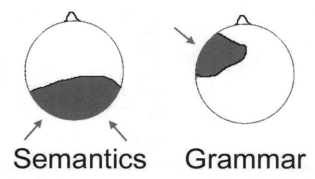

Semantics   Grammar

Figure 3.3   Helen Neville and colleagues found that semantic processing activates both the right and the left hemispheres of the brain, whereas grammatical processing usually recruits the left hemisphere only. The nose indicates the front of the head. This is a view from the top. Source: adapted from figure 2 in Neville, Helen J. and Bruer, John T. (2001), in *Critical Thinking About Critical Periods*, edited by Donald B. Bailey, Jr., John T. Bruer, Frank J. Symons, & Jeff W. Lichtman. Baltimore: Paul H. Brookes Pub Co. Copyright © 2001 by Paul H. Brookes Pub Co. By permission of the authors and Brookes Publishing.

Further research from Neville's lab has indicated that there seems to be a sensitive period for learning grammar but not for learning vocabulary. The same brain systems are used for learning vocabulary whatever age the vocabulary is learned. So, whether a child starts to learn the English language at age four, seven, or twelve years, the same brain systems are used for processing semantic information—these are located within the *posterior* regions of the left and right *hemispheres*. In contrast, the way the brain processes grammatical information changes with the age at which the person is first exposed to the language. The studies showed that people who learned English as a native language or as a second language between one and three years of age recruit the left side of the brain when processing English grammar. But people who learned English later, usually as a second language (for instance, deaf people who learn American Sign Language before learning English), end up recruiting not only regions in the left hemisphere, but also similar regions in the right hemisphere. In fact, the older the first exposure to the English language, the more *bilateral* the brain activity.

This change in brain activation in people who learn English early, compared with people who learn it later, indicates that delaying exposure to the English language leads the brain to use a different strategy when processing grammar. Indeed, people who learn the language later and who showed bilateral activation during language processing performed worse on grammar tasks. This does not mean that these people cannot improve on English grammar, but the results suggest that the bilateral brain activation indicates an unusual and possibly harder way of learning.

One clear implication for education from this research is that there may be a finite time for the most efficient type of grammar learning. After the age of 13, we are still able to learn grammar, but we will probably be less efficient and use different brain strategies than if we had learned grammar earlier. Neville's research suggests that the earlier grammar is learned, the faster it is acquired.

This research has implications for teaching first and second languages. Delaying exposure to a language leads the brain to use a different strategy when processing the grammar of that language. Learning a second language after 13 is likely to result in a less automatic mastery of the grammar of this language. In most European countries and in the USA, second language learning usually starts at about 13. This is simply too late if grammar and accent are to be mastered as efficiently as possible.

The same applies to deaf children who need to learn sign language. Deaf children are sometimes prevented from using sign language due to a fear of it interfering with their ability to learn a spoken language. However, sign language has a very specific grammar system and so if children do not learn sign language early on, the chance of them being able to master it later is reduced.

· Learning to read and write

After naturally learning a spoken language, how does the young child cope with the unnatural skill of reading and writing? Of course, in most countries the printed word has become a part of our natural environment. This is a prime example of how culture, which at first slowly introduces artificial inventions, eventually becomes ubiquitous and therefore "natural." To understand written words, children must appreciate that an object can be represented by certain sounds and that these can be represented by lines on a surface. Both reading and writing are established most readily on a foundation of good spoken language.

Categorizing words and learning the alphabet involves attending to sounds of speech. This has been convincingly demonstrated by researchers at the Haskins laboratory in Connecticut. Peter Bryant, a developmental psychologist at the University of Oxford, found that young children of preschool age enjoy nursery rhymes, and suggested that this demonstrates an implicit awareness of the sound and rhythm of spoken language. If you tell a three year old: "Jack and Jill went up the STAIRS" the child will most likely laugh at you and correct you: "Jack and Jill went up the HILL." Nursery rhymes are easy to remember, because they rhyme. Words that start with the same sound also make nice little "poems"— Peter Piper, Fee Fie Fo Fum. . . . Appreciating rhymes is one thing, but appreciating the sounds that make up the rhyme is another.

When comparing different languages, Usha Goswami, at the University of London, found that in languages other than English, rhyme plays a less important role. From this point of view, it is unlikely that rhyme sensitivity is a necessary prerequisite for becoming literate. Instead, it may be a sign (in some but not all languages) of the speech system becoming developmentally mature.

Learning phonemes and learning letters tend to go hand in hand, and speech sounds may become an object of learning because of the letters that represent them. It is hard to know what comes first. Whether reading development can be accelerated by raising awareness of phonemes without letters is doubtful. Can brain research throw any light on the processes underlying rhyming, awareness of phonemes, attention to the visual shapes of letters, and reading and writing skills? Probably, but the studies have not yet been done.

In brain-imaging studies, rhyming skills have been tested in adults (does B rhyme with T?—yes. With S?—no). The brain regions that are active when you answer such questions are part of the system that the brain uses for reading and for language in general. This subpart of the language system is also active when you try to remember a telephone number, a string of sounds that you may rehearse silently to remember. Thus a large proportion of the brain's language system seems to be dedicated to sound processing.

In the deaf, the part of the brain's language system that processes speech does not respond to sounds but responds to signed gestures instead. Remember that the constituents of language need not necessarily be sounds or voice but can be manual gesture.

Writing

As vocabulary and grammatical competence increases, children become able to give a continuous account of events—to "tell a story." This narrative form of talk is related to the independent expression of language needed for writing. Children who have competent narrative skills learn to read and write more readily than children who have not established these skills. Few children will have established the skills involved in writing before the age of four, no matter how good their conversational language or how exposed they are to books and other forms of writing.

Although children can use plastic letters and keyboards to start writing, to write on paper children need to be able to coordinate and control their finger movements. The brain's *motor cortex*, which controls hand and finger coordination, is not usually fully developed until at least five years, and studies suggest that hand and finger coordination is slower to develop in boys than in girls. Development continues throughout the primary school years. Because there are large individual differences in the speed of acquiring fine motor coordination, it is pointless to be cross with a young child who makes little progress in writing simply because they can't control their hand movements. Whether or not coor-

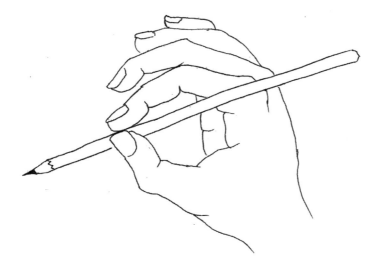

Figure 3.4   Fine finger coordination, as well as the coordination of hand and arm, which are all necessary for writing, develop during the first five or so years of life.

dination should be accelerated through handwriting or through other kinds of finger exercises is an open question.

Dyspraxia

Some children have inordinate difficulties, probably because of some brain abnormality, in motor coordination. This is termed *dyspraxia* and is seen in their inability to do up buttons, to hold a pencil properly, and to throw and catch balls. Since large parts of the brain are dedicated to maintaining posture and preventing ourselves from falling over on uneven or slippery ground, even a small brain abnormality may show itself in poor motor control. This obviously affects handwriting ability.

Numbers and sums

According to the renowned Swiss psychologist, Jean Piaget, babies do not develop any kind of number sense until they are at least four or five years old. Piaget showed that before this age children fail the "number conservation test." In this test children are shown a row containing six glasses and a second row of six bottles. The objects in each row are equally spaced and the rows are the same length. The children are asked which row contains more objects and most three-year-olds will reply that they are the same. If the row of glasses is then spread out so there are bigger gaps between each of the glasses, and the child is asked the same question, most children reply that the row of glasses contains more objects. So three-year-old children seem to think that number depends on how big something looks. Piaget claimed that this demonstrates that young children do not "conserve" number.

Piaget's theories have had a great deal of influence on Western education systems. It is often assumed that any mathematical learning before the age of about six is merely rote, without any deep understanding of the concepts learned. Some people have argued that teaching math at an age when children lack a real understanding of mathematical concepts can cause them to become wary or afraid of mathematics. Therefore, children often spend many years learning about sets and subsets, which, according to Piaget, are a prerequisite for a deeper concept of number.

Since Piaget's theories were first published, a mass of research has demonstrated that his view of young children as lacking a number concept is simply wrong. The problem with Piaget's tests is that they often overlooked what children were actually capable of. When young children's mathematical concepts are tested without asking explicit questions about them, they seem to do much better. This reminds us of the important distinction between *implicit* and *explicit* knowledge. Implicit knowledge can be hidden.

Using an ingenious revamped version of the Piaget conservation experiment described above, in the 1960s the cognitive psychologists Jacques Mehler and Tom Bever, then working in Boston, demonstrated that three-year-old children can implicitly "conserve" number. They showed that certain experimental situations can elicit the same results as Piaget: children as old as four often answer that longer rows contain more marbles than shorter rows, even if the shorter row actually contains more marbles than the longer row. However, if the marbles are replaced with candy (in this study M&Ms were used) and no verbal response is required—children are told to choose one of the rows to eat—children as young as two take the row with the greater number of M&Ms, whatever its length. So children clearly do have some concept of number at a much younger age than Piaget proposed.

Even babies can add up

More recent studies reveal quite clearly that even very young babies have some concept of number. However, it seems clear that this is limited to very small numbers: 1, 2, 3. Nevertheless, even this tiny set of numbers is sufficient to demonstrate that they can add and subtract spontaneously.

Karen Wynn at Yale University carried out a number of clever experiments that demonstrate that even five-month-old infants have some understanding of addition and subtraction. In one study, she showed babies a toy that was then hidden behind a screen. The babies then saw her hiding a second toy behind the screen. A few seconds later, Wynn removed the screen and timed how long the babies looked. If removing the screen revealed only one toy (the "impossible" outcome) the babies looked for much longer than if there were two toys (the "possible" outcome). In other words babies are surprised if the number of toys does not add up. This study demonstrates that young babies have some understanding that $1 + 1 = 2$.

Learning to count

Usually by about three years, children begin to count and start to apply number words to objects (e.g., "I have three dolls") and actions ("I climbed four steps"). According to development psychologists Sue Carey and Liz Spelke, at Harvard University, this is a crucial step and allows the tiny initial set of numbers to be extended to—eventually—infinity. Children's understanding of counting is poor when asked to compare two or more sets of objects. However, when tested with one set at a time, children as young as two or three understand that counting occurs in a fixed order and the last number counted represents the value of the set. When very young children first learn number names, as in "One, two, buckle my shoe," they are not actually counting. A deep understanding of the significance of counting does not develop until the end of the child's fourth year. Until three or four, children do not seem to realize that counting has anything to do with knowing "how many." This understanding seems to develop through teaching informally by parents and siblings, and formally by teachers.

According to Rochel Gelman and Randy Gallistel, at the University of California, children are equipped with innate principles of counting even when they lack the names for numbers. Even before three, well before they have had any explicit teaching, children will answer correctly when asked how many times a character appeared in a television program, or how many times a whale splashed into the sea. Gelman has shown that three-and-a-half-year-old children always detect counting errors. For example, they notice when an adult recites numerals out of order, forgets to count an item, or counts an item twice. By the fourth year, children generalize counting rules to novel situations. Just as it has been proposed that we are born with a disposition to learn the rules of grammar, so it has been suggested that we are born with an ability to learn about numbers.

Using fingers

Before they have had any formal teaching, children develop aids to help them add and subtract. They use their fingers as counters. Three year olds add two sets of numbers by counting the first set on the fingers, then the second set on different fingers, and then counting all the raised fingers. They quickly progress to going through the same counting routine without the need of their fingers. By the age of about four or five, children work out that adding two numbers is easier if you start to count upwards from the largest number. If asked "What is 2 and 5?" children often inverse the problem, and count two numbers up from 5, which takes less time than counting five numbers up from 2. This demonstrates that, before being formally taught, children develop quite naturally the concept that a + b is the same as b + a.

Children's early ability to add and subtract objects is based on their experience with objects and might be a precursor to the more formal, abstract type of addition and subtraction learned in school.

What in the brain makes us numerate?

Only a few days after birth, babies can tell the difference between two and three objects. How is this possible? The brain must be equipped with some kind of number concept, which develops during gestation. This must be the case because it is hard to see how babies could learn about number from the environment in the first few days of life. The French neuroscientist Stanislas Dehaene has suggested that already before birth the brain develops, through genetic control, a module specialized for identifying numbers. Just as the newborn brain is equipped with a start-up visual system before exposure to visual stimulation, so the brain may be equipped with a start-up kit for a number system.

This idea also explains why some rare people simply have no concept of number and find it incredibly hard to understand even the most basic math problems. They are known as *dyscalculic*.

If almost all young children have some basic concept of number and counting, this does not necessarily mean that it is essential, or even beneficial, to start teaching young babies math. While basic mathematical abilities appear to exist in young children, and are much more sophisticated than Piaget imagined, they are strictly limited to very elementary arithmetic. If the number of objects to be counted or sets to be judged is increased to more than about three of four, children start to make errors.

A deep knowledge of counting of numbers is largely the result of coaching by adults in the primary school years and so may be considered a clear example of cultural transmission.

Chapter 4

the mathematical brain

Brain scientists have studied how the brain processes mathematical calculations and have found that different brain regions are specialized for "guesstimates" and exact calculations. Patients with brain damage who have suddenly lost their math skills have revealed a great deal about these processes, as have children who never acquired math skills in the first place. These studies have also shed light on left–right brain differences and on gender differences. Studies involving patients with brain damage have indicated that the *parietal lobe*, which is involved in seeing and remembering where objects are, is associated with knowledge of numbers and their relations.

A brain region for mathematics

It has been known for a long time that certain brain-damaged patients are no longer able to read Arabic numerals. It seems bizarre, but these patients might read 9 as 5 or 38 as 48. Of these patients, certain have been reported who, although they often confuse components of numbers, never confuse the decimal quantity (the base) of the number—they do not read 30 as 300. Other patients have exactly the opposite pattern—they never confuse single numerals, but will confuse the base of numbers, so might read 36 as 360. This is an example of a *double dissociation* (see Appendix). In the first case, there is a deficit in the selection of individual number words, which is intact in the second case. In the second case, there is a problem in the conceptual understanding of quantity, which is intact in the first case.

Brian Butterworth at the university of London is one of the scientists who study such patients to discover the brain basis of math. The existence of these two types of patient suggest that there is a region of the brain that is in some way specialized for quantity (sometimes called *number grammar*), while a different region is specialized for the selection of number words. In this chapter, we will describe some of the key experiments that have helped scientists understand which parts of the brain are involved in mathematical concepts and calculations.

There is little point in searching for one brain region that "does" mathematics. There are different aspects of math, for example, quantity and number. Take reading numbers: there are two types of number we can read—number words ("five") and numerals or digits ("5"). The ability to read these can be selectively impaired as a result of damage to different brain regions. Some patients can read number words but not digits and other patients have the opposite problem. Generally, damage to the visual cortex on the left side of the brain causes problems in word reading, whereas damage to visual cortex on the right side causes problems in digit reading. Thus the brain seems to have several systems that deal with the different aspects of number and quantity, which normally work together, integrating all this information so it makes sense as a whole.

Calculation in the parietal lobe

Since the late 1980s, Stanislas Dehaene and Laurent Cohen in Paris have studied brain-damaged patients and have shown that different mathematical problems can occur as a result of damage to different brain regions. One of the first patients they studied, called Mr M, suffered a large brain hemorrhage and lost function in part of the back of his left hemisphere, in particular the left *parietal lobe*.

His lesion was large and left him with many disabilities, including profound arithmetic problems. Not only was he completely incapable of performing the simplest sum (such as $2 + 2 = 4$), he was also unable to recognize numbers presented visually. On the other hand, the researchers noticed that when trying to name numbers, he could often come up with the right answer, after some time, by counting from one up to the number that was presented. He used the same method of counting from one upwards to reach numbers that had meaning to him, such as the age of his daughter. Clearly, Mr M still retained a *representation* of the number, but he found it impossible to retrieve and name numbers immediately from the presentation of a digit or a question requiring an exact number as an answer.

Now, although Mr M's calculation was poor and he could not instantly recognize numbers, the doctors who worked with him found that he did not have the same problem in estimating quantities. For example, Mr. M knew that ten is larger than five. The only difficulty he had with comparing numbers was when he was asked to compare close numbers, such as 34 and 36. Mr M was also able to approximate time and quantities—when asked how many days are there in one year, he said that a year contained "about 350 days." He said that an hour is "about 50 minutes," and a dozen eggs is about "6 or 10." His answers are not exactly right, but they are not far off. He could not add 2 + 2 but on the other hand he knew for sure that the answer is not 9.

Dehaene and Cohen concluded that although the left parietal damage had caused this patient to lose his calculation abilities, it had not harmed his ability to approximate. This patient, and others like him, suggest that the processes required to perform exact calculations reside somewhere in the left hemisphere, possibly in the parietal lobe, which in the case of Mr M was damaged. A different region of the brain, likely to be the right hemisphere, which in Mr M's case must have been still intact, seems to underlie approximation of number.

Although patients with parietal lobe damage have serious problems with recognizing and calculating numbers, they often have fewer problems when something nonnumeric has some kind of numerical order, such as days of the week or letters of the alphabet. Mr M, for example, knew instantly that A comes before C in the alphabet and that Tuesday comes before Thursday. Only the representation of numbers as exact indices of quantity seemed to be impaired. Mr M had particular problems subtracting numbers—even simple sums such as 5 − 2 baffled him.

The number line

Dehaene has suggested that this might be because subtracting numbers requires thinking about numbers represented on a "number line," going from one to infinity, from left to right (or right to left depending on which country you come from), higher numbers appearing to the right of lower numbers. Most of us find it easy to imagine this number line, and many of us will have learned about numbers using a physical representation of such a number line—an abacus, for example.

The abacus is still used widely today and is an extremely useful technique to learn about numbers, in particular about how to add and subtract numbers. Imagine not being able to think about numbers on such a number line. Without memorizing every single possible subtraction and addition it might be very difficult to subtract and add numbers. This is exactly what Dehaene and Cohen have proposed happened in Mr M's case (and other patients with parietal lobe damage). Mr M is no longer able to imagine numbers as representations in space, on a number line, which is why he finds subtraction and addition so difficult.

The parietal cortex, space, and quantity

The parietal cortex (see Figure 4.1) is critically involved in representing where things are in the environment—this ability is called *spatial representation* and is

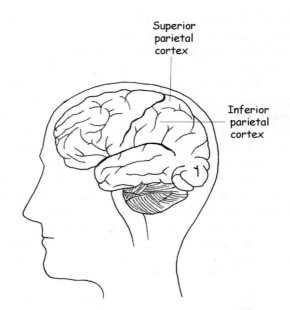

Figure 4.1   The parietal cortex, which can be divided into superior (higher) and inferior (lower) sections is involved in spatial manipulations and in arithmetic and number understanding.

crucial in everyday life. Without it we would find it extremely difficult to pick up objects, to guide ourselves round our environment, to remember where anything is, and to pay attention to particular parts of our surroundings.

According to Vincent Walsh at the University of London, the parietal cortex plays an important role in the representation of magnitude. This applies not only to numbers and quantities but also to time and space. Spatial representation is relevant to math. Ever since Euclid and Pythagoras, arithmetic and geometry have been linked. If you think about it, the number line that we use for counting, adding, and subtracting involves imagining numbers as objects in space. In Western cultures, zero is generally thought of as existing at the leftmost point on the line, and the further along to the right of the line you go the bigger the numbers get. Cultures in which the alphabet is written from right to left, for example, Arabic or Urdu-speaking cultures, have a number line running from right to left.

People generally show high correlations between mathematical ability and spatial ability on aptitude tests. In other words, people who have very good spatial ability—who have a good sense of direction and easily remember their way around complicated environments—often, but not always, have good mathematical skills as well. Perhaps they have a particularly well-developed parietal cortex. Perhaps even at birth there are differences; or perhaps differences are

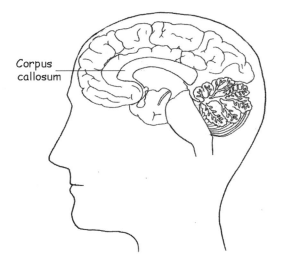

Corpus
callosum

Figure 4.2 The corpus callosum is a mass of fibers that lies in the middle of the brain and connects the two hemispheres, allowing them to communicate with each other instantly and continuously.

linked to specific experiences. Evidence from brain imaging studies is in principle available to answer these questions. But these studies have yet to be done.

The two sides of the brain

As well as implicating the parietal lobe in calculation, the study of Mr M also suggested that the different sides of the brain (the *hemispheres*) might be responsible for different components of mathematics and quantity. The idea that the two hemispheres have different functions is an intriguing possibility that has interested scientists for many decades. Normally the two sides of the brain work together, continually comparing and processing information that is transferred from one side of the brain to the other by a mass of fibers connecting the two hemispheres, called the *corpus callosum*.

To study the different sides of the brain, scientists have investigated patients whose right and left hemispheres are no longer connected together and therefore work independently of each other. Such patients, of whom there are very few in the world, have had their corpus callosum surgically removed or lesioned, normally as an attempt to cure intractable epilepsy. As a result, their brain is effectively split into two halves—hence the name split-brain patients. Although the operation is fairly successful at reducing epileptic seizures, these days it would not be carried out because it is such a drastic procedure. Lesioning just a small section of the corpus callosum seems to have as much benefit as cutting the whole thing. In split-brain patients, the two halves of the brain work in isolation because they are no longer able to communicate with each other. Studying split-brain patients has revealed a huge amount about the different roles of the two cerebral hemispheres.

Remember from Chapter 1 that information transmitted to the right side of the body, such as a touch on the right arm or the sight of something on the right side, is processed by the left side of the brain. Normally the information processed in one hemisphere is quickly—within a few milliseconds—sent to the other hemisphere via the corpus callosum. Because this information transfer is not possible in split-brain patients, the workings of one of their hemispheres in isolation can be investigated by presenting a stimulus to the opposite side of their body. For well over a century, we have known that language resides in the left hemisphere in most people. While this is true for people who are right-handed, it is not usually the case for left-handers—language is normally housed in both hemispheres in these people. If an object, say an apple, is presented to the left side of a split-brain patient (who is looking straight ahead), this information only gets to the right hemisphere, and the patient is unable to name the object. The patient has no such naming problem if the apple is presented to the right side, in which case the visual information is sent to the left (language) hemisphere.

Quantity comparisons

Split-brain patients are unable to compare numbers when one number is presented to one hemisphere and the other number is presented to the other hemisphere. They have no way of integrating this information, so the comparison question is meaningless. However, if the two numbers appear together on the same side, the patient has no difficulty judging which is smaller. This is true for both sides. Comparison is slightly slower for the right hemisphere than the left, but the difference is minimal. This shows that both hemispheres are able to recognize and compare digits. Comparison between quantities does not rely on language. If it did, the right hemisphere would be unable to compare quantities.

Guesstimates

However, the right hemisphere is unable to identify written numerals such as "sixty-four." The right hemisphere knows what 6 means, that it is less than 8, that it represents six dots, but this knowledge completely disintegrates for the word "six." Neither can the right hemisphere alone name digits and perform arith-

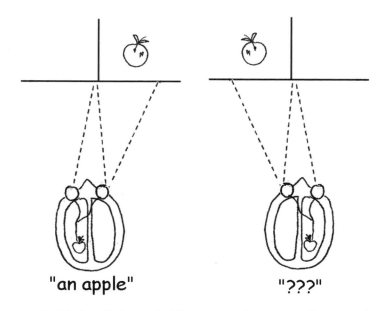

"an apple"   "???"

Figure 4.3 Split-brain patients have had their corpus callusum surgically cut, usually as an attempt to treat intractable epilepsy. The result is that their two hemispheres are separated and can no longer communicate with each other. They can name objects presented to their right visual field because these are processed by the left, language, hemisphere of the brain. Objects presented to their left visual field cannot be named because the right hemisphere is incapable of producing language. Eyes and nose indicate the front of the head. View from the top.

metic. The left hemisphere can add up 2 + 5 but split-brain patients find this impossible if the sums are shown to their right hemisphere. The left hemisphere can do multiplication whereas the right hemisphere cannot. This is not surprising. Multiplication is strongly linked to language in most societies. In most cultures children learn multiplication by rote learning times tables. Thus only the left (language) hemisphere knows its times tables!

Nevertheless, the right hemisphere can approximate. Split-brain patients know that obviously wrong sums such as 4 + 6 = 23 are incorrect even when flashed to their right hemisphere. So it seems that the right hemisphere approximates while the left hemisphere calculates. No wonder, then, that Mr M, who had massive damage to his posterior left hemisphere, was unable to calculate but had no difficulties approximating.

Left-brain/right-brain?

Research on split-brain patients has given us great insight into the workings of the two cerebral hemispheres. This knowledge has infiltrated into mainstream culture, but, unfortunately, the research has often been overinterpreted with abandon. There is a now widely held belief that the two sides of the brain control different "modes of thinking" and that each person has a preference for one of these modes, that is, that one hemisphere dominates over the other. People are referred to as "left-brained," "right-brained," or even "whole-brained." You can even find "hemispheric dominance inventories" that you can fill in to see whether you are left- or right-brained, and then do exercises to change this. This is pop psychology but not scientific psychology. While it is true that one hemisphere dominates over the other in terms of our experience of the world and our actions, both sides of the brain work together in almost all situations, tasks, and processes. In other words, you are not right- or left-brained. You use both sides of the brain.

It has been argued that education currently favors left-brain modes of thinking, which are logical, analytic, dominant, and accurate, while downplaying right-brain modes of thinking, which are creative, intuitive, emotional, and subjective. While encouraging education to involve a wide variety of tasks, skills, learning, and modes of thinking is probably a good thing, it is purely metaphorical to call these right-brain or left-brain modes. People with no right hemisphere are not devoid of creativity. People with no left hemisphere, although most will be unable to produce language, can still be analytical. Some will still be able to talk—language is housed in the right hemisphere of a small minority (about 7%) of people.

Whether left-brain/right-brain notions should influence the way people are educated is questionable. Most neuroscientists question the validity of categorizing people in terms of their abilities as either a left-brain or a right-brain person. In terms of education, such categorization might even act as an impediment to learning.

Imaging mathematics in the brain

So far, we have discussed research on mathematical understanding in people with damaged brains. Brain-imaging studies have shown that the parietal lobe is activated during calculation in people with normal, healthy brains. The first imaging study to show the involvement of the parietal lobe in math was carried out in Sweden in the 1980s. Since then, many further imaging studies, using different imaging techniques and different types of task, have supported this pioneering result. The parietal lobe, in particular the *inferior* (lower) part in the right hemisphere, is activated when participants compare numbers, and when they subtract and add numbers. As we have discussed, the parietal lobe is critically involved in knowing where things are in space. Its involvement in calculation fits with the notion that calculation contains a spatial element.

The *inferior parietal lobe* is activated for both multiplication and comparison. In fact its level of activation seems to depend on the difficulty of the mathematical task

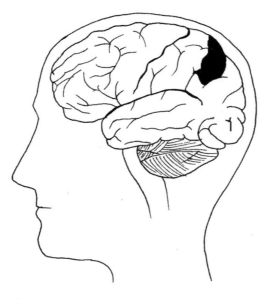

Figure 4.4   The parietal cortex is activated by mathematical calculations.

in both cases. Apart from the parietal lobe, some further differences are found when participants perform multiplication rather than comparisons. During multiplication there is a shift in brain activation toward the left hemisphere whereas, during comparison, activation is in both hemispheres with a slight preference for the right. This fits with the notion that multiplication, but not comparison, is dependent on regions in the left hemisphere that are associated with language. As we have already mentioned, multiplication in almost all educational systems is learned by rote, which is similar to learning the vocabulary of a language.

A basic ability to compare numbers and a basic quantity representation system is present very early on in development and even in other species. Behavioral studies have revealed that number perception, discrimination, and elementary calculation abilities are present from a very early age, as we mentioned in Chapter 3. The ability to compare numbers depends on a nonverbal representational system located primarily in the parietal lobe. For comparison and quantity estimations, there is no need to convert the numbers into words, which would rely on the left hemisphere. As was demonstrated in the experiments with split-brain patients discussed above, both hemispheres are capable of doing the job of comparing and estimating numbers.

Calculation, approximation, and language

Recent evidence lends further support to the idea that exact calculation is dependent on language, while approximation relies on nonverbal visual and spatial brain networks. Stanislas Dehaene, Liz Spelke, and colleagues trained bilingual volunteers to make both exact calculations and estimations in one of their two languages. The researchers then tested the volunteers in both languages. Performance on the exact problems was faster in the language the volunteers used when they first learned to calculate than in the second language, even if they currently used this language a lot. In contrast, performance on approximations was equivalent in both languages. The brain-imaging evidence supported these behavioral results: the parietal lobe in both hemispheres showed greater activation for approximations than for exact calculations. Additional activation was found during exact calculations in the brain's language areas.

Evidence suggests that fluency in arithmetic in adults is likely to depend on a constant interplay between quantity, visual, and verbal representations of numbers. Rote calculations are performed largely using the verbal system, while approximations of calculations are made using the quantity system.

Gender differences and mathematics

Many studies have shown evidence for gender differences in mathematical ability. However, if they exist, these differences are clearly not purely biological. There are variations in the size of the gender effect between cultures. While boys outperform girls in both China and the USA, girls in China perform better than boys in the USA. This is not a biological difference between the Chinese and the Americans—when Chinese girls are taught in the USA their mathematical ability declines to the level of American girls.

If there are sex differences in math, there is also a great degree of overlap between boys and girls—many girls in all countries do better than many boys. A recent analysis of findings from many different studies found that the gap between boys and girls had been reduced by half over 30 years, a clear indication that gender differences are at least partially socially induced. Over the past few years in the UK, girls have generally outperformed boys in national math exams (and in many other subjects) at age 16 and 18. This trend for girls to outperform boys in math in high school is also now occurring in the USA.

Research on gender differences in the brain has demonstrated some subtle differences between male and female brains. However, many of the results are equivocal and there is little agreement as to what the differences mean. Even less is known about the timing of the development of any neurological gender dif-

ferences. One of the most consistent findings is that male brains are more voluminous in the *temporal lobes*, including the *amygdala* and *hippocampus*. This has
recently been replicated in a large study carried out by Tina Good and colleagues
in London investigating structural brain differences between the sexes. Good and
colleagues also found that the *anterior cingulate cortex* is more voluminous in
women. The *orbitofrontal cortex* has also been reported to be larger in women
than men in a recent study by Ruben Gur and colleagues in Philadelphia. Both
the anterior cingulate and orbitofrontal cortex have strong involvement in emotional processing in social and nonsocial contexts. Their increased size in women
compared with men may reflect the sex differences in emotion processing. For
example, women tend to outperform men on tests of emotional perception and
emotional sensitivity.

The idea that female and male brains have evolved to take on different roles
has been expanded recently by Simon Baron-Cohen from Cambridge University,
who argues that men have a tendency to analyze and construct systems while
women are inclined to empathize. Baron-Cohen suggests these sex differences
arise more from biological than cultural causes. The important point to remember, though, is that although many men have a typically "male" brain, and many
women have the typically "female" brain, there is much overlap between the two
genders.

In terms of brain activation differences between male and female brains, a
fairly consistent finding is that the left *planum temporale* (a language area) is more
highly activated during language tasks in men than in women. Although still controversial, one possibility is that men's brains are more *lateralized* (or asymmetrical) than women's brains, which use both hemispheres during language tasks.
This might correspond to reported sex differences in verbal tasks: several
researchers have found that women outperform men on verbal tasks. In contrast,
men seem to be better at spatial tasks than women.

These sex differences have been linked with hormonal differences. A study by
Doreen Kimura and colleagues at the University of Western Ontario investigated
spatial abilities in women during their monthly hormonal cycles. The major
finding was that women's spatial ability was inversely related to the level of estro-
gen, the female sex hormone. A more recent study found that testosterone, the
male sex hormone, improves spatial memory and increases hippocampus size in
both male and female birds.

There are brain differences between genders, but even bigger differences
between individuals. Spatial abilities have been traditionally considered a domain
of male excellence. A number of women and some men of our acquaintance
freely confess to being poor at reading maps and not being able to remember
routes. Math involves spatial manipulation, which might explain why boys have
historically often outperformed girls on math, and girls generally do better at
languages than boys in exams.

Research on cognitive and brain differences between the sexes suggests that there is a grain of truth in the well-known gender stereotypes. If confirmed, this might have repercussions in the teaching of skills that involve spatial or verbal skills, for example math and languages, respectively. Of course we are not talking about average levels of ability here but extreme ends of high and low ability, regardless of gender, even if the proportion of boys and girls in these extremes may differ. One strategy might be to develop computer software that bypasses the need for skills in individuals who lack them. This would be much like glasses for nearsightedness.

Dyscalculia

Quite different from gender differences is the observation that some people are really very poor at numbers indeed. They can be male or female and it is at present not known how frequent such cases are. The distinctive feature about the cases is that numeracy fails to develop despite excellent teaching and rich environmental input. Brian Butterworth at the University of London has studied such cases and found that they can run in families. Affected members may not be able to estimate which of two numbers, 26 and 31, is bigger. They also cannot tell at a glance whether two or five matches have fallen out of a box.

One must suspect that a subtle brain anomaly is behind such a specific and persistent problem, and this problem is often referred to as *developmental dyscalculia*. Of course, severe and persistent difficulty with math need not be due to neurological problems but can occur for other reasons, including anxiety. Whatever the cause, education strategies informed by psychological and brain studies of number processing could help in circumventing or rehabilitating the deficits. These strategies would be different if the causes are different, and this is why it is important to look for causes.

In children with *dyscalculia* the ability to acquire arithmetic skills is moderately to severely impaired. These children can have difficulty understanding even very simple mathematical problems both at school and in other contexts, such as when calculating the cost of items in shops, counting change, or working out how long a number of activities will take. Children with dyscalculia describe math and calculation as a different language that they do not know. Math and the concept of number is as incomprehensible to a dyscalculic child as Chinese is to someone who has never learned the Chinese language. Not surprisingly, dyscalculic children often become very frustrated and anxious in math lessons and elsewhere when any kind of calculation is required. Their mathematical impairments are especially frustrating because these children are often motivated and have average, or even high, intelligence. Dyscalculia sometimes occurs in children with dyslexia. It is unknown why or how these two disorders are sometimes linked.

Developmental dyscalculia can arise for several reasons. Clearly, the brain is *hardwired* to calculate—newborn babies have basic numerical abilities. Young babies can distinguish between small numbers of objects and even seem to be able to do basic math. They know that one doll plus another doll equals two, and not three or four, dolls. There seems to be an innate understanding of the number concept. One of the most prevailing hypotheses to account for dyscalculia put forward independently by two of the world's experts in mathematical ability and the brain, Stanislas Dehaene in Paris and Brian Butterworth in London, is a lack of this innate number sense.

This might be because one of the principal start-up mechanisms for fast learning of quantity and number is missing. This sort of mechanism is often called a *module*. The module may fail to develop properly because of early brain damage or genetic disorganization of the underlying neural circuitry. In the adult brain, studies of brain-damaged patients and brain-imaging experiments have indicated that the left and right parietal cortex, which is involved in visuospatial processing, is associated with knowledge of quantities and their relations. Parietal lobe lesions in adults, caused by stroke or brain damage, can lead to dyscalculia. Some children seem to suffer from an early deficit of the parietal lobe quantity representation and therefore lack an intuition of quantity. Alternatively, or in addition to this possible parietal lobe deficit, the connections between quantity and exact number concepts may fail to develop properly. For instance, a child may learn the subtraction algorithm by rote, yet fail to connect it to his or her intuitions of quantity, resulting in large errors.

Teaching dyscalculic children mathematics

Whether dyscalculia is caused by damage to a particular brain region or failure of development of connections between components of the brain's mathematical system, education strategies need to be informed by psychological and neuroscience studies of number processing. In cases where a neurological fault exists, it would be obviously wrong to assume a simple problem of motivation. Here strategies are needed to circumvent the missing skill.

Our assumption is that a failing start-up mechanism for fast learning does not prevent slow learning. And, indeed, it is here that remedial teaching can contribute greatly. The principle is teaching by patient and slow repetition of foundational elements that are normally taken for granted, and by providing explicit rules. This involves major effort and is not the same as installing the missing intuitive and implicit rules. But it is something highly practical. In the end the dyscalculic individual will be able to perform and check basic operations.

Further brain-imaging studies are needed to show just what compensatory processes are used by individuals who have made good progress. Such knowledge could inform the design of better teaching programs. Speculatively, we assume that general intellectual resources are needed for good compensation. Not every child has enough of these and it is not fair to ask for extra effort to be made continuously. We shall mention the costs of compensation whenever we talk about developmental disorders. There is an alternative: full support by outside means. In the case of dyscalculia, we have electronic calculators already, and there may be other devices that help with guesstimates. Brain science can become an ally of those designing and testing future programs. These may have long-term effects on brain reorganization, just as much as conventional education is bound to have.

Chapter 5

the literate brain

The consequences of literacy for our social, political, and economic lives are enormous. To be deprived of the written word would be an intolerable restriction for most of us, and yet being able to read and write is an artificially taught skill. Being able to read and write for those who are literate is as natural as speaking and listening. In this chapter, we will describe recent brain research on literacy, and show that literacy has profound consequences for the shaping of the human brain. In the next chapter, we will consider the burden of being dyslexic in a literate society.

A brief history of writing

Many people hold the invention of writing to be one of the greatest cultural inventions in the history of humankind. Writing started in Sumer, part of Mesopotamia (present-day Iraq), and independently in China, about 5,000 years ago. Its spread throughout all cultures has been rapid, and its spread to individuals has accelerated recently so that universal literacy as a basic human right can be contemplated. The course of the history of writing has not been smooth, and there are different ways of representing language in visible form. Some very ancient examples of writing are pictorial, and the most ancient examples, found in Mesopotamia, were clay models. So if you were trading six sheep with a business partner in another town, you could send an intermediary. He would carry, along with the sheep, a sealed mold which contained six small clay sheep. This method ingeniously allowed both a record of what was transacted and also guarded against dishonesty.

It can readily be imagined that this method could be simplified by reducing clay shapes to simple scratches in clay. These scratches would harden and could represent all sorts of objects and events that could be read a long distance away

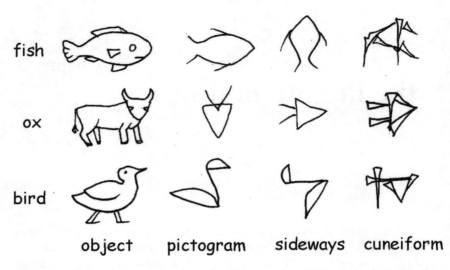

fish

ox

bird

object   pictogram   sideways   cuneiform

Figure 5.1 The most ancient examples of writing were clay models of objects or animals. These were simplified to scratches in clay. First the exact object was drawn, then more stylized representations of the object were used.

from where they originated, and what is more, a long time apart. In this way, writing hugely enhanced the ability to transmit knowledge across generations.

Before writing, spoken language existed for tens of thousands of years. Speech, even if well phrased and strong in emotional impact, does not leave a permanent record. Writing does. Speech depends on memory and, while it can be transmitted in song and in epic form, it remains a transient mode of communication. When laws were formulated it was useful to cut them into stone. Thus one of the earliest codes of law, the famous code of the Babylonian King Hammurabi (eighteenth century BC), is written in cuneiform writing on hard granite and can be seen today in the Louvre in Paris. The code was respected as a rule book to define criminal offenses and set limits to their punishment. An example is translated as follows: "If any one be too lazy to keep his dam in proper condition, and does not so keep it; if then the dam break and all the fields be flooded, then shall he in whose dam the break occurred be sold for money, and the money shall replace the [grain] which he has caused to be ruined." This was a permanent record for everyone to see as a warning and to refer to if necessary.

However, writing does not convey precisely the same things that speech conveys. It is a code that transmits only certain aspects of language and not others. For instance, written language does not convey the melody or prosody of spoken sentences. Usually it does not convey the stress patterns of words: we have to guess whether to say pro*ject* or *pro*ject and use information from context.

Figure 5.2 Herodes Atticus, a wealthy patron of the arts in ancient Greece, hired 24 slaves, each given the name of a letter, to help his son learn the alphabet.

Old Egyptian hieroglyphics and Chinese, for instance, primarily map abstract signs and rudimentary pictures onto language meaning. Other languages have developed writing systems that primarily map visible signs onto the sounds of speech. Here, two very different paths have been taken. Several Indian languages use a syllabary: each syllable that exists in the language has a recognizable symbol. For example, you have individual symbols for ki, ka, ke, ku; bi, ba, be, bu, and so on. This works when the total set of syllables is relatively small, that is, no more than a hundred or so.

As the examples ki, ka, ke, ku and bi, ba, be, bu show, the syllable is capable of being segmented into smaller constituent sounds: consonants and vowels. You can do with far fewer different symbols, say about 20 to 30, to represent as many syllables as you want. Furthermore, you can use these symbols to write down any word from any language, by ear, even if they don't contain the syllables you are used to. You are using tiny speech fragments, *phonemes*, instead. The first big invention of the alphabet was to introduce symbols for consonants, and this is credited to the Phoenicians on the Mediterranean coast. These people had knowledge of Egyptian hieroglyphics but refashioned them to represent the most important speech sounds in their own language.

The Greeks must be credited with the second big invention of the alphabet, the introduction of graphic signs for vowels. This only slightly increased the set of letters in the alphabet and happened around 500 BC. From then on the alphabet has been adopted by more and more languages while the number of letters has hardly had to be increased. The Romans decreased the number of letters, and the order they used to recite the alphabet is the order we still use today.

The very beginnings of schooling from Greek and Roman times involved learning the alphabet. In around 150 AD, a fabulously wealthy patron of the arts, Herodes Atticus, who built a theater in Athens that can still be seen today, had a son who had trouble learning the alphabet. This son was considered a good-for-nothing with very poor memory. The father hired 24 slaves for his son, each being given the name of a letter. Presumably, the young Atticus eventually learned their names and at the same time, he learned the alphabet. A major step in his education was thus achieved. Atticus may well have been the first dyslexic recorded in history.

The legacy of the alphabet

Learning the alphabet is still the basis of literacy. Even Chinese children are now generally taught the Roman alphabet, as a getting started exercise before the arduous task of gradually learning thousands of symbols. These symbols each have a rich history and represent a mixture of different aspects of language. They are not the same as "words" in the Western sense, but elements of meaning. These elements usually need to be put together in compounds to serve as words. These words allow rich interpretation including historical allusion and puns with other words. Chinese poetry is renowned for containing many layers of meaning, while being highly economical in its written form.

Japanese children have to learn three different writing systems: the Chinese logographic system, referred to as Kanji; the Japanese syllabary, referred to as Kana; and in later school years, the alphabet, referred to as Romaji. Anything less would be considered uncultured! In fact, it would make them not fully literate, as they need to use all systems to understand different literary genres and names of people and places. Given the ease of translating the alphabet into type via a keyboard, many Japanese and Chinese speakers use an alphabetic version of their language by preference.

Even though the alphabetic writing system had such a triumphal history, it is not necessarily the simplest system to learn. Learning to use the alphabet is not equally easy for everybody. The small minority who experience serious difficulty while learning to read and write suffer from dyslexia. They never quite achieve the same degree of effortless reading and writing as the majority of people. Perhaps they would be better off if they could use a writing system that is based on a syllabary. Possibly so, because the intuition of what a syllable is comes easily to almost everybody.

Writing is generally simpler in alphabetic systems since the number of symbols is small, and fortunately, only a few letters are confusing. There are the infamous mirror-reversible letters, b, d and p, q. Almost all children have problems learning and remembering which is which, but get there eventually. The letters are confusing because the brain is used to operating in a three-dimensional world, and operating in the two-dimensional world on paper is a novelty. Think three-dimensionally, and imagine b, d, p, q as solid objects: They are one and the same object rotated in space. Thus, the brain of the young child, when first coming across such shapes, gets into a conflict—a recipe for confusion.

The origin of the letter shapes that we use today goes back to the earliest beginnings of writing when Phoenician and Greek scribes borrowed and modified shapes from Egyptian hieroglyphics. Remarkably little has changed in the shape of letters since the Romans cast them into the form that is particularly suited to stone inscriptions. Many still consider this form as the most beautiful, and the font known as Times New Roman may well be the most widely used in current word processing.

Visible language in the brain

Visible language creates a new world of objects, symbols, or letters, which have a lawful relationship to the sound of speech. The mappings between symbols and speech have to be learned, and this learning has a lasting impact on the brain. Thus the brain of the literate person is different from that of the illiterate. Literate people just need to look at print to know what it says. In fact, they decode it automatically, even if they have no intention of reading it. The demonstration that reading is automatic and involuntary is given in the following famous example. The Stroop paradigm was named after a Dutch psychologist who lived in the first half of the twentieth century. He presented people with a list of words written in different colors and asked them to name the color of ink that the words were written in. He measured how long it took them to name the color of the ink for each word. The trick was that sometimes the word was a color name that was different from the color ink it was written in (for example, the word "BLUE" might be written in red ink). When the color of the ink was different from the color the word named, people were slower than if there was no such mismatch. This is because before you name the color of the ink you involuntarily read the word, and the meaning comes to mind unbidden. Once you have learned to read, you cannot help but read words.

In general, it is much faster to read a word than to name a picture. Many people find this astonishing, since as children they were naming pictures well before they were able to read words. Once you can recognize print, the world never looks the same again. When print is in front of your eyes, you are compelled to read it. So is learning to read a kind of "brainwashing"?

Comparing literate and illiterate people

If literacy is a kind of brainwashing, then it would follow that the literate and the illiterate brain are organized differently, and this might have consequences for all sorts of things. For instance, literacy may have consequences for how speech is processed, even when it is only heard. However, comparing literate and illiterate people is not easy in places where schooling is not only universal, but compulsory.

Psychologists in Portugal realized that they had the opportunity to study people who are illiterate for historical and sociopolitical reasons. In Portugal, schooling did not become compulsory until the middle of the twentieth century. In remote rural areas in particular, children did not go to school and might even have thought of school as some kind of evil torture that they were glad to escape.

Researchers Luz Cary, José Morais, and their colleagues identified people who were illiterate and had remained illiterate all their working lives. They also identified people who had somehow been able to take advantage of opportunities offered later in life to acquire a moderate amount of reading and writing knowledge. These moderately literate people had remained in the same rural places, doing the same, usually agricultural, jobs. This meant that a fair and stringent comparison between these two groups could be made, a comparison that is truly about the effect of literacy on the brain, and not about the effect of schooling during childhood.

Cary, Morais, and colleagues conducted a number of psychological experiments with these two unusual groups of people. These experiments used spoken language, and sometimes pictures, and they showed a number of surprising differences. The consequences of literacy were particularly strong when it was necessary to break up the sounds of speech, that is, to manipulate *phonemes*. For instance, "what is 'told' without the 't'?" The answer "old" was easy for the literate, but not for the illiterate individuals. This work showed for the first time that the idea of breaking up words into smaller sounds becomes meaningful if one can think of these sounds as letters. After all, it is these phonemes that map directly onto letters.

Think of two groups of children each playing with a toy village. One group has ready-made wooden houses while the other has houses constructed out of Lego bricks. Those who have the Lego brick houses will consider the town as infinitely modifiable, whereas the children with the wooden houses will think of their houses as fixed and whole. For them, the concept of being able to remove pieces from each house and to change the shape of the houses makes no sense.

Brainwashing through literacy is real. Once you have got hold of the principle of the alphabet, your whole perception of speech changes. You are aware that the sounds of words can be broken up and put together again.

Another effect of the alphabetic principle was seen in a study by Alexandre Castro-Caldas and colleagues where again literate and illiterate individuals took part. They were asked to repeat back real words and made-up nonsense words. Everyone could repeat the real words well, and there was no difference between the literate and illiterate group. However, there was an intriguing difference when they repeated nonsense words. The illiterate people tended to turn these into real words. So, for "banona," which does not mean anything, they might say "banana," which has a meaning. Why did they not simply repeat the nonsense words, like the literate group? The literate group were not fazed by nonsense words, because they were already familiar with such entities. After all, the names of the letters are nonsense words, for instance, "eff" and "aitch." Moreover, once you know the alphabetic principle, you have a recipe for making up words that do not exist. When you do not know this principle, made-up words can only be thought of as existing, but unknown, words.

How different is the literate brain?

These same individuals, then in their sixties, were flown from their rural home in Portugal to the Karolinska Institute in Stockholm to have their brains scanned by Martin Ingvar and colleagues.

When repeating nonwords, the illiterate volunteers activated more strongly the *frontal lobes*, the all-purpose problem-solving areas of the brain, and in particular, those regions that are known to be involved in the retrieval of memories. The literate volunteers activated more strongly the left *temporal lobe*, the area of the brain specifically engaged in language processing. This was expected, because the illiterate people treated the nonsense words like real words, which they had misheard or which they did not know. Hence, they sometimes turned them into real words, and generally searched for such words in their memory. The literate people treated the nonwords, quite nonchalantly, as possible but not real words. There was no need to search their memory or consider turning them into real words.

This unique experiment gave a first direct demonstration of the changes in the brain that are due to literacy. It showed that the literate brain reacts differently even when only listening to speech.

To reiterate, speech sound is a key factor in reading. Skilled readers, who read words automatically, often have the experience that the sound of the word springs to mind unbidden. You might think that reading silently is a purely visual task, but this is not the case. The processes the brain uses when reading silently are remarkably similar to the processes used when reading aloud.

Does the brain's reading system depend on the language of the reader?

It is not merely the case that becoming literate changes the brain. The specialized demands of particular languages, such as English, Italian, or French, make specific demands on writing. Even though all these languages use the same alphabet, they have historically developed quite different writing systems.

Theoretically, the alphabet guarantees that you can immediately pronounce a word that is written in another language, but in practice, the writing system of each language involves extra rules for pronunciation. Some writing systems have more complex rules than others. Compare Italian to English, for instance. Italian has a very transparent and regular orthography: what you see is what you say. Sound out letters bit by bit, and the whole word will come out more or less as it should sound: Napoli, Milano, tortellini. In English, by contrast, the correspondence between words and sounds is far from simple and it would be foolish to rely on sounding out letters bit by bit. Where would that get us with " biscuit," "yacht" and "Leicester"? Even worse, the same letter combinations can have very different pronunciations in English. The word "wind," for instance, sounds differently in "The wind was blowing a gale," and "We need to wind up the clock."

With English you have to build up a store of word sounds linked to their precise spelling patterns, or you are lost. What difference does this make to the brain? Remember that even when you read silently, the visual form of the word cannot be divorced from its sound. Some people remember spellings by sounding out what they see—as if it were Italian. For instance, if they see the written word "parliament," they actually hear in their head "par-li-a-ment." Many people, even those who are excellent spellers and don't need to use this particular trick, nevertheless, smile at rhymes of words that are not spelled the same way. For instance:

> *There was an old woman of Gloucester,*
> *Whose parrot two guineas it cost her. (anon.)*

The reading system of the brain and its fine-tuning

To study the brain's adaptation to these differences in spelling rules, a European collaborative study was carried out by researchers Eraldo Paulesu in Milan, Jean-François Demonet in Toulouse, and Uta Frith in London. As a first stage, they scanned skilled readers of English and of Italian while reading simple words either aloud or silently. This revealed that the regions that make up the reading system of the brain are exactly the same for Italian and English readers. This system, which has also been demonstrated in studies by other research groups with speakers of English, occupies large areas of the left hemisphere of the brain, the side dedicated to language and speech. This common system is shown in Figure 5.3. The system can be divided into three connected parts, one at the front in the *frontal lobes*, one in the middle in the *parietotemporal cortex*, and one at the back in the *temporal lobes*.

We will come back to these different regions in the next subsection. Figure 5.3 shows the subtle differences found between Italian and English readers. Although the three regions activated were the same, the relative weight given to them during reading was different. The second picture shows the area that was more active for Italian readers. The third picture shows the area that was relatively more active for the English readers. The reading system is fine-tuned to the particular demands of the writing system in question.

In a subsequent study, French-speaking readers were scanned under identical conditions. They activated exactly the same system as the other two language groups, but as far as the fine-tuning was concerned, they sided with the English readers. French, after all, has a rather complex writing system, more akin to English than to Italian. This is especially noticed when trying to spell from dictation. For instance, the sound for *c'est* and *ces* and for *mais* and *mes* is exactly the same.

What do the three regions of the reading system do?

A surprising amount is known about the brain's reading system. Over the past 150 years, many patients who suffered brain damage in the left half of the brain, usually as a result of stroke, have been observed. Some of these patients lost their ability to speak; others lost only their ability to read and to write. This knowledge helps us to piece together the function and purpose of the three regions of the reading system. It allows us to understand why these areas, rather than others, have been recruited by the brain for the culturally acquired task of literacy.

The most frontal region is named *Broca's area* in honor of Paul Broca, a French pioneer in neurology. He reported the historically groundbreaking case of "Tan,"

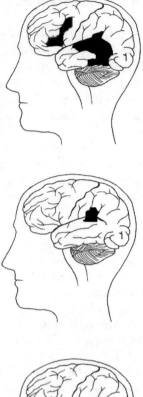

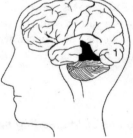

Figure 5.3 The brain's reading system in English and Italian. The top figure shows the whole reading system for both languages combined. The middle figure shows the region associated with sound–letter translation being more active in the Italian readers. The lower figure shows the word form area at the back being more active in English readers.

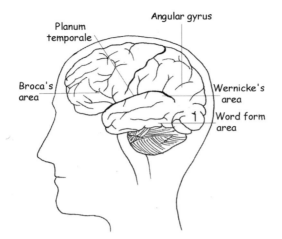

Planum
temporale

Angular gyrus

Broca's
area

Wernicke's
area

Word form
area

Figure 5.4   The brain's reading system comprises several different areas. *Broca's area* in the frontal lobe is involved in the production of spoken language. *Wernicke's area* is in the temporal lobe and is involved in the decoding of language. The *angular gyrus* is in the parietal lobe and has many functions, amongst which is the association of spoken and seen words. The *visual word form area* lies at the base of the left temporal lobe and is involved in processing the spelling, sound, and meaning of words.

a man who, after a stroke, could only utter the word "tan" and had otherwise lost his speech completely. Although there are individual differences that make the exact boundaries of Broca's area uncertain, there is full agreement that speech depends on this part of the frontal lobe. In the European study described above, Broca's area was activated both when volunteers read words out aloud and when they read silently. It is as if the brain is prepared to utter the words at a moment's notice.

The middle region of the reading system includes *Wernicke's area* and the *angular gyrus*. The nineteenth-century German neurologist Carl Wernicke was interested in language and its basis in the brain, and found patients who could speak but could not understand language. The area that is damaged in these patients, which lies along the *planum temporale* of the left hemisphere, is known as *Wernicke's area*. The *planum temporale* was of special interest to the American neurologist Norman Geschwind, who in the 1960s noticed that it was bigger on the left than the right in most brains he had the opportunity to study. Numerous studies of patients showed that when this region was damaged, the patient could no longer name letters or translate a written word into speech. This area seems preeminently important for learning the alphabetic code. The *angular gyrus*, in the parietal lobe, lies halfway between Wernicke's area and the visual

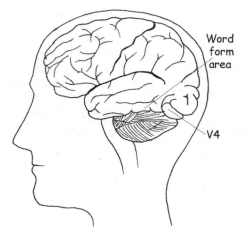

Figure 5.5 The *word form area*, which is involved in processing the spelling, sound, and meaning of words, lies adjacent to V4, the visual area responsible for processing color.

cortex. It has many functions amongst which is the association of spoken and seen words.

What about the third area, at the base of the left temporal lobe? Wernicke also had patients with damage at the *base* of the left temporal lobe, and these patients had great difficulties spelling and recognizing whole words. They could, nevertheless, still sound out words from their letters. He suggested that this region might control access to a thesaurus, where the spelling, sound, and meaning of each word is stored. Neuroscientist Stanislas Dehaene and his colleague Laurent Cohen in Paris confirmed that the area at the base of the left temporal lobe is indeed concerned with whole words. They call it a *visual word form area*. Cathy Price and colleagues in London have found that this region is also active when people name pictures or sounds, such as "doorbell" or "foghorn."

The fine-tuned reading system

We have seen that the reading system can be divided into three parts and each part has a distinctive role. The frontal part of the reading system, Broca's area, is the brain's basic speech production system. The middle part, Wernicke's area and the angular gyrus, is active during the translation of letters and sounds. The area at the back, the word form area, situated at the bottom of the temporal lobe, is the region involved in storage and retrieval of whole words.

Now, at last, we can explain the differences in the weighting of the different regions of the reading system of Italian, English, and French readers. We can explain this fine-tuning by the exact requirements of the English, French, and Italian writing systems, respectively. In English and French, it is more important to recognize whole word forms than to translate letters to sounds. In Italian, this is less important, because the sound of the whole word is easily derived from the piecemeal translation of letters to sounds. Accordingly, Italian readers activate the translation area more than English and French readers. English and French readers activate the word form area more than Italian readers.

Nevertheless, readers of both languages use both areas, and this suggests that reading relies on more than one process. One fascinating aspect of different alphabetic writing systems is that they have not gone entirely one way or another in a twofold choice: either using the principle of always translating small units of sound to letter ("s-i-t" for "sit"), or using the principle of distinctive spellings for whole words ("cough" and not "c-o-f"). English is a good example of how both these possibilities are mixed together. It turns out that both principles are mixed in most languages, even if not in such a dramatic fashion as in English.

The remarkable automaticity of reading that has been demonstrated with the Stroop paradigm allows readers to do two things at once. They identify the whole word, but at the same time they translate the letters into sounds, piecemeal. It makes sense that one or the other process is weighted a little more heavily according to which writing system is used. Therefore, when learning to read English or French, more work is done by the region responsible for whole word recognition. When learning to read Italian, more work is done by the region that is responsible for letter–sound translation.

Is the reading system an add-on to the speech system?

What is more important, the sound elements of the word, or the sound of the whole word? The skilled reader has a simple answer to this question: obviously both are important. The illiterate person, on the other hand, will go for the whole word sound and may not even know what is meant by sound elements of a word.

The alphabet makes readers aware of something of which they are otherwise unaware: the possibility of cutting up words into tiny sounds. We have already compared this to Lego bricks used in a toy village. We have seen how this allows the combination of sounds without meaning, consonants (b, m) or consonant clusters (sp, str) and vowels (a, o), beginnings of syllables and ends of syllables (str-ing, str-and, h-ing, h-and), and so on. This results in a huge explosion of combinatorial possibilities. In principle, you can write down any made-up word that you can think of.

The same combinatorial explosion underlies speech itself. Unlike in the case of written language, the brain has had millions of years to evolve speech. The processes are deeply embedded and we are entirely unaware of them. The alphabetic system that has come to be the predominant writing system in the world's languages is parasitic on the ancient human speech system. But to master it, we need to become aware of the combinatorial process. As we shall see in the next chapter, this is not equally easy for all readers.

Mixing colors and words

The automatic integration of sound and sight is seen not only in reading, but also in a particularly fascinating "condition" called *synesthesia*. People who are synesthetes mix different sensations. It is not really a condition because it happens to people who have no brain abnormality. One person tastes a bitter taste whenever he hears a doorbell. Another can smell strawberries whenever she touches cotton clothing. The most common form of synesthesia involves associating a color with a particular letter or word. Most people with this form of synesthesia associate every letter and every word with a particular color. One synesthetic friend always "sees" the color pink when she hears the letter L or any word beginning with an L, whereas Qs are associated with green for her.

Until recently it was believed that synesthesia is very rare, but more recent estimates suggest that as many as 4 or 5 percent of the population may have some kind of synesthetic experience.

No one knows what causes synesthesia but there are several explanations. One explanation is that the combination of senses is a consequence of childhood associations. In the case of color–word synesthesia, perhaps these people are remembering the colors of the alphabet letters hanging on their walls or the magnetic letters on their fridge from when they were young. But this does not explain why synesthetic people claim really to "see" (not just think of) colors when they read letters.

An alternative idea is that synesthesia is caused by overactive connections between the region of the brain that processes colors, called V4 (visual area 4), and the area of the brain that stores words (the word form area). These two areas lie very close to each other at the back of the brain and it is possible that signals are passed from one region to the other.

Synesthesia is a phenomenon that tells us how rich our experience of written language is. It also gives us a glimpse of the amazing facility of the brain to combine different experiences, and in particular to mix sight and sound. The visual form of the written word immediately evokes the sound of the word, at least in normal readers. We take this for granted, but perhaps it is just as amazing as the ability of synesthetes to evoke a color every time they hear a word.

Chapter 6

learning to read and its difficulties

How does the brain change when you learn to read and write? Why do some children have such difficulties learning to read? These are the questions we will turn to in this chapter. Brain research designed to answer these questions is still at an early stage. One reason is that the scanning techniques have not yet been well adapted for children, because children find it hard to remain absolutely still in the scanner. Even tiny movements make the scanned picture difficult to interpret. Thus the main findings so far have come from adult volunteers. This is true for skilled readers as well as for readers who suffer from dyslexia.

Learning to become musically literate

No study exists as yet in which the same individual has been scanned before and after learning to read. However, Lauren Stewart at University College London has scanned adults before and after they learned to read music.

Music has been written down since the invention of a notational system by Guido d'Arezzo early in the eleventh century. As a result, it was possible for people to perform music they had never heard before. Thus music could be transmitted over time, and this allowed musicians to perform the same original composition in different places. The effects of music notation on cultural transmission are similar to those of written language. The spread of notation has been rapid and universal. However, unlike with literacy, only a small proportion of the population is taught to read music. The adult volunteers in the following experiment could not read music but were eager to learn.

Stewart scanned adult volunteers using *fMRI* techniques before and after she taught them to play the piano and read music. Because she wanted to make sure that simply doing the same task twice did not confound the effects of teaching, she also included a control group who could not read music and were not taught and were scanned at the same times. After three months, 15 volunteers had

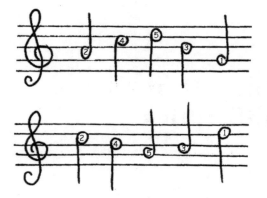

Figure 6.1   A cartoon of the stimuli used in Lauren Stewart's musical Stroop experiment. The notes indicate keys on the keyboard, the numbers indicate which fingers should be used. In the upper line, notes and finger numbers are congruent, while in the lower line they are incongruent. Participants were asked to ignore the musical notation and use the finger notation. Musicians showed interference from the musical notation. Source: adapted from figures 1 and 4 from Stewart et al. *NeuroImage* 20 (2003); 71–83. Copyright © 2003 by Elsevier Science. By permission of the authors and Elsevier Science.

reached the equivalent of a Grade 1, as defined by the British Associated Board of the Royal Schools of Music.

Stewart demonstrated that they could now read music automatically by using a Stroop paradigm, which you may remember from Chapter 5. Here, numbers indicating fingers (1 = thumb, 2 = index finger, and so on) were superimposed on real notes. The students were told to ignore the notes and play a keyboard simply by using the numbers with the appropriate fingers. Sometimes the numbers ran counter to the notes: for instance, when the note sequence went up, the numbers went down. In this case, the task was more difficult; the notes interfered even though the volunteers were instructed to ignore them. Just as in the case of literate people, who can't help reading a printed word, so the now musically literate people could not help but read the musical notes on the stave. This interfered with their ability to follow the superimposed number sequence.

Changes in the brain after learning to read music

Thus Stewart's teaching had achieved its aim to instill knowledge of music notation, knowledge that sprang to mind automatically when notation was present. How was this reflected in the brain?

One tiny area in the parietal lobe of the brain, shown in Figure 6.2, had now become a hot spot. The same region remained inactive in people who had not

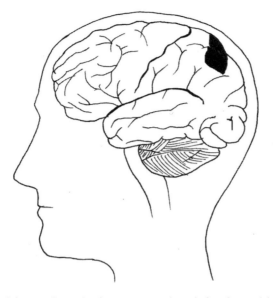

Figure 6.2 The right superior parietal cortex was activated after the participants learned to read and play music.

been taught. Why the parietal lobe? This area specializes in locating objects in space and time and is also implicated in math, in particular, representing magnitude (see Chapter 4). The newly acquired skill of music reading must have taken advantage of this preexisting specialization.

The next question was how to capture changes in the brain that occurred as a result of being taught to read music. Stewart had given this question a lot of thought. Did the experiment just described actually capture the critical changes? Perhaps all we saw before training was brain activity associated with doing an impossible task (trying to sight-read) and, after training, brain activity associated with doing a task successfully. But we want more than comparing a blind attempt with an informed attempt. We are interested in the brain area that has become active because of the training, not because of the change in task.

To nail this difficult problem, Stewart used an ingenious paradigm that worked by stealth and that had been introduced previously by researchers who wanted to make the reading system of the brain visible. Stewart showed the students musical notation both before and after training, but on neither occasion did this actually relate to the task they had to do. The volunteers had no difficulty performing the task, which was to search for a protruding line in a grid, even before musical training. The ingenious part of the task was that, on half the occasions, the protruding line was superimposed on a graphic pattern that looked

Figure 6.3 A cartoon of the implicit music reading task used in Lauren Stewart's fMRI study. Participants had to indicate whether a single line was protruding from a grid. In the upper row the stimuli are real musical notes, while in the lower row they are not although looking very similar. For non-musicians, these two types of stimuli make no difference. Their brain activation was the same. After training, the budding keyboard players could not ignore the musical stimuli even though this did not help the task they were given. Their brain activation before and after training shows a change in a particular brain region. Source: adapted from figures 1 and 4 from Stewart et al. *NeuroImage* 2003; 20: 71–83. Copyright © 2003 by Elsevier Science. By permission of the authors and Elsevier Science.

superficially like musical notation, but was in fact meaningless. This is shown in Figure. 6.3.

Would the brain register a difference? Before training there was no difference in brain activation with the two types of material. However, after training, a change was seen in the same area of the parietal cortex that was active in the study already described. We need not have worried: the activation of the parietal cortex was indeed due to training and not to change of task.

However, this stealth experiment revealed one additional hot spot in the parietal lobe that was strongly activated after training. This area is known to be highly active when you are getting ready to make a complex motor response. So it seems that the students in Stewart's experiment were actually preparing to play the notes. They were not aware of this, just as they were not aware of translating one spatial code into another: vertical position on the stave to horizontal position on the keyboard. The notes that they saw had set in motion a whole string of neural events, unwittingly and we might say unnecessarily, given that the task was simply to find protruding lines. Just as in the Stroop experiment, musical notes had acquired a significance that could not be suppressed. The meaning they had was strongly manifested in a readiness to play them on the keyboard.

Learning to read words

No study exists as yet where the same children are scanned repeatedly as they learn to read. However, Guinevere Eden and her team at Georgetown University in Washington, DC carried out an fMRI study of readers of different ages (from 6 to 22) and different levels of reading skill. Just as in Stewart's study, the participants were asked to detect randomly placed protruding lines, which were overlaid on two different stimulus materials. These were either simple words or strings of squiggles that looked rather like letters. Remember that once you have learned to read, you can't help but read words that are in front of you, even if you are not asked to. Just as in the music reading experiment, by looking at the effect of automatic reading, the researchers were able to catch an indirect glimpse of the reading system.

Even among the youngest readers, reading induced neural activity in left hemisphere areas. This activity was increased in older readers and, within each age group, was greater for the more advanced readers. In contrast to this left-sided increase in activation, activity *declined* in right hemisphere areas during this same time period. The researchers concluded that the lengthy process of learning to read involves a switch in activity from right to left: left brain structures become increasingly tuned to reading-specific tasks, while the right hemisphere contributions, which may have more to do with processing visual aspects of text, become less important.

The left hemisphere regions, whose activity increased most with increasing reading skill, were right in the middle of the brain's network for reading, which we discussed in the previous chapter. This makes sense: what budding readers need to learn, and indeed have to be taught to learn, is the mapping between sounds and letters. As we saw in Chapter 5, this is the main responsibility of the regions around the *angular gyrus* and the *planum temporale* of the left temporal lobe.

Learning to read in the classroom

In recent years, many studies have been carried out on how best to teach children to read and write. There is a general consensus that methods that combine attention to spoken words and the close mapping of letters and their sounds are most efficient. As we have seen in the previous chapter, insight into letter–sound correspondence goes hand in hand with being able to read. Some children need more than one start as they may not be ready for this insight when they first enter school. Their brain may be a bit slower to develop than that of the average child, but this does not necessarily make them dyslexic. If these children are given another opportunity to learn to read at a later age, say seven years, they do fine. In some countries, the age at school entry is seven years, and this would make it

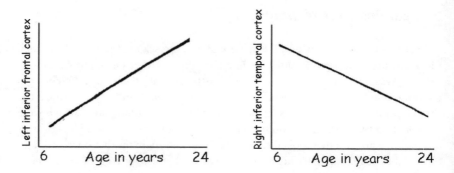

Figure 6.4   Activity in the left hemisphere increased with age during a reading task, whereas activity declined in right hemisphere areas during this same time period. Source: adapted from figure 6 from Turkeltaub et al. *Nature Neuroscience* 2003; 6(7): 767–73. Copyright © 2003 by Nature Publishing Group. By permission of the authors and Nature Publishing Group.

easier for the slower developing children to learn to read. In complete contrast, there are those who advocate that waiting is not the best option and that children of kindergarten age should be trained in phonological skills and letter knowledge in readiness for entering school. We cannot say which of these options is better, and for whom.

When children are older, say seven to nine years, it is easier to teach them explicit spelling rules. There have been periods in the past where such explicit teaching and learning was frowned upon, as good readers and spellers are typically unaware of the rules. However, some children, who have less intuitive access to the sound of speech and its mapping to letters and are less attuned to the regularities of the spelling system, benefit from explicit rule teaching. Significant improvements in spelling and reading have been shown in these cases, but not necessarily an improvement in the experience of emotional stress. There is always the worry that even when children know the rules and can recite them when requested, they will not actually apply them.

Dyslexia

Some children find reading difficult even after effort and training. Dyslexic children have severe difficulties in learning to read, while they can be bright and very capable in other respects. Dyslexia is surprisingly common, affecting an estimated 5 percent of the population, and runs in families. We now know that these problems have a genetic origin and a basis in the brain. But how can reading be part of our genetic make-up?

In the previous chapter we argued that written language learning subplot of the development of spoken language. It is plausible, therefo dyslexia the primary stumbling block to learning to read and write is 1 speech. Many dyslexic children indeed also have some problems in s, guage and verbal memory. For instance, they have problems in repeating and remembering novel words but have no problems in understanding the meaning of words.

Many teachers and researchers feel that narrowing down the problems of dyslexic children to speech is oversimplifying the issue. These children very often have attention deficits, some have visual problems and confuse letter shapes, and others have hearing problems. Many have motor coordination problems and actually find it hard to grip a pencil in the proper way and draw neat lines. Are all these problems connected and are they, in fact, the ultimate causes of the difficulties in learning to read?

Recent studies by Franck Ramus, Uta Frith, and colleagues at the University of London have investigated this question, and the answer is a surprisingly clear "No." These studies confirmed that a proportion (varying between 10 and 60 percent depending on the sample tested) of dyslexic children have additional visual, hearing, or movement difficulties. Interestingly, so did some nondyslexic children and many dyslexic children had no such problems. Moreover, when the reading skill of the dyslexic children with the additional sensory and motor problems was compared with the reading skill of the children without such problems, there was no difference. Thus, frustrating as the additional problems are, they are simply additional to dyslexia and do not cause the reading difficulties.

Ramus's studies also showed that almost all the dyslexics, whether children or adults, had speech-processing difficulties, but hardly any nondyslexics had these difficulties. The group of dyslexic adults that he tested had learned to read as accurately as the average population, but they were still slow readers and way behind with tasks that challenged them to manipulate speech sounds.

Supported by effective teaching, children can make great strides in overcoming the reading and spelling difficulties associated with their dyslexia, when the wish to learn is strong and when a good teacher is available. However, they do not grow out of being dyslexic. Reading usually remains slow and effortful; spelling almost always remains error-prone. Verbal memory and the ability to repeat and learn novel words remain relatively poor. This is what one would expect of a developmental disorder with a basis in the brain: compensatory learning can happen, but the underlying problem does not go away.

The difficulties for each dyslexic person are different and cause a slight or severe disruption of the learning process. Each individual has his or her own pattern of strengths and weaknesses. If verbal skills are not your forte, you may be good at lateral thinking and do well in fields such as the arts, creativity, design, and computing. Common sense suggests that individual strengths need to be identified and taught to enable dyslexic people to make use of their talents.

How is dyslexia recognized?

So far, no unique biological marker for dyslexia exists. There is no blood test, or genetic test, for dyslexia. However, understanding the specific brain functions that underlie dyslexia will allow researchers to come up with better diagnostic tests for younger children. Children at genetic risk could then receive early intervention that would help them learn to read. It makes sense that early intervention, before the child becomes too anxious about reading or develops an aversion to it, is helpful. In many cases, remedial action involves gentle overcoming of such anxieties and systematic rebuilding of confidence. Good teachers tend to be good therapists in recognizing when motivation is a major issue, and have ingenious methods of making the task of learning as rewarding as possible. Nevertheless, it would be far preferable to start before negative feelings about written language have built up. This is why the "wait and see" approach is not always a good idea and why early diagnosis is highly desirable.

Dyslexia is a strongly heritable condition. If one parent has dyslexia, the child has a high probability of being dyslexic too. This probability is estimated to be between 25 and 50 percent, depending on the diagnostic criteria that are being used. The diagnosis of dyslexia is often based on a formula where someone's performance on a reading test is seen as lagging significantly behind their performance on tests of general ability and other cognitive skills.

The fact that a child can't read or spell is not a sufficient reason for diagnosing dyslexia. Because of the lack of biological tests, we are dependent on highly visible behavioral signs and symptoms and, just as in the case of autism, as we shall see in the next chapter, these are extremely varied.

One of the important lessons of brain research is that the behavior that you see on the surface can have very different causes. There are many reasons for difficulties in learning to read and write, other than a subtle abnormality in brain development. These cases need different approaches. Sometimes, transient emotional and social problems have to be resolved, which may not be easy. Sometimes, merely looking at print is an unpleasant and even punishing experience, due to visual problems. But in many cases, problems with speech processing can de demonstrated. Unfortunately, brain-imaging studies, which might elucidate the nature of the problem, are still scarce.

What precisely is the problem with speech processing?

Learning to read using an alphabet involves processing the sounds of words and learning what each sound means. This is often referred to as *phonology*. Maggie Snowling from York University in the UK was one of the first researchers to study

and identify phonological problems in dyslexic children. Children and adu
dyslexia find it difficult to process and classify language sounds. The impa
in phonology is thought to be due to a subtle abnormality in brain develc
and directly linked to poor learning of both spoken and written languag_.

Snowling found that even in preschool years, before they read and write,
dyslexic children can be picked out by their delayed speech development. She
showed that dyslexic children acquire word names more slowly than do other
children and, already at age three to four, their ability to remember words is poor.
Very often, people are ready to blame a delay in speaking or reading on lack of
stimulation, but this is not warranted here. The children studied came from
homes where they were surrounded by books and strongly encouraged to learn
to read.

First studies of the brain in dyslexia

Norman Geschwind, the neurologist who studied the causes of sudden loss of
reading and writing skills in patients who had suffered strokes, was also interested in people who had been dyslexic all their lives without having had an acci-
dent to cause brain damage. His laboratory benefited from the generosity of a
few dyslexic people who had died and donated their brain for research. In these
brains, the *planum temporale* on the left was much the same size as the same
region on the right. Normally, the left planum temporale is larger.

These first findings of anatomical differences gave a great boost to the idea
that developmental dyslexia was a brain disorder and perhaps resembled the cases
of so-called *acquired dyslexia*. This term is used to describe reading problems that
arise after brain damage in a previously perfectly normal reader. Could the
anatomical differences in these people be effects rather than causes of reading
disability? Possibly, but since these early studies, evidence has been found for
brain differences that have existed from even before birth. Geschwind's succes-
sor in Boston, neurologist Al Galaburda, found that small clusters of nerve cells
in dyslexic brains were not in the right place. During the early development of
the brain, some cells had wandered to the top layer of the cortex and were visible
as minute scars. These scars were common in the medial temporal regions, the
center of the reading system, which is also concerned with speech processing. It
is possible that these scars have some role in causing dyslexia and, in addition,
visual, auditory, and motor impairments.

Other brain abnormalities have been found in anatomical brain-imaging
studies of dyslexic people. One of the more consistent findings is that the layer
of *white matter*, which lies underneath the brain surface and contains all the
myelin-covered fibers that connect the nerves together, is thinner in the brain's
reading system in dyslexics. Perhaps there are weaker connections between the

three different regions of the reading system, rather than any specific anatomical abnormalities in the regions themselves.

The dyslexic brain during reading

A number of brain-imaging studies, carried out in the UK and the USA, have found that, during reading, dyslexics have reduced activation in the major components of the reading and speech- processing system of the left hemisphere of the brain. Perhaps the most striking demonstration comes from a study with adult dyslexics who were asked to read aloud very simple and familiar words that they could read accurately while lying in the scanner. These dyslexics were part of the large European study conducted by Eraldo Paulesu, Jean-François Demonet, and Uta Frith in Italy, France, and the UK, which we discussed in the previous chapter. This study showed, for the first time, that the underlying difficulties in phonology are the same regardless of language.

As Figure 6.5 shows, regardless of language, dyslexic readers have reduced activation in the most posterior of the three main regions of the reading system of the left hemisphere. Several other studies have found the same results. Recently, Eamon McCrory, Cathy Price and colleagues from the University of London found that this region is less active in dyslexics even when they only had to name pictures. This *word form area* is associated with the processing of form and sound of the whole word. It is the area that was identified as being particularly important in English and French, as we discussed in the previous chapter. No wonder, then, that English and French dyslexics suffer more when learning to read than Italian dyslexics. Italian dyslexics can learn to read and write accurately and may never be suspected of being dyslexic. But their difficulties are real, even if they are hidden: compared to their peers their reading is much slower, their verbal memory is poorer and they find it difficult to do tasks that challenge the ability to process speech sounds.

Teaching dyslexic people to read

There is no complete cure, but the effects of dyslexia can be greatly ameliorated with patient teaching and learning. If it is true that dyslexic children have a serious stumbling block in processing *phonemes* and relating them to their spelling, then they cannot be expected to learn just like normal children. They will inevitably need specialized teaching. If you can't learn to read normally, how is it best to learn? Is it possible that dyslexic children compensate by recruiting general abilities, such as attention and intelligence? If you can't learn the mapping from sound and words to letters the fast way, you can learn in a different, slower way.

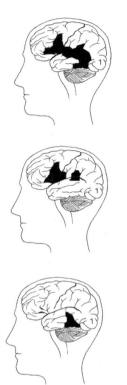

Normal reading
system

Reading system
in dyslexics

Difference between
normal readers and
dyslexics

Figure 6.5 Brain scans were conducted on volunteers from each of the UK, France, and Italy while they were reading. Three parts of the reading system of the left hemisphere are activated during normal reading—this is shown in the top image. Only two areas are activated in dyslexics—shown in the middle image. The spot where the main difference between the two groups was found is the third region of the reading system, in the temporal cortex, shown in the lower image. Dyslexics in all three languages showed the same reduction of activity in this region, which plays an important role in understanding whole words.

If so, then teaching procedures need to be slower than the normal ones and more explicit in pointing out sound–letter relationships.

Teachers have long used such methods and these have often proved successful with dyslexic readers. These methods establish connections between the internal images of letters, words, and sounds. Just learning to recite the alphabet, knowing in which order the letters come up, is a major achievement in learning. Letters and their sounds have to be repeated again and again to make sure that the code is known. After learning the alphabetic code, the work is by no means over. Another phase of learning has to happen. This is aimed at setting up an inner lexicon of written word forms. This lexicon is huge in English, because many spellings are unique and have to be remembered and learned by rote. This is a slow process for dyslexics, who find precisely this type of learning hard.

There are many excellent remedial programs and some of these have been experimentally shown to be effective. Charles Hulme, Maggie Snowling, and Peter Hatcher at York University have shown that structured intervention, where sounds are linked with letters and text reading is practiced, is highly effective. Many remedial programs emphasize piecemeal letter-to-sound mapping, similar to the method that is effective in the regular Italian orthography. However, those English words that are impossible to read by this method must be introduced with sufficient health warnings so as not to confuse the child. Computer programs have been designed to act as particularly patient teachers and to present carefully those words that could be mapped correctly when using the piecemeal method.

With successful teaching, the difficulties of dyslexics can become camouflaged. We don't usually check how long someone takes to read text when they read silently. It is not easy to measure the effort that highly skilled dyslexics have to expend while reading. In reports on the success of teaching programs we rarely hear about this aspect. We see scores that indicate improvement in the accuracy of reading—but not necessarily in the speed. As far as we are aware, no teaching program has succeeded in both increasing reading speed and decreasing reading effort. Modest improvements, of course, are expected as a result of sheer practice over the years. This is not the same as the incredibly fast and automatic access to the word lexicon that the normal reader enjoys. To create an analogy, imagine having to look up words in a dictionary by going through the alphabet, letter by letter. Now compare this to clicking on a word on the computer and instantly seeing its meaning, its sound, and its correct spelling.

Effects of remedial teaching on the dyslexic brain

Some researchers argue that it is possible to strengthen regions of the brain that are particularly concerned with the processing of speech sounds. They try to do this by repetitive but still motivating exercises that involve attentive listening to modified sounds. Paula Tallal and colleagues at Rutgers University have claimed that such exercises improve both spoken and written language processing, and have produced computer-based programs. Other researchers have produced programs for exercising visual and motor skills and they also claim that such programs are successful with dyslexics. Not everybody is convinced of these claims.

Two imaging studies have given us information about the changes in the brain after more traditional remedial teaching. One study by Sally Shaywitz and her team at the University of Yale compared three groups of young adults. One was a group of normal readers, the second was a group of dyslexics showing relatively little improvement, and the third was a group of dyslexics who showed excellent improvement. Just as in the European study, the well-compensated dyslexic readers still showed abnormal brain activity during reading: reduced activation of the so-called word form area, at the base of the left temporal lobe. The unimproved readers activated areas of the brain's memory systems more than areas of the reading system. This suggests that they use a less efficient way of recognizing words, while the reading system proper was engaged in the brains of the improved readers.

Guinevere Eden and her colleagues at Georgetown University scanned young dyslexic adults who had been randomly divided into two groups. One of the subgroups, but not the other, received an intensive training program designed to improve reading skills. This training consisted of explicitly teaching the sounds of words and word parts for three hours per day for eight weeks. The training dramatically improved the dyslexics' reading skills. All the people who received the training improved their reading skills, whereas the people in the subgroup who received no training did not. The trained subgroup even formed a book club at the end of the training period.

Moreover, the brain activity in this group reflected their improved reading skills. Intriguingly, brain scans taken after the training showed that the right parietal lobe of the trained group became active during reading. It seems that the trained group compensated for the weak performance of their left parietal lobe by using their right parietal lobe, an area that is known to integrate sights and sounds. Matching and learning word sounds and spelling involves auditory-visual integration. This integration is automatically given for normal readers through the specialized areas of the reading system in the left hemisphere, in particular the word form area that, as we have already seen, is less active in dyslexics. Eden's study suggests that dyslexics can boost integration of the sight and sound of words by recruiting another region of the brain.

These results emphasize the fact that the adult brain is capable of change and that it is worth trying to train people with dyslexia even as adults. The fact that this change is not a cure for dyslexia does not detract from the success. Reading and spelling appears to remain effortful for dyslexics, and this must not be underestimated. However, compensation comes at a cost. It would be a mistake to think that it is just a matter of time until practice establishes normal performance. Normal performance? No. Good performance? Yes!

disorders of social-emotional development

Little Andrew is having a severe temper tantrum. He refuses to button his shirt, he refuses help, and he will be late for school again. Is it a case of not being able to, or is that he simply will not button his shirt? Can we tell the difference between motor coordination problems, as in dyspraxia, and completely different issues, such as avoidance of an unpleasant task or attention seeking?

What do social and emotional problems have to do with the brain?

Let's assume that Andrew's problem is an emotional one. He can, but he won't, do up his buttons. Is his emotional problem caused by his genes or by his environment? There is no doubt that there are many entirely environmental reasons for developmental difficulties, and these reasons can usually be established during a proper systematic assessment. We do not wish to dismiss temporary difficulties that affect learning and development, but we believe that brain science has as yet little to offer their understanding.

Here we are concerned with biologically caused problems where we believe brain science has made advances. When talking about this topic, we have noticed that there is often a reluctance to acknowledge the relevance of brain science, especially when we are considering problems that are manifest in areas of social and emotional development. Perhaps there is an underlying assumption that this sort of problem should have an explanation in the social and emotional relationships of the person.

To think about complex emotions and social understanding in human beings as grounded in biology still seems a bit far-fetched. Yet brain research suggests that we need to change these preconceptions. Many brain disorders that primarily affect social-emotional understanding are now being recognized for what they are, and as conditions that can be improved. Indeed, the first tentative examples of how knowledge from brain science can be used in teaching have come from the study of developmental disorders. This is already the case for the disorders discussed in earlier chapters, dyslexia and dyscalculia.

Autism

Autism is a highly varied developmental disorder typically characterized by difficulties in communication and social interaction and by restricted interests and inflexible behavior. The cause of autism is most likely a genetic predisposition that impacts on brain development before birth. The signs and symptoms appear gradually, and can only be fully recognized from about the second year of life. Autism comes in many degrees, spanning a whole spectrum, and can occur together with both low and high intelligence.

You can find children with autism who do not speak a word, never look at you, and generally behave as if they were alone in a world of things, not in a world of people. At the other extreme you can find children who talk at you continuously, but you may be hard pushed to understand what they mean. It is the failure of perfectly ordinary emotional communication that is the core feature of autistic disorders, at all ages and all levels of ability. You can sense this failure regardless of whether the individual dazzles you with encyclopedic knowledge and logical analysis, or whether he or she seems supremely indifferent and quite incapable of understanding you.

Because of the wide variety of different forms of autism and their gradual recognition, the number of diagnosed cases has risen enormously in the last decades. According to recent studies, autistic disorder is estimated to affect six people per 1,000—that is 0.6 percent of the population.

Asperger syndrome

Some individuals on the autistic spectrum are affected very mildly, and their early development is not strikingly abnormal. This means that their diagnosis is late, usually after age eight, and their early problems are only recognized with hindsight. For these cases the label *Asperger syndrome* is now commonly used. The often high intelligence of these children and their desire to learn social rules can camouflage the extent of their social communication problems.

Teachers today are likely to find children with Asperger syndrome in their classrooms. The child may not have a diagnosis yet, but to identify the possibility and to refer the child to a specialist can be the first step toward real help. Not only teachers, but the other children in the school, need to know about Asperger syndrome and how it restricts simple everyday communication.

There are many harrowing stories, for example those collected by Clare Sainsbury in her book with the evocative title, *Martian in the Playground*. They give insight into the plight of children with autistic spectrum disorders who are so clever and, in many ways, so well adapted that they are not diagnosed until they are adolescents or adults. One woman told us about the terror and unpredictability she experienced during school. Yet no one ever suspected anything was wrong as she was academically extremely successful. She never complained about the bullying that went on. She did not even realize that it was bullying and should not happen. She would have liked to have friends, but she was unaware of the importance of giving space to others and trying to listen to their interests rather than talking nonstop about her own interest in computers. She could not understand why the other children complained about her "weird" and "annoying" behavior.

Another example is an adolescent girl who desperately wanted to gain a friend and started to imitate a popular classmate, down to wearing the same outfits and getting the same haircut. She had no idea why the popular girl avoided her even more than usual.

Unusual talents

What day was August 11, 1974? Julian, a gentle adult with autism, can tell you within a couple of seconds that it was a Sunday. In fact, Julian can rapidly work out the day of any date, yet he scores very poorly on IQ tests. Incredibly accurate memory for facts, an extensive vocabulary, and self-taught reading skills are not uncommon in autistic children with low measured IQ. Musical talent, poetry, and art can be some of the *bright splinters of the mind*. This phenomenon has been explored for many years by Beate Hermelin at the University of London, who wrote a fascinating book with this title. To many people this phenomenon suggests that the brain is specialized into different modules, and only some but not all brain systems are disrupted in autism.

Modules of the mind

One controversial and still speculative idea, which we have mentioned before in this book, is that the brain of the newborn infant comes equipped with various *start-up mechanisms*. These enable fast-track learning in particularly important domains. In autism, one or more of these *modules* may be faulty.

What start-up mechanisms are we talking about? We presume that there is such a mechanism for learning language, for learning numbers, for learning music, because all these abilities develop quickly and can exist in relative isolation from other types of learning. This isolation means that they act like modules in a complex machine. A module can break. It is possible to be highly intelligent and creative and yet have absolutely no ear for music. On the other hand, a single module can survive while many others are damaged. It is possible to be very slow at learning anything except music, and this can be shown as a bright splinter of the mind. But since we are talking about development, where one thing hinges on another, even a minor malfunction in a single module is likely to have huge consequences. The broken module may prevent others from developing in the manner of a domino topple.

For the idea of start-up mechanisms to work, it is necessary to assume that there are neural structures that are geared toward processing a particular kind of stimulus and to facilitate a particular kind of learning. This is like different organs that do different jobs to digest different things—fats, proteins, and so on. We also assume that there is, in addition, an all-purpose mind-machine that is not specifically geared to particular stimuli, but can cope with almost anything. This is like a general learning system that simply responds to associations of experience. Again speculatively, we suggest that this general mechanism might take over if a module is faulty. It would make any learning different from normal fast learning, but still feasible.

These ideas are controversial. Some researchers prefer to think that specialization is an outcome of development and not its starting point. Annette Karmiloff-Smith, from the University of London, for instance, suggests that brain development is not explained well by start-up kits and modules, but that instead, experience itself will lead to the gradual development of modules in the adult brain. This is very likely true for modules such as reading that are acquired late. It is perhaps less likely for modules such as number or speech that seem to be present very early. Once techniques are available to look at the functioning of the living brain in response to different stimuli at different ages, we will learn more about the origin, development, and function of modules.

How the speculative idea works for autism

What module breakdown might give rise to the social problems in autism? There are many different theories put forward to explain the symptoms of autism, and here we will only describe one of them, popularly known as a "lack of theory of mind" or "mind-blindness." *Theory of mind* is a shorthand description for the human capacity to attribute wishes, feelings, and beliefs to other people to explain their behavior. A new word for this capacity is *mentalizing*. Another term, used by Simon Baron-Cohen from Cambridge University, is *empathizing*.

So, for instance, when observing that the driver in front suddenly stops, you assume that he wished to stop perhaps because he believed there was an obstacle in the road. It doesn't matter if it turns out that there was no obstacle after all. It is the thought that counts when you try to explain someone else's behav-

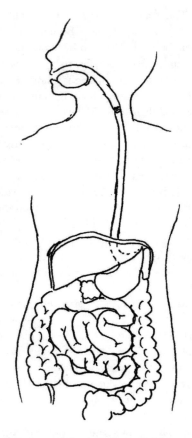

Figure 7.1   For the idea of start-up mechanisms to work, it is necessary to assume that the brain is specialized for processing different types of information. This is like the digestive system where different organs are specialized for processing different nutrients.

ior. Mentalizing or empathizing is something we do automatically and with the greatest ease. Perhaps this is because our brain has a module for it. It might be this module that is faulty in autism. Let us briefly consider the evidence that this is the case.

The mind-blindness theory of autism

The *mind-blindness* hypothesis of autism was proposed by Simon Baron-Cohen, Alan Leslie, and Uta Frith at the University of London in the 1980s and has been

Figure 7.2 Because autistic children do not attribute intentions or desires to other people's actions and speech, they often take things literally.

developed since by many other researchers. The main proposal of the mind-blindness theory is that the intuitive ability to understand that other people have minds is missing in autism. This missing ability has a basis in the brain and is manifest in different ways at different ages.

Imagine what it is like to be mind-blind. An exquisitely detailed and largely accurate portrayal of what it must be like to be mind-blind is given in the recent best-seller, *The Curious Incident of the Dog in the Night-time*. The author, Mark Haddon, narrates his book from the point of view of a teenage boy with Asperger syndrome who sets out to solve a puzzling incident. The hero, Christopher, works out this puzzle even though he has no understanding of what other people know or believe about the incident. He has to find out everything by himself.

Experiments have established that normally developing children very rapidly acquire the ability to mentalize and, by age five, have an understanding of very complex social scenarios, such as false beliefs, pretence, deception, and white lies. Not so children with autism. They are unable to understand that other people can have different beliefs from their own. One of the first problems noticed in children with autism is a lack of joint attention, as shown normally in pointing and looking intently at the same thing as another person. Another is lack of pretend play. Most normally developing babies clearly attend to what another person is attending to and start to use make-believe in play from about 18 months. Pretence involves understanding that belief is different from reality and therefore depends on having a theory of mind.

Figure 7.3 Pretend play, for example, pretending a banana is a telephone, involves under-standing that belief is different from reality. Most infants start to use make-believe in play from about 18 months, whereas infants with autism are severely delayed in their use and understanding of pretend play.

As children with autism get older they too can get an idea that belief is different from reality. However, this idea dawns on them about five years later than most children.

Mentalizing in the brain

The idea of a faulty mentalizing module has support from brain research. Several brain-imaging experiments have revealed which brain regions are active when normal adults engage in automatic mentalizing. These regions are all part of the *social brain*.

In nonautistic people, different tasks that involve inferring people's intentions, beliefs, and desires activate three key regions of the social brain: the *medial pre-frontal cortex*, the *superior temporal sulcus*, and the *temporal poles* adjacent to the *amygdala*. We still know little about the precise functions of these regions but some preliminary suggestions have been made. The medial prefrontal cortex is involved in monitoring internal mental states of both the self and other people. The superior temporal sulcus is important for recognizing and analyzing people's

Figure 7.4   The brain has evolved to interact with other brains. Sideviews with fronts facing each other.

movements and actions. The temporal pole is involved in processing emotions. Their consistent activation in all sorts of mentalizing tasks suggests that these three brain regions play key roles in mentalizing.

In several recent studies, very able people with Asperger syndrome have been scanned while they perform mentalizing tasks. These studies have demonstrated that the three brain regions involved in mentalizing are connected more weakly in people with Asperger syndrome than in normal control participants, and are therefore less active.

Does this mean that there are specific brain regions that develop abnormally in autism? Some preliminary evidence for this exists from anatomical studies. The findings so far suggest that the proportion of gray and white matter in parts of the brain involved in mentalizing is subtly different. These tiny anatomical abnormalities may be a sign of abnormally developing connections. The parts mentioned as trouble spots most often in recent research are the *temporal lobes*, *frontal lobes*, and the *cerebellum*. Some evidence suggests that it is poor connectivity between different regions that is particularly characteristic of autistic brains.

Only recently has evidence been found that the brain in many people with autism is bigger and heavier than the brains of nonautistic people. The size seems to be normal, or even smaller than normal, at birth but an increase is noticeable after the first year of life. As we described in Chapter 2, in normal brain development, connections between brain cells (*synapses*) at first multiply, and are then pruned away according to how much they are used. Perhaps appropriate synaptic pruning does not occur in autism.

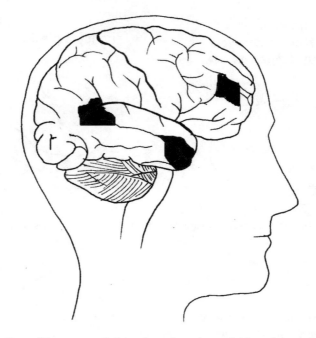

Figure 7.5 Many different mentalizing tasks activate the medial frontal cortex (at the front), temporal poles (the middle activation), and the superior temporal sulcus (the activation toward the back of the brain).

Overcoming mind-blindness

Lacking the *innate* basis for mind reading does not necessarily preclude the ability to *learn* about mental states. Earlier, we speculated that a general all-purpose learning mechanism can come into play when a module is faulty. Parents and teachers can help in this. An awareness and understanding of mental states can be accumulated gradually by explicitly teaching the person about mental states using logic, memory, and detailed explanations of events that have happened and what they mean. Clearly this requires a lot of motivation, patience, and effort on the part of both the student and teacher.

Unfortunately, as far as we know, compensatory learning does not occur simply by being around and copying another person. Compensation can be achieved by learning explicit rules about the social world by reading and study-ing examples. Different situations and contexts have to be rehearsed separately. In order for a person with autism to learn about other people's intentions and

feelings, the implications of actions, facial expressions, gestures, and w
to be spelled out, even if they seem obvious to most people.

Here we would like to make a more general point. What does it i
teach someone with a developmental disorder that may involve a faulty n
It is a bit like teaching most people about complex mathematics. A small nu .ver
of people seem to have an intuitive grasp of complex mathematical concepts,
which they seem to "see" without much, if any, conscious effort. Most people do
not have this intuitive grasp of mathematics but that does not preclude them
from learning it the slow way. However, this requires effort, motivation, and
explicit teaching.

Attention deficit hyperactivity disorder (ADHD)

On a recent train journey during the school holidays we happened to sit opposite a mother and her three sons aged between four and nine. They were typically boisterous and clearly looking forward to their outing. The middle boy,
however, was a little more than boisterous. He was continually hopping from
one seat to another, demanding that his brothers change seats with him and that
they run up and down the carriage. He clearly annoyed his brothers, who were
trying to read their comics. The middle boy also annoyed his mother after he
managed to put his hands into air vents on top of the window and made them
completely black. Instead of stopping after his mother had wiped his hands clean,
he immediately sought out the same air vents and slid his hands in again. The
poor mother was exasperated. She offered him sandwiches to distract him, but
this did not last long—he was not hungry and only took one bite. She threatened
to take him right back home, but again—no effect. He just carried on with his
restless activities.

This boy seemed bored but unable to do anything about it. His brothers found
things to do that kept them occupied, at least for a while. Unlike them, he could
not find such absorbing entertainment. His attention was not held by a strong
intention to do one particular thing. Instead it was continually "grabbed" by fleet-
ing external and often unsuitable stimuli.

Attention deficit hyperactivity disorder (ADHD; or ADD: attention deficit disorder) is a disorder characterized by inappropriate impulsiveness, attention problems, and in some cases, hyperactivity. A frequent symptom is social impairment,
as manifest in lack of friends, because these children tend to behave in a way that
not only adults but also other children find difficult. They find it hard to join in
cooperative group activities and often jump the gun or are waylaid by distrac-
tions that disrupt the group activity. In most cases, the symptoms are caused by
subtle dysfunctions in brain development, and research suggests that, like autism,
ADHD may have a genetic basis.

ADHD starts in childhood, but typically persists into adulthood. Although only recently recognized and labeled, ADHD is being diagnosed with increasing frequency in both children and adults in Europe and the United States. It is estimated that over 5 percent of school-aged children in the USA are diagnosed with ADHD. Many individuals who are now diagnosed as having ADHD may have previously been labeled hyperactive.

ADHD is usually diagnosed when various symptoms, including difficulty sustaining attention, playing quietly, and listening, and excessive talking and fidgeting, are present together for at least six months to a degree that is maladaptive, inconsistent with developmental level, and causes significant impairment at school and/or at home. The problem is that many perfectly normal young children to some extent fit the symptom profile. The ability to sustain attention and to keep still for long periods of time develops gradually and almost all children are naturally distractible, boisterous, and active.

One prerequisite of the ability to sustain attention is that parts of the *frontal lobes* have reached a certain level of maturity. Because the frontal lobes develop over a very extended time period, as will be described in Chapter 8, and develop more slowly in some children than in others, there is a significant risk of overdiagnosis of ADHD.

Misdiagnosed children would be those who are just a little delayed in reaching the necessary degree of maturity. At present, it is unknown to what extent environmental input is facilitating or delaying the development of what we might call "self-control." It stands to reason that experience is necessary to form habits of sustained attention, and adults may foster the control of behavior by verbal commands and by reminding the child how important it is to do this and that, and by suitable rewards. Role models may well have an impact on the tuning of self-control.

The brain in ADHD

One of the first brain-imaging studies on ADHD was carried out in the mid-1990s by Xavier Castellanos and his colleagues from the National Institute of Mental Health in Bethesda. This study demonstrated subtle structural abnormalities in the brain circuit whose function is to inhibit thoughts and actions. The researchers used MRI (see Appendix) to scan the brains of a large group of boys with ADHD, aged between 5 and 18, and another group of similarly aged boys without ADHD. The results showed that *prefrontal cortex* and regions of the *basal ganglia* (see Figure 7.6) were smaller in the boys with ADHD than in the boys without ADHD.

The *prefrontal cortex*, located at the front of the frontal lobe just behind the forehead, is believed to play an important role in planning, decision making,

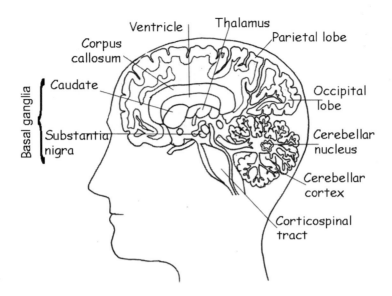

Figure 7.6 The basal ganglia are a set of structures in the middle of the brain, which are involved in movement control and coordination.

attentional control, and the *inhibition* of inappropriate behavior. The *basal ganglia*, a network of structures located deep inside the brain, are involved in generating movements. The basal ganglia are intricately connected with the prefrontal cortex and whether they generate a movement depends to some extent on the commands sent to them from the prefrontal cortex. The prefrontal cortex sends commands to start and to stop movements—in other words, as well as deciding when and how to act, it is also responsible for stopping action from occurring.

The controlling brain

Inhibition is a crucial function of the frontal lobes, which develop gradually throughout childhood and adolescence. It is this inhibitory control that stops us from saying or doing exactly as we feel, depending on the social context. Young children, whose frontal cortex is not fully developed, find it much harder to inhibit actions and speech and tend to act impulsively regardless of social context. We remember when one child strode up to her aunt and told her quite confidently that her parents always dreaded the aunt's visits. Needless to say, this caused a fair bit of embarrassment, and it was a long time before the aunt's next visit!

All children are disinhibited to a certain extent. But severe and prolonged difficulties with inhibiting actions and staying mentally focused are the primary symptoms of ADHD. It is possible that frontal inhibitory control is not working efficiently in ADHD, perhaps because the frontal lobes develop at a slower rate in children with ADHD than in most children. That could explain why many children can have ADHD-like symptoms to a certain extent—such symptoms are a normal consequence of frontal cortex immaturity. The brain-imaging study by Castellanos and colleagues suggests that the malfunctioning prefrontal cortex in children with ADHD might account for why these children continue to find it difficult to inhibit behavior and sustain attention.

Treatment of ADHD

ADHD is often treated with drugs, such as Ritalin and classes of amphetamine. These increase the amount of *dopamine* and *noradrenaline* in the brain. Stimulating these chemical systems induces feelings of energy and euphoria in adults. These drugs are very successful at treating hyperactivity and attention problems. Many people are surprised that the choice of drug is a stimulant and not a sedative. It is not yet known why stimulating drugs are so effective in treating the symptoms of ADHD.

Medication does not cure ADHD but it can help the child function better at school and at home. It is generally thought that medication is most efficient when used in conjunction with other types of therapy. There are various other treatments including cognitive therapy and family therapy, which can help children improve their self-control and attention and help the child's family learn how best to cope with and control their child's behavior. There is some research showing that, in a small number of people, certain types of food, including artificial colors, flavors, and preservatives, can aggravate ADHD. These may be real effects, but they are very small. Focusing on dietary regimes should therefore not come at the cost of educational measures that strengthen behavioral control.

Conduct disorder

Before the frontal cortex is ready to perform a stop-and-start function in the normal child, other people, usually adults, have to perform this function instead. Here the idea is that the child follows these external commands. Not all children do this, and no child does it all the time. When the external control is not working, or the child appears to be unable to use external controls, then conduct disorder, or "defiant and oppositional" disorder, can be diagnosed. This type of disorder is often associated with ADHD. Only in a minority of children is this a persistent problem that later develops into serious antisocial behavior.

Much thinking has been devoted to the social reasons for conduct disorder, and far less to the biological reasons. Many psychologists and teachers talk of attention-seeking behavior and believe that parental style is a source of the problem, so that improvement can be achieved by special instruction to parents. Often parental style cannot be held responsible, but even in these cases, behavior modification programs can be effective.

A disorder of empathy and moral sensitivity

The acclaimed Brazilian film *City of God* portrayed life in a severely deprived favela, where gangs of young boys have to fend for themselves by robbery and other criminal activities. Guns were easy to come by, as were drugs, and killings and other acts of violence seemed the inevitable experience of almost every child. The law of the street as shown in the film was kill or be killed. And yet all the boys, except one, held on to some moral code or code of honor. The exception was a boy who took pleasure in killing and did not know mercy. He was successful as a gang leader whose members were mortally afraid of him. This gang leader acted in a way that could not be excused by the environment that he lived in—the others suffered equally and did not sink to his cruelty. Amongst all the violent youths in his town, he was the only psychopath. (Note that we use the terms "psychopath" and "psychopathy" rather than the more recent "antisocial personality disorder" to emphasize the lack of empathy in this condition.)

Psychopathy in adults is a condition that sometimes starts with conduct disorder in childhood. James Blair, a developmental neuroscientist at the National Institute of Mental Health in Bethesda, proposed that there is a neurodevelopmental disorder that leads to psychopathy in adulthood and may well have a genetic basis. This may be rare and the disorder is currently diagnosed rather crudely, with clinical questionnaires, just like ADHD and conduct disorder. Blair suggests that the brain basis of psychopathy is poor functioning of parts of the *amygdala* (see Figure 7.8).

The amygdala normally responds to expressions of sadness and fear in other people. This quite automatic and unconscious response then leads to an aversive response. We do not like to see other creatures suffer or be afraid. When we see fear or hurt in someone's eyes and we are the cause of it, this can act as a signal to stop what we are doing. This is like a reflex that Konrad Lorenz described in fighting dogs and other animals: there are certain signals, termed *submission cues* (for example, displaying the neck), that tend to make the winning animal stop and shrink back from doing further damage. Blair argues that the same reflex exists in humans and that this reflex is vital for learning about moral behavior. We instinctively know that we should not cause distress to other human beings.

Figure 7.7 Most people feel empathy towards others who are upset. Empathy is lacking in psychopaths.

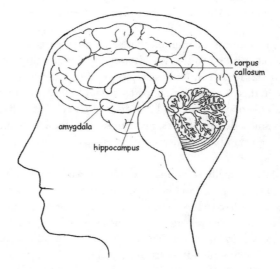

Figure 7.8 The amygdala is situated deep inside the brain and is involved in processing emotion.

We therefore learn to judge as morally wrong those things that result in somebody being hurt.

Even young children implicitly make moral judgments. They can distinguish moral wrongdoings from other kinds of wrongdoings that do not have a victim. This is known as the "moral–conventional" distinction. For instance, children know that it is wrong to talk in class. However, they can say it is OK to talk in class when the teacher gives express permission for it. In contrast, when young children are told that the teacher gives permission to damage someone else's property or to hurt someone, most will still insist that it is wrong to do so. This ingenious manipulation has led to a test to probe into moral understanding.

Children learn about the wrongness of moral transgressions, such as hurting or stealing from others, directly from the negative reactions of siblings and peers as well as from parents and teachers. Conversely, conventional transgressions, such as wearing dirty shoes in the house or not putting a toy back in a drawer, are explicitly taught. An understanding of morality and its transgressions seems normally to develop quite naturally in the course of interaction with siblings, peers, and adults. If children can be identified early as being unresponsive to others' distress or fear, then common sense would dictate that it is particularly important to instill rules of moral conduct and tools for self-control.

Smetana's test for "moral–conventional" distinction (conventions can be broken, but moral rules cannot) has been given to children with conduct disorder, and a small minority are unable to make this distinction. This is also true for individuals who have been diagnosed as psychopaths. It may well be that the children who do not intuitively feel that moral transgressions are worse than conventional transgressions will grow up into adult psychopaths if not given appropriate guidance. In these cases, social adversity, aggression, and impulsive behavior are often contributory circumstances.

However, other individuals with the same or worse degree of adversity, and with disinhibited behavior, are capable of empathy, and the crimes they commit are far less callous than those committed by psychopaths. Furthermore, they show remorse, while psychopaths do not feel remorseful about their deeds. "He was in my way," a psychopath said when asked why he hit a child to the ground. Another psychopath who was not violent, but who constantly deceived people and took advantage of their trust, said, "It's their own fault for believing other people all the time."

Misfortune seldom comes alone

One of the most common observations in clinics is that children can often be diagnosed with more than one disorder. The word coined for the coincidence of several conditions is *comorbidity* (from *morbus*, meaning illness). Sadly, having one illness does not protect you from getting another. However, the frequent coincidence of attention deficit disorder and dyspraxia with other developmental disorders needs some comment. Is it coincidence? The numbers seem too big for this, although a proper prevalence study of comorbidity has yet to be done.

One theory is that the neurological abnormality that causes developmental disorder comes in two forms. In one form, it attacks only one start-up module. This would result in pure cases of autism, or of dyslexia, coexisting with high intelligence and good use of language. The analogy is a revolver with a single bullet that hits one very precise target. Remember that even such a pure case will not be entirely pure, because the missing module is likely to have a domino effect on mental functions that normally depend on it. In another form, the neurological abnormality is much less focused. Here, the analogy is to a shotgun with shrapnel, which affects a wider target area with somewhat unpredictable effects. The most common effects would be on the brain's most labor-intensive computations. These are movement control and the control of attention.

Disorders of social-emotional development are a challenge for education

That developmental disorders can be caused by a subtle brain abnormality is still not generally accepted. A minority of children with developmental disorders are severely affected and need a very different approach to teaching from normal. This approach has to do with coping and overcoming problems. The idea is that compensation may be possible, even if a cure is not possible as yet. Many hold that only education can make a substantial difference to the quality of life of affected individuals. Education does not cure the conditions, but it can certainly improve them.

Chapter 8

the adolescent brain

Adolescence is a time characterized by huge hormonal and physical changes. It is also when we undergo real changes in identity. During puberty children's personalities can seem to change. A 14-year-old girl we know, who was an outgoing 10 year old without any concerns about herself, became intensively self-aware and self-reflective as soon as she reached puberty. Her new-found interest in boys was something she hid from her parents. Her mother told us that she started to keep a diary in which she confided her feelings, thoughts, and dreams. In the company of adults she was coy, but in the company of her peers she was outgoing. In photographs she no longer smiled unselfconsciously, but looked sullen and posed or avoided the camera altogether. She always wanted to look different: prettier and thinner than she thought she was. At the same time, she became better able to plan her schoolwork, focus her attention, and think in a strategic manner. She also became more popular with a different set of girls at school. Her mother was surprised when she had a birthday party and invited a girl in her class who she didn't particularly like but who she felt would hold it against her if she were not invited. Four years earlier, she had refused to invite the same girl to her 10th birthday party.

Much is changing in the body and seems to be changing in the brain during puberty. These are not just hormonal changes and upheavals. Despite common anecdotal and autobiographical accounts, there has been surprisingly little empirical research on the development of cognitive skills and the brain during puberty and adolescence. In the past three or four years, a handful of pioneering experiments have looked at the development of brain and cognitive processes during the adolescent years.

What changes after puberty?

We all know that, after puberty, children seem to become more aware of themselves and other people around them, their opinions and emotions. Worry about appearance and concern about what other people—especially peers—will think seem to become profoundly important, much more so than before puberty. Much of this has to do with growing sexual interest and a self-conscious awareness of the opposite sex. But social awareness in general seems to show a massive change. A friend of ours recounts how, when his daughter was 10 years old, he could always get her to stop messing about with her younger sister in the supermarket by promising to sing a song right there and then. It would always work—both his daughters would instantly be quiet to hear him sing their favorite song. As soon as his older daughter turned 13, there was a complete turn around. He found that the only way to stop her messing around with her little sister in shops was by threatening to sing. Now, she couldn't think of anything more embarrassing than her dad singing in public, and would immediately be quiet!

Another of our friends talks about how her son became completely fearless, at least in front of his friends, after he turned 14. She told us that she'd recently had a phonecall from her son's school to inform her that her son and his new friends had been caught playing a game called "Chicken." This is a rather popular game where they all egg each other on to run across a busy road just in front of an oncoming car. The boy's mother had noticed that he had also begun to show off on his bike and new skateboard in front of his friends, taking risks on the main road, where he was not supposed to go. A couple of years before, her son was scared of the roads and would always ask her permission to go out. We see this as an example of how powerful emotions such as fear can change from being negative to rewarding and how peer pressure can start to determine behavior.

What had caused such a big change in these two children? We all have experience of the changes that occur in our minds and personalities after puberty and yet there is surprisingly little scientific evidence about cognitive and neural development during this important period of human life.

The first experiments on adolescent brains

Why do we know so little about brain development during adolescence? There are two main reasons. First, the notion that the brain continues to develop after childhood is relatively new. Experiments on animals, starting in the 1950s, showed that sensory regions of the brain go through *sensitive periods* soon after birth, during which environmental stimulation appears to be crucial for normal brain development and for normal perceptual development to occur. These experiments and concepts were discussed at length in Chapter 2. Based on these experiments, the very idea that the human brain might continue to undergo change after this sensitive period in early childhood seemed highly improbable.

It was not until the late 1960s and 1970s that research on postmortem human brains revealed that some brain areas, in particular the *frontal cortex*, continue to develop well beyond childhood. The frontal cortex is the area responsible for so-called *executive functions*, such as the ability to inhibit inappropriate behavior, plan, select actions, hold information in the mind, and do two things at once. Pioneering studies, mainly carried out by Peter Huttenlocher in Chicago in the 1970s and 1980s, demonstrated that the frontal cortex is the latest brain region to develop in the human brain. He collected numerous postmortem brains from children, adolescents, and adults, and found that the frontal cortex was remarkably different in the brains of prepubescent children and postpubescent adolescents.

There were two main changes in the brains before and after puberty. First, studies from the late 1960s revealed that although the volume of brain tissue remains stable, there is an increase in *white matter* in the frontal cortex after puberty compared with before. What does that mean? As neurons develop, they build up a layer of *myelin* on their *axon* (the long fiber attached to each brain cell, see Figure 1.6, p. 12). Myelin acts as an insulator and increases the speed of trans-mission of electrical impulses from neuron to neuron. Now, myelin is made up of fatty tissue and appears white under the microscope. Therefore as myelin is added to neurons, the cells appear less gray and more white when observed with a microscope. This finding means that the transmission speed of neurons in the frontal cortex might get faster after puberty.

It was Huttenlocher who discovered the second difference in the brains of pre-pubescent and postpubescent children. His studies revealed a large decrease in the density of synapses in the frontal cortex after puberty. As explained in Chapter 2, there is an initial wave of synaptic proliferation (*synaptogenesis*) that occurs just after birth and continues in most brain regions until about one year of age. At this point, synaptic densities in most brain regions are at their maximum. After these early peaks in synaptic density, synapses that are not used start to be pruned back, whereas synapses that are used are strengthened. In the frontal lobe, however, synapses continue to proliferate throughout childhood. This can be seen in Figure 8.1.

It seems that only after puberty does synaptic pruning begin in the frontal cortex. This vigorous synaptic pruning occurs after puberty and throughout adolescence in the frontal lobes, and results in a gradual decrease in synaptic density in this region. Remember from Chapter 2 that synaptic pruning is essential for the fine-tuning of functional networks of brain tissue and of perceptual processes. The results from the frontal cortex suggest that fine-tuning

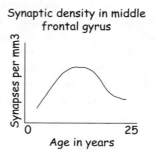

Figure 8.1   In part of the frontal lobe called the middle frontal gyrus synapses continue to proliferate throughout childhood, and are gradually pruned throughout adolescence. This results in a gradual decline in synaptic density during the teens. Source: adapted from figure 3 in Huttenlocher et al. *International Journal of Neurology* 1983; 16–17: 144–54. Copyright © 1983 by *International Journal of Neurology*. By permission of the authors.

of cognitive processes of the frontal lobes only takes hold in adolescence. One exciting but purely speculative possibility is that sensitive periods might accompany the fine-tuning of self-control and similarly high level executive functions, just as they do for fine-tuning of face and voice perception.

Viewing the adolescent brain with MRI

The second reason that we know very little about brain changes during adolescence is that, until recently, the structure of the human brain could be studied only after death. Nowadays, noninvasive brain-imaging techniques, particularly Magnetic Resonance Imaging (*MRI*; see Appendix) can produce high-quality images of the living human brain. MRI works on the principle that water is magnetic and gives off a signal in a magnetic field. Because of their different water content, different structures (bone, cerebrospinal fluid, white and gray matter, for example) appear distinct in the MRI image. This gives a high-resolution, three-dimensional photograph of the human brain.

Frontal cortex changes during adolescence

In the past few years, several MRI studies have been performed to investigate the development of the structure of the brain during childhood and adolescence in humans. One of the first MRI studies, carried out by a group of researchers led

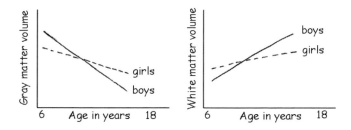

Figure 8.2 Overall there is a gradual decrease in gray matter and an increase in white matter in the brain during adolescence, in both boys and girls. Source: adapted from figure 1 from De Bellis et al. *Cerebral Cortex* 2001; 11(6): 552–557. Copyright © 2001 by Oxford University Press. By permission of Oxford University Press.

by Elisabeth Sowell and Paul Thompson in UCLA, scanned the brains of a group of children whose average age was nine years, and a group of adolescents whose average age was 14. Just as the cellular studies performed 30 years earlier had demonstrated differences in white matter between the brains at two age points, so did the brain images in this MRI study. The brain images showed higher gray matter volume in the frontal cortex and parietal cortex in the younger children. The older group, by contrast, had a higher volume of white matter in the same regions.

The researchers concluded that the progressive loss of gray matter and concomitant increase in white matter that occurred between childhood and adolescence represented both a postpubescent decrease in synaptic density and a simultaneous increase in axonal myelination. Fewer synapses and more myelin on axons would result in more white matter and less gray matter in the MRI scans.

These findings have been replicated by several studies since 1999, both by the UCLA team and by another group led by Jay Giedd at the National Institute of Health in Maryland. Both groups have confirmed that the amount of white matter in the frontal cortex increases after puberty.

As can be seen from Figure 8.2, the increase in white matter with age is slightly different in boys and girls. This MRI study, carried out by Giedd and colleagues, revealed that in boys the increase in white matter in the frontal lobes is sharper and peaks later than in girls.

Development is not always gradual. A large-scale MRI study published in 1999 found evidence for a complex "nonlinear" relationship between age and gray matter density. In this study, the brains of 145 boys and girls ranging in age from 4 to 22 years were scanned using MRI. Instead of a simple linear decrease in gray matter with age, there was a dip in neural maturation that coincided with

Figure 8.3   "My myelin is increasing in my frontal lobes."

puberty. At puberty, gray matter volume in the frontal lobe showed a temporary increase. This study found evidence for a peak of gray matter density occurring at about 12 years, followed by a decline in gray matter after puberty.

The researchers attributed the temporary increase in gray matter to a second wave of synapse proliferation at the onset of puberty. The gradual decrease in gray matter density that follows puberty was attributed to postpubescent synaptic pruning occurring in the frontal lobe. In other words, the researchers suggested that there is a sudden increase in the number of synapses at puberty, giving rise to an excess of synaptic connections. At some point after puberty, there is a process of refinement such that these excess synaptic contacts are eliminated, or pruned. This results in a decrease in synaptic density, which appears in MRI as a decrease in the amount of gray matter, in the frontal lobes of older adolescents.

Why is it so important to learn about the brain changes in adolescence and what will be revealed in the future? One of the most devastating mental illnesses, schizophrenia, typically has its onset in the late teens to early twenties. However, often people who later develop schizophrenia have social and behavioral problems during their teenage years. Knowing more about brain development and changes in brain chemistry during adolescence might one day prevent the tragic course of this mental illness.

It is equally important to know about brain development during adolescence for teaching and learning in the classroom. Learning in the teenage years is essential to a successful career. Yet many young people are simply not motivated to learn at school and college. It should be possible to find ways of making learning at this stage of life more rewarding, and brain research might have a role to play in this.

Brain changes continue after adolescence

So when does the brain reach maturity? Recent MRI studies indicate that it may be much later than the end of adolescence. The UCLA group scanned the brains of children aged 7 to 11 years, adolescents aged 12 to 16 years and young adults aged 23 to 30 years. This study again showed evidence for a decrease in gray matter between childhood and adolescence in the frontal cortex, as was found in previous studies. But remarkably, the results of the study also revealed that the amount of white matter in the frontal lobes continued to increase well into the 20s and up to the age of 30.

A study published by the same group in 2003 expanded on these results. Sowell and her colleagues carried out a large-scale MRI study of 176 healthy individuals between the age of 7 and 87 years. They analyzed gray matter density changes in each person's brain. The analysis revealed a reduction in gray matter density in the frontal and temporal cortices, which was accompanied by an increase in white matter, consistent with earlier MRI and cellular studies. But, although the decrease in gray matter is most dramatic from childhood into young adulthood, this study revealed that white matter volume continues to increase well beyond this stage and even up to the age of 60.

So, while early cellular studies in animals described in Chapter 2 suggested that changes in the brain more or less cease early on in infancy, more recent postmortem studies of human brains and recent MRI studies have revealed an extended period of brain development, in particular in the frontal cortex. Taken together, the results provide consistent evidence for the developing nature of the adolescent brain. The main changes that have been observed are in the amount of frontal gray matter, which seems to increase from age 7 to roughly 12 and declines thereafter, and a simultaneous increase in white matter.

And it seems that the brain continues to develop well into adulthood. This is a pretty impressive finding after the decades of research suggesting that there are critical periods in brain development during the first few years of life, after

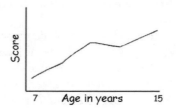

Figure 8.4   In one study, performance on executive function tasks was shown to improve with age, as shown in this graph. Source: adapted from Anderson et al. *Developmental Neuropsychology* 2001; 20(1), 385–406. By permission of the authors and Lawrence Erlbaum Associates, Inc.

which time no further development can occur (see Chapter 2). These days, this concept seems far from accurate—recent studies point to a brain that naturally undergoes large waves of development well into the teens and doesn't even stop there.

What about changes in behavior and cognition after puberty?

Given the continued developmental changes in the frontal cortex during adolescence, it might be expected that cognitive abilities that rely on the functioning of the frontal lobes should also change during this time period. The term *executive function* is a phrase used to describe the capacity that allows us to control and coordinate our thoughts and behavior. It includes the ability to direct our attention, to plan future tasks, to inhibit inappropriate behavior, and to keep more than one thing in mind at once. In fact, these tasks are what an executive director of a company typically has to do. These skills are believed to rely heavily on the frontal lobes. We know this because damage to the frontal lobes dramatically impairs executive function skills, and brain-imaging studies reveal activation of the frontal lobes during these types of task.

Since MRI studies have demonstrated major changes in frontal cortex throughout adolescence, executive function abilities might be expected to improve during this time. In other words, selective attention, decision making, and response-inhibition skills, along with the ability to carry out multiple tasks at once, are abilities that might improve during adolescence. If you think about typical 10 year olds and compare them with typical 15 year olds, this idea seems quite possible. Children certainly do seem to become better at inhibiting inappropriate behavior, doing two things at once, and planning, as they get older. However, only a handful of studies have systematically investigated the changes in cognitive skills during adolescence.

Behavioral studies by Vicky Anderson and her colleagues in Australia investigated executive function during adolescence in a large group of 11 to 17 year olds. A range of paradigms was used to explore the progression of a variety of executive functions that required selective attention, multitasking, and problem solving. The results showed a steady improvement in performance on many executive function tasks with age during adolescence. This progression was attributed to the continued myelination of axons in the frontal cortex.

But the steady linear pattern of development reflected in this Australian study was not found in a recent behavioral study that used a rather different paradigm. This study was carried out by Robert McGivern and his team at San Diego State University and involved a "match-to-sample" task. In this task, volunteers were shown pictures of faces showing particular emotional expressions (happy, sad, angry), or words describing those emotions ("Happy," "Sad," "Angry"), and were asked to specify, as quickly as possible, the emotion presented in the face or word.

In a third condition, volunteers were shown both a face and a word and had to decide whether the facial expression *matched* the emotion word. The rationale behind the design of the task was that the face/word condition places high demands on frontal lobe circuitry, since it requires working memory and decision making. So one would expect better performance in older children. The computer-based task was given to a large group of children aged 10 to 17 years and a group of young adults aged 18 to 22 years.

The analysis of the time it took the participants to answer the questions revealed an intriguing result. At the age of puberty onset, at 11–12 years, there was actually a decline in performance in the matching face and word condition compared with the younger group of children. The 11–12 years olds were about 15 percent *slower* on this condition than the younger group. The results suggest that there is a dip in performance on this kind of task at the onset of puberty. After puberty, from age 13–14, performance improved until it came back to the prepubescent level by the age of about 16 years.

The researchers linked this pubertal dip in performance with the proliferation of synapses that occurs at the onset of puberty. Remember that one MRI study, described above, showed that the frontal cortex develops in a nonlinear fashion, with a slowdown in brain development during puberty followed by rapid development throughout adolescence. The nonlinear development may well correspond to brain reorganization. This involves increased synaptic proliferation in the frontal lobes, followed by synaptic pruning and strengthening. If so, the teen frontal lobes undergo a phase of waxing and waning, reminiscent of the toddler brain (see chapter 2).

It is possible that the excess of synapses at puberty, which have not yet been incorporated into specialized functional systems, result in poorer cognitive performance for a while. Only later, after puberty, are the excess synapses pruned into specialized efficient networks. During this time, what is perceived as important in the social world around us also changes and leaves its imprint on the pruning process. But this is still speculation.

It must be remembered that this pubertal dip in performance has been found in just one study so far. Many more studies that replicate and extend this result are needed before we can say that the pubertal dip is a robust and consistent finding.

Viewing the adolescent brain in action with fMRI

Functional neuroimaging is a useful tool to investigate the brain activation patterns associated with executive function. Functional MRI (*fMRI*) techniques allow real-time imaging of the human brain at work and is a noninvasive and safe way to investigate the function of the brain in children. fMRI has been used only in a handful of studies investigating the neural bases of cognitive development using tasks designed to tap specifically into *frontal cortex* function.

One fMRI study that investigated neural development of executive functions during adolescence was performed in 1997. The researchers used a version of a so-called "Go/No-Go" task, which involves inhibiting a response when a certain stimulus is shown. In the study, volunteers were presented with a series of letters and required to press a button upon seeing each letter, except when the letter X appeared. Volunteers were instructed to refrain from pressing any buttons if they saw the letter X—the "No-Go" stimulus. This task requires executive action: the command to inhibit a habitual response.

A group of children between 7 and 12 years old and a group of young adults between 21 and 24 years old took part in this study. The results showed that in both children and adults, several regions in the frontal cortex were activated during the task that required inhibiting the normal response. While the location of activation was essentially the same for both age groups, there was more activation in children than in adults. This increased activity in the children's brains was located in the *prefrontal cortex*, the part of frontal cortex that lies just behind the forehead.

By contrast, adults showed more activity in a different, lower, region of the prefrontal cortex. The activation in the higher part of the prefrontal cortex was negatively correlated with accuracy on the task: participants who performed best (that is, the people who managed to remember not to respond to the letter X in the Go/No-Go task) had the lowest levels of prefrontal activation. The opposite pattern was found in lower region of the prefrontal cortex, in which activation increased with improvement in performance on the task.

The higher and more diffuse activity in the higher region of the prefrontal cortex in children suggests that the task is harder for children. There is a heavier dependence on this region in children compared with in adults. The researchers suggested that during adolescence, the network recruited for this task is modified until adulthood, at which stage activation of a smaller, more focal, region of the prefrontal cortex is used to perform the same task.

A different fMRI study looked at verbal fluency in children whose average age was about 11 years, and adults whose average age was 29 years. The verbal fluency task requires participants to generate different words starting with the same letter as quickly as possible. It is a fairly demanding task that relies on prefrontal cortex. The results of this study revealed that children performed worse on the task and had on average 60 percent greater activation in the prefrontal cortex than did adults. Of course, children know fewer words, but also their frontal cortex is less developed. It is more active, perhaps to compensate for the less developed neural circuits.

Implications of brain research for teenagers

These are some of the first studies that have investigated development of the brain and cognition during adolescence. They speak of a major reorganization of the parts of the brain that continues to develop throughout the adolescent years and beyond. The effects of this reorganization seem to be greater control and better planning of the complex actions necessary in both work and social life.

The idea that young people who have reached sexual maturity should still go to school and be educated is relatively new. And yet the research on brain development during adolescence shows that secondary and tertiary education are vital. The brain is still developing during this period: it is adaptable, and needs to be molded and shaped. Perhaps the aims of education for older adolescents might well change to include strengthening of internal control, for example, self-paced learning, critical evaluation of transmitted knowledge, and meta-study skills.

If 0–3 years is seen as a major opportunity for teaching, so should 10–15 years. During both periods, particularly dramatic brain reorganization is taking place. This may well be a signal that learning in certain domains is becoming ultrafast during these periods. In previous chapters, we talked about "modules" and "start-up mechanisms" in the baby's brain. In the adolescent brain, these start-up mechanisms may no longer fulfill an important function. Instead, modularization of culturally transmitted skills that were learned in the absence of start-up mechanisms may be the predominant activity. Thus, ice skating, piano playing, reading, calculating, computer programming, and so on, have to be housed in the brain as legitimate inhabitants and be given space. They are just as legitimate as natural skills, such as walking, eating, speaking, singing, and communicating with each other.

Chapter 9

lifelong learning

Learning occurs at all ages and it is never too late to learn. The brain has continued *plasticity*—that is, an ability to adapt to changing circumstances and acquire new information—until old age, when this ability diminishes. In this chapter, we describe research that reveals the flexibility of the adult brain.

The plastic brain

Research in the past few years has shown that the adult brain, at least in certain regions, is almost as malleable as a child's brain. Brain *plasticity* means the ability of the nervous system to adapt continually to changing circumstances. This happens in everyone's brain whenever they learn anything new—a new language, a new skill, a new route home, and even when they see a new face. Plasticity also refers to the way the brain adapts and finds new ways of learning after an injury has occurred, such as after a stroke. Also when parts of the body are damaged, even elderly people can learn to compensate for the damage.

Thirty years ago, scientists believed that the structure of the brain develops during childhood and once the organization of the brain has emerged, there is very little room for changes and for plastic alterations. As we saw in Chapter 2, these beliefs prompted the argument that young children should be educated and stimulated as much as possible because after a certain age it would be too late to learn. We now know that this reasoning is flawed. There is enormous capacity for change in the adult brain, limited only by the natural decline of old age.

As we shall see, changes in the brain generally occur as a function of use. Use it—or lose it. Generally, unlike computers, we cannot learn a new skill and keep it up for ever without practicing it. The brain continuously adapts to its environment. Research on plasticity in the adult brain has benefited from brain-imaging techniques such as fMRI and PET, and from studying the recovery of brain function in patients with brain damage.

Remembering your way around

The *hippocampus* is a seahorse-shaped structure deep inside the brain that is essential for spatial navigation and spatial memory. The hippocampus is the part of the brain that helps you remember where things are and how to find your way home. Research on rats has demonstrated that so-called "place cells" in the hippocampus fire away when the rat moves around its environment: each cell responds to a specific location. This research on the rat hippocampus, which was carried out in the 1970s by John O'Keefe at the University of London, was the first to suggest that the hippocampus creates and stores maps of space.

Recent functional imaging studies, also carried out at the University of London by O'Keefe in collaboration with Neil Burgess and Eleanor Maguire, have confirmed that the hippocampus stores spatial memories in humans, too. In one experiment, volunteers were scanned while navigating round a virtual town—their task was like playing a video game in which they had to move around a complex city, negotiating streets, houses, rooms, people, and objects. Prior to the experiment, participants had learned the layout of the town from playing the game for a couple of hours. In the scanner, participants were given a list of objects located in the virtual town (such as a book on a table, a red door and a dustbin) and had to find them by remembering where they were located and moving the joystick towards them.

When the researchers later analyzed the brain scans they found that the hippocampus was greatly activated during this spatial memory task. Now this was quite a difficult task and some participants did better than others at remembering where in the town the objects were located. What might have been the reason for these individual differences in spatial memory? One result from the study was that hippocampal activity increased with accuracy of navigation. The better the navigators, the more hippocampal activity they had. This suggests that the activity in the hippocampus is directly related to, and may cause, better spatial memory. However, we cannot rule out the reverse—remembering more may cause more activity in the hippocampus.

These video game experiments provide clear evidence that the hippocampus is crucial for spatial memory in animals and humans. What has this to do with brain plasticity? Well, the question is: what happens in the brain when you become an expert in navigation? To answer this question, the London-based researchers turned to a group of people who had learned to become experts in spatial navigation.

Learning to be a London cab driver

London black-cab drivers have to be expert navigators. Every day they have to get from place to place, remembering the complex layout of London streets,

Figure 9.1   London is a vast and complicated city to navigate. This map shows a tiny portion of central London.

avoiding one-way systems, dead ends, all costly mistakes. Most of them are extremely adept at this. Indeed, in order to obtain a license to drive a black cab, you need to pass a test called "The Knowledge," which involves memorizing the "A to Z" of about 25,000 London streets and hundreds of landmarks. The cabbies are tested on The Knowledge by being asked how they would get from one place in London to another—they have to recite the exact route they would take, including whether any streets are one-way, access-restricted, and so on. So how do black-cab drivers accomplish this feat?

Eleanor Maguire and her colleagues scanned the brains of these expert navigators. The brain activity of London cab drivers was recorded while they reported a complex route they would take to get from one area of London to another. For example, they were asked to explain in as much detail as possible how they would get from Shepherd's Bush to Parliament Square. They were all good at this task.

The area that was activated while the cabbies were reporting the route was the hippocampus. This was of course expected. But the researchers found more than this. They compared the structure of the cab drivers' brains with brains of noncab-driving men of the same age. There were significant differences between the hippocampus size of the London cab drivers and the noncab drivers. The posterior hippocampus was much larger in cab drivers than in the other men. Furthermore, the size of the posterior hippocampus was exactly related to the time

Figure 9.2   London taxi drivers have to have outstanding spatial memory.

the person had been driving cabs, suggesting that its size depends on how much a person has used their spatial memory. This is important because it argues against the possibility that people who happen to be born with a large posterior hippocampus have better spatial navigation skills and are therefore more likely to become cab drivers. Maguire's results suggest it is the other way round: the more you use your spatial navigation skills, the bigger your posterior hippocampus becomes.

Another equally important finding in this study was that a different part of the hippocampus (the anterior hippocampus) was smaller in cab drivers. Its size was also related to the amount of time the person had been driving cabs. But this time, the relationship was reversed. In other words, the longer a person had been a cabbie, the smaller his anterior hippocampus became. This suggests that when one part of the brain develops and grows through experience there might be costs to other parts of the brain. This is just as well as otherwise our heads might explode!

Navigation systems now available for personal use in cars mean that anyone, however practiced or knowledgeable, can find a route. This is good news for the spatially challenged! It will be interesting to see if London cabbies of the future use navigation systems instead of their hippocampus.

Hippocampus size in birds changes as function of use

The hippocampus is known to remain plastic well into adult life. The hippocampus in birds changes in size, especially in birds that parasitize other birds' nests, so have to know and remember where things are. Hippocampus size is related to how much parasitizing a bird does. Thus it seems that the hippocampus can change in size according to how much the bird uses it to remember where nests are located. The size of the hippocampus appears to wax and wane according to how much it is used.

Learning to be a musician

What makes expert musicians skilled at music? Recent research by Christo Pantev at the University of Münster in Germany has shown that the part of the brain that processes sound (the *auditory cortex*, which is located near the surface of the brain next to the ears on both sides) in highly skilled musicians is enlarged by about 25 percent compared with people who have never played an instrument. Just as with the cab drivers, enlargement is correlated with the age at which musicians began to practice. This work again indicates that the reorganization of the auditory cortex is use-dependent. The longer musicians have been playing an instrument, the more they will have used and stimulated their auditory cortex.

It is not only the sound-processing part of the brain that changes in musicians. The regions of the brain that control movement and touch also change as a function of use. Thomas Elbert at the University of Konstanz in Germany studied violin players to look at brain plasticity. Professional violin players use the fingers of their left hand to play the strings of their violin, their left hand fingertips being stimulated often for several hours a day. The researchers wanted to find out what happens to the parts of the musicians' brains that *represent* finger movements.

Remember from Chapter 1 that the opposite side of the brain controls movements and processes sensations from the side of the body where the movement or sensation occurs. Each finger on your left hand, and indeed every left part of your body, is represented in a part of the top of the brain on the right called the sensorimotor cortex. This is called the *sensory homunculus* (see Figure 9.3). The reverse is true for the right side of the body, which is represented in the left sensorimotor cortex.

How does this organization occur? Brain cells tend to organize themselves into networks that become specialized for different kinds of information processing. When the finger touches a surface this sensory stimulus activates neurons in the sensorimotor cortex in the opposite side of the brain. The representation of the left-hand fingers is in the right sensorimotor cortex, and vice versa. The high level of activity reinforces the connections between the group of excited neurons. Each time the same finger is simulated, the connections between the activated network of neurons become stronger and stronger, and eventually the group becomes specialized for processing touch on that particular finger.

It follows that the representation of the left-hand fingers is in the right hemisphere of the brain, and vice versa. Back to violin players. Elbert's research

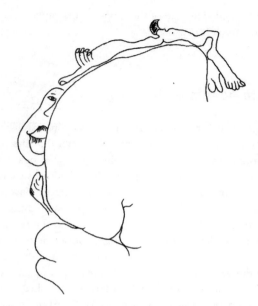

Figure 9.3 Each part of the body is processed by a different part of the sensorimotor cortex. This is called the *sensory homunculus*. The whole body is mapped out in the brain, and the larger the area given to a particular body part, the more sensitive that body part is.

showed that the left-hand representation in the right hemisphere of the brain is enlarged in many string players compared with people who have never played a stringed instrument. In contrast, the finger representation is not enlarged in the left hemisphere of these violin players. This is not surprising since the right-hand moves the bow and there is much less movement and stimulation of the right-hand fingertips.

Elbert also found that the earlier in childhood someone starts to play the violin, as long as they continue to practice, the larger their right hemisphere's finger representation. This research suggests that the brain assigns a quantity of synapses to the processing of the fingers in accordance with how much the fingers are used. On the other hand, one crucial finding from this research is that it is not just people who have been playing the violin all their lives who develop larger representations of their fingers through playing. If adults start playing the violin, they also change their finger representation.

But as people who stop playing eventually lose their flexibility, it is likely that the synaptic connections are reset again. An analogy is with a gymnast's body. With practice, gymnasts' bodies change, but not for ever. Lack of practice will change their bodies again: limb flexibility will be lost; muscles will weaken. They can be retrained, however. The brain is similar: use it or lose it.

Brain changes are rapid

It is not just skilled musicians who have been training for years whose brains change according to use. Studies have shown that in just five days the sensory and motor areas of the adult brain can adapt according to how they are used. Alvaro Pascual-Leone and colleagues studied the role of plastic changes of the human motor system in learning to play the piano. Nonpiano-playing adults learned a five-finger exercise on the piano for two hours a day over the course of five days. The area of the brain responsible for finger movements became enlarged and more active in these participants compared with control participants who had not learned the piano exercise. So a relatively short amount of practice can make a significant difference to the brain.

Even when arbitrary associations are learned, this learning is associated with rapid brain changes in adults. Désirée Gonzalo and Ray Dolan at the University of London trained volunteers to associate arbitrary visual symbols with certain sounds. When participants had learned that a sound was paired with a specific color, visual brain areas—as well as auditory areas—started to respond to that sound. It was as if the visual areas anticipated that the visual stimulus would usually occur with the sound. The opposite pattern also occurred—the auditory cortex, which is specialized for processing sound, showed responses to a color associated with a particular sound.

These findings highlight the possibility that sensory brain regions, which are traditionally thought to respond exclusively to information in one sensory modality, can also respond to stimuli in other sensory modalities. Moreover, these adaptive responses can be induced very rapidly. The participants in this experiment had been learning the color–sound pairs for just a few minutes before they had their brains scanned.

Brain changes need to be maintained by practice

Professional musicians have to practice for many hours a day, however skilled they already are. So, there is no resting on your laurels even when you have achieved a high degree of skill and after clear changes in the brain can be demonstrated. A recent study, carried out by Arne May and colleagues at the University of Regensburg, Germany, scanned people's brains before and after they had learned to juggle. The brains of people who learned to juggle, practicing with three balls at least one minute a day for three months, had changed. Two regions had increased in size—the *midtemporal area* and the left posterior *intraparietal sulcus*, which both process visual motion information. But three months later, during which time the people stopped juggling, these regions had returned to their normal size. Just like the gardener landscaping a garden, so the teacher has a never-ending job to do.

Plasticity as a compensatory mechanism   ΠΡΟΣΟΧΗ)

There are many examples of plasticity occurring as a compensatory mechanism in people who have lost some function. Gemma Calvert and her colleagues at Oxford University have shown that compensatory plasticity occurs in deaf people whose auditory cortex (the region of the brain that usually processes sound) does not deal with sounds. The auditory cortex of deaf people who can lip-read actually starts to respond to mouth movements. This is extremely useful because deaf lip-readers need to be especially sensitive to mouth movements. Instead of becoming redundant, the auditory cortex starts to respond to other signals that the deaf person needs to process and understand.

Similarly, the auditory cortex of deaf people who communicate using sign language starts to respond to hand movements. These are striking examples of the brain's capacity to adapt to changing circumstances.

Similar adaptive changes occur in blind people who read Braille. In blind people the visual cortex is no longer used to process visual stimuli. However, studies by Christian Buchel in London and Norihiro Sadato in Japan showed that, instead of that huge part of the brain remaining dormant, the visual cortex starts to respond to the sensory signals that are available: the feel of Braille. This is especially remarkable because the regions of the brain that normally respond to touch (the *somatosensory cortex*) are far away from the brain's visual cortex (see Figure 9.5). Nevertheless, Braille reading with the fingers takes the place of seeing and, as a consequence, the visual cortex takes over the job of processing tactile information. Such findings highlight the adaptive capacity of the brain to modify its function according to use.

Another adaptive change can happen in the brains of Braille readers. Some Braille readers use just one finger and others use several fingers at a time to read Braille. As we discussed above, normally each finger is represented individually in the brain's *sensorimotor cortex*. However, in people who use several fingers simultaneously to read Braille, instead of having several separate representations of the different fingertips, they develop one large, merged representation of all the fingers of the Braille-reading hand in the opposite side of their brain. When these people read Braille with their fingers, masses of information from the fingertips is sent to the centers of the brain where all that information is merged. One consequence of this merged finger representation is that these people perceive all the tactile information from the different fingertips at the same time. Therefore, unlike most people who can easily distinguish sensations on individual fingers, these Braille readers are not able to determine where the

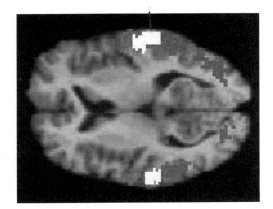

Figure 9.4   Auditory cortex is activated both when people hear speech and when they lip-read speech. The common activation in auditory cortex for hearing and lipreading is shown in white. This is a slice through the middle of the brain, viewed from above. Source: figure 2 from Calvert et al. *Science* 1997; 276 (5312): 593–6. Copyright © 1997 by AAAS. Reprinted by permission of the authors and AAAS.

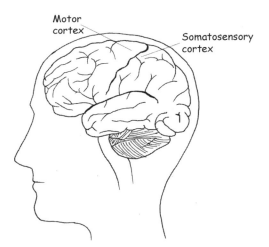

Figure 9.5   The region of the brain that normally responds to touch (the *somatosensory cortex*) is far away from the brain's visual cortex. Nevertheless, Braille reading with the fingers takes the place of seeing and, as a consequence, the visual cortex takes over the job of processing tactile information.

information comes from. If one of the three fingers is touched, Braille readers who use three fingers are not sure which finger is being touched.

An analogy of this phenomenon is with most people's toes. Normally the toes are not represented separately in the brain. We do not use our toes independently and therefore the representation of them in the brain is merged. If one toe is touched, because of their merged representation in the brain, it is very difficult to tell which toe is being touched.

One-fingered Braille readers, in contrast, do not have a "fused" representation of the fingers. Instead, the finger used for Braille reading has an enlarged representation. Three-fingered Braille readers are often better Braille readers than one-fingered Braille readers.

This kind of adaptation can occur in adults. The amount of adaptation is smaller in people who learn to read Braille as adults compared to those who start as children, particularly before the age of 10. But there are still significant adaptive changes of the finger representation in the sensorimotor cortex of the adult learner's brain.

The brain is capable of "relocation of function"—brain cells can change the specific job they perform depending on how much they are used. As we just described, when blind people read Braille, the part of their brains that would normally process vision now processes touch. The brain will repair itself, at least to a certain extent, after a stroke. Many stroke victims, with physiotherapy and effort, can regain much of their lost motor function, some within a matter of weeks after the stroke. The brain is able to reallocate resources, so that functions that used to be controlled by the damaged part are now controlled by a different, working, part. This useful strategy makes use of cortex that was originally meant for another, if related, purpose. This abundance of evidence that the brain remains plastic and flexible in adulthood has great implications for lifelong learning. It may be the case that not all brain regions can be refunctioned—but this is not yet known.

How is the brain plastic?

The adult brain clearly cannot be thought of as fixed. Even in adulthood, the connections between neurons are not fixed and can, and do, change as a function of use. All the communication between neurons occurs at the synaptic junctions (see Chapter 1, Figure 2.1, and Appendix for details). So-called *dendritic spines*, which are tiny protuberances on the dendrites of the neuron, make contact with the synapse of the nearest neuron (or neurons). They make contact by facilitating transmission of chemicals across the synaptic gap. Under certain conditions, these dendritic spines can shrink away and break contact; under other circumstances they (or new ones) grow to make new contact.

Research by Leif Finkel and Gerald Edelman from Rockefeller University has demonstrated that neurons do not act in isolation; they interact with many other neurons and form neural networks. Neurons organize themselves into groups and each group becomes specialized for processing a specific type of stimulus. For example, when one finger is touched, the touch stimulus is processed in a neural network in the *somatosensory cortex*. The touch information activates one group of neurons more than other groups. Within this group, the high level of activity causes the connections between the neurons in the group to be reinforced. Each time the finger is touched in the same way, the same group of neurons is activated, and the connections between them are strengthened each time. Repeatedly stimulating the group of neurons makes the connections among the activated group of neurons become stronger and stronger. Eventually the group becomes specialized for processing the sense of touch on that one finger.

This kind of process was proposed over half a century ago by Canadian neurophysiologist Donald Hebb in his book, *Organization of Behavior*. He wrote: "When an axon of cell A is near enough to excite a cell B, and repeatedly or persistently takes part in firing it, some growth process or metabolic change takes place in one or both cells such that A's efficiency as one of the cells firing B is increased." What this means is that when one neuron sends signals to another neuron, and that second neuron becomes activated, the connection between the two neurons is strengthened. The more one neuron activates another neuron, the stronger the connection between them grows. Some neuroscientists remember this by the phrase, "What fires together, wires together!"

With every new experience, your brain slightly rewires its physical structure. This idea about how neurons rewire with experience is known, after its proponent, as *Hebbian learning*. Hebbian learning is a theory—it is a concept about how neurons can learn by slightly rewiring their connections. Work with living neurons has revealed a possible mechanism by which Hebbian learning can occur. This is known as *long-term potentiation* or LTP. LTP is defined as an enduring (lasting over one hour) increase in the efficiency of a synapse that results from incoming neuronal activity. LTP results in stronger connections between nerve cells and leads to long-lasting changes in synaptic connections. These changes in connections are thought to be responsible for learning and memory. Tim Bliss and Terje Lomo, working at the Mill Hill Medical Research Centre in London, discovered LTP in the hippocampus in 1973.

Another description of LTP comes from research with aplysia, a seaslug, by Eric Kandel of Columbia University. This demonstrated that the animal's neuronal connections grew stronger as it learned to associate a food it disliked with the presence of a beam of light. Kandel and colleagues found that if two connected neurons are stimulated at the same time, the amount of chemical signal passing from one neuron to the other can double.

So not only does the physical structure of the brain change slightly with experience, learning also modifies the brain's chemical characteristics. Whether this is permanent has yet to be verified. But clearly, for optimal adaptation, not all learning should be permanent.

Exercise and the brain

Emerging new research in animals and humans suggests that physical exercise may boost brain function, improve mood, and increase learning. Physical exercise triggers chemical changes in the brain that spur learning in mice.

In one study carried out by Henriette van Praag, Fred Gage, and Terrance Sejnowski in California, genetically identical mice were separated into two groups. One group was housed in cages with food and water only, while the other group also had access to a running wheel. Mice love to run—the mice that had access to a wheel ran on average 3 miles (5 km) a night. After six weeks in the two environments, the mice were tested for their ability to learn their way round a complicated maze. The mice who had had access to the running wheel were better at learning than their sedentary peers. Because the mice were genetically identical, the difference in their learning must be due solely to differences in their environments. The only aspect of the environment that differed between the two groups was the amount of physical exercise the mice were able to do. From this experiment, at least, we can conclude that exercise seems to be good for learning.

The brains of both groups of mice were then examined for the number of cells and the ability of those cells to sustain LTP. As we described above, LTP is proposed to be the basis of laying down long-lasting memories. The number of brain cells in the *hippocampus* (one of the brain regions responsible for learning and memory) of the mice who had wheels was almost double the number in the inactive mice. Furthermore, the brain cells of the mice that ran were better able to sustain LTP than the sedentary mice. The increased number of cells in the hippocampus and the enhanced LTP can explain how exercise improves learning.

Adult brains can grow new cells

What is most fascinating about these findings is that they undermine the notion that the adult brain cannot grow new cells—all the mice in this study were adults. This is not just true for mice, but is also true of certain regions of the adult human brain too. A recent study carried out by the same Swedish and American researchers found that new cells can divide and grow in the adult human hippocampus. This overthrows the dogma that we are born with all the brain cells we will ever have and no more can ever grow. Of course, it is not just a case of growing more and more cells. In fact, we all lose brain cells, and rapidly from

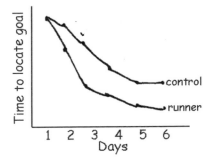

Figure 9.6   After six weeks, mice who were allowed to run were quicker at locating a goal in a maze than mice who had no wheel to run in. In addition, the amplitude of LTP in the hippocampus was higher in the runners. Source: adapted from figure 1 in van Praag et al. *Nature Neuroscience* 1999; 2(3): 266–70. Copyright © 1999 by Nature Publishing Group. By permission of the authors and Nature Publishing Group.

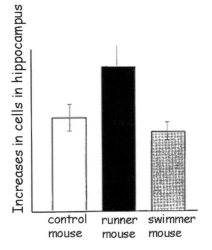

Figure 9.7   The number of synapses in the hippocampus was increased in mice who were allowed to run. This was not true for mice who did no exercise (control mice) or for mice who were allowed to swim. Source: adapted from figure 2 in van Praag et al. *Proceedings of the National Association of Sciences* 96(23): 13427–31 (1999). Copyright © 1999 by National Academy of Sciences, USA. By permission of National Academy of Sciences and the authors.

about age 40. But the new research shows that there may be ways of replacing at least some of the lost cells in some brain regions.

Exercise therapy

Exercise has a positive effect on mood-altering brain chemicals. Indeed, exercise on its own can function for some people as an antidepressant. Exercise is frequently used as a treatment for depression and other mental health problems. It has been found to be effective at improving mood in about 60 percent of people with depression, and this increases to over 80 percent if exercise is combined with another sort of treatment. Physical therapy can speed up the recovery process for people who have suffered strokes or brain damage. Furthermore, daily physical activity improves learning and overall mental capacity in patients recovering from strokes or head injury as well as in healthy elderly people. However, it is difficult here to know what is cause and what effect: perhaps these patients exercised more because they were recovering, rather than vice versa.

Exercising and educating

We have known for a long time that exercise improves general wellbeing and health. Current health advice everywhere emphasizes that physical exercise is the normal state that human beings are designed for, and hence is good for you. More and more people have taken up some kind of physical exercise regime and gyms have sprung up all over the place as more sedentary lifestyles have developed. Some companies even have their own gym because regular physical exercise has clear benefits in terms of the health and energy levels of employees. There seems to be another advantage of exercise: it makes the brain more efficient at learning.

The positive effects of exercise are likely to be the same in children's brains. Through increasing the ability of blood cells to absorb oxygen, exercise does not just improve muscle, lung, and heart function; it also improves brain function. A study in England demonstrated that children who do just five minutes of basic exercise (jumping on the spot, waving arms around and so on) before class do better in the class. Apparently, they have more motivation and learn material more efficiently than when they don't exercise before class.

Exercising the brain

Of the one hundred billion neurons in your brain, it has been speculated that you lose about one thousand neurons each day after you reach 40. This may be a

Figure 9.8 Monkeys can be taught to use a rake to collect food. This is the first time tool use in monkeys has been trained.

good thing or a bad thing—we don't know. For example, it might be that losing cells is a necessary part of learning.

More and more evidence is surfacing to validate the idea of use it or lose it. "Exercising" the brain daily is of course what we do by being alive! Using our brains in unfamiliar ways may encourage new connections to form. Solving different kinds of problems will produce different kinds of thought processes as you search for solutions.

Teaching and learning applies to all ages and includes cultural knowledge in different domains as well as emotional, social, communication, and motor skills. Neuroscientific ideas and findings are of potential relevance in all these domains, but the achievements of brain research in these areas are still sparse.

Hidden powers of the brain

Up until very recently, researchers who have studied monkeys have never observed these animals using tools. This is unlike chimps, which can catch insects from tree bark using a stick. Tool use seemed to be a major step in the evolution of humankind and a very special accomplishment of the brain. It was generally assumed that most animals, including monkeys, could never be trained to use tools. But in evolution, new abilities do not usually appear out of the blue. They often build on existing latent abilities.

Atsushi Iriki at Tokyo University refused to believe that monkeys could not be trained to use tools. He had noticed that occasionally they would grasp a branch with fruit to bring it nearer. This is hardly using a tool, but it is something to build on. Iriki's goal was to give insight to monkeys about the use of a rake. And in a remarkable series of studies he achieved this aim.

With the rake that Iriki provided, the monkeys could capture food that was otherwise out of their reach. Amazingly, after a long training period of about three months, the monkeys were able to use a rake as a tool. They could even use a rake to grab another rake with a longer handle when they needed to retrieve food far away. Their knowledge had become generalizable and it looked very much like insight. Now the monkeys use a rake naturally and spontaneously when it is useful. Convincing videos document this success.

At the same time as the monkeys became aware of the rake's power as a tool, changes in their brain occurred. Cells in *parietal cortex* only became active after the function of the rake had been learned.

Interestingly, Iriki also learned how to train the monkeys more quickly. He now only needs two weeks to accomplish the great feat. There is a reason that the training period cannot be shortened further, and this has to do with the time needed for the brain to modify its responses.

Given that no one would have believed tool use could be trained in monkeys, it has to be asked what hidden powers the *human* brain houses. Perhaps the ability of our brain to process language in written form corresponds to the release of brain powers, never realized until then.

learning and remembering

Different types of learning and memory

One of the contributions to education that neuroscience is capable of making is illuminating the nature of learning itself. It is unlikely that there is one single all-purpose type of learning for everything. In terms of brain structures involved, learning mathematics differs from learning to read, which differs from learning to play the piano. Each memory system relies on a different brain system and develops at a slightly different time. Remembering who you are differs from remembering where you are.

Episodic memories of particular events or episodes in your life, for example your first day at school or your most recent birthday, are processed in different brain areas from *semantic memories* of names, numbers, dates, and facts. These two types of memory are distinct from *procedural memory* for skills like tying shoelaces and walking. These types of memory, and more still, are processed separately in the brain and, as we shall see, they can exist in isolation from one another. Learning can be *implicit* or *explicit*. That is, we may sometimes be unaware that we are learning, and on other occasions we may be highly aware.

Implicit forms of memory

Different memory systems rely on different brain systems and develop at different times. The most basic type of memory is one that we are not even aware of and which we have little control over. This type of memory is called a *conditioned response*. You might have heard of the Russian physiologist Ivan Pavlov whose experiments with dogs early in the last century established the psychological theory of the *conditioned response*. Pavlov's dogs salivated whenever they heard a bell that they had previously learned to associate with being given food. This is a type of conditioned response, over which the dogs had no control.

Figure 10.1   Ivan Pavlov found that dogs would salivate whenever they heard a bell that they had previously learned to associate with being given food.

Conditioning can also occur if a certain food makes you sick. After that, just the smell or thought of the food can make you feel ill, and you will usually avoid eating that particular food. Just one bad experience with the food can make you avoid it forever. Through evolution this has been built into the brain. It is, after all, a matter of life and death. If you cannot learn to avoid poisonous foods, you could be in trouble.

A well known conditioned response that has been studied in humans is called the "eye-blink response." A small puff of air to the eye causes the eye to blink; if a tone is played at the same time as the puff of air, after a few trials the tone alone will elicit an eye-blink. The brain has learned to associate a tone with an irritating puff of air. Such conditioned responses are believed to be controlled, at least in part, by the *cerebellum*. Even very young babies show conditioned responses.

A similar type of memory is called *conditional learning*. This occurs when an action is learned in order to produce a response. Babies start to develop conditional learning from about three months. Three-month-old babies will quickly learn that kicking a mobile animates it, or that crying usually results in the immediate appearance of a parent!

Leading on from this is memory for motor skills and movement, which is called *procedural memory*. This ability relies on the *basal ganglia*. These deep brain structures are not fully developed at birth, but by about three months of age they are already functioning. At the same age, infants start to show procedural learning. They slowly begin to learn that grasping a toy in a certain way allows them to hold and manipulate it for example. Gradually the procedures they naturally learn become more sophisticated and include crawling, standing, and eventually walking. These are all very complicated things for the brain to learn, and it is hardly surprising that such a large proportion of the brain is dedicated to learning and carrying out movement skills like these. The brain regions involved are largely different from those responsible for learning facts and remembering events.

It is clear that babies can learn without awareness right from the start. Children tacitly know a lot about the world they live in well before they can talk about it. In adults too, much knowledge appears to be implicit. Try explaining exactly how to ride a bike without getting on one. There are many components to riding a bike that we simply cannot describe. This is an example of implicit procedural memory, but we probably learn all sorts of facts and sequences implicitly too. These implicitly learned pieces of information might contribute to feelings of instinctiveness when, for some reason, we choose one thing over another without really knowing why.

Teaching often involves making implicit or procedural knowledge explicit. Teachers have to explain how to read, how to paint, and how to play the violin, for example. Knowing how or when to make rules explicit is likely to be an important determinant of effective teaching. When can explicit teaching replace implicit learning? Is a degree of prior implicit learning always helpful? It is possible that a reciprocal dialectic between implicit learning and explicit teaching most efficiently supports learning.

The power of implicit learning

Many years of research on implicit learning have shown that people are able to learn information in the absence of awareness. The brain can process and store information without us knowing about it. In explicit learning, we learn information consciously and know very well that we have learnt it. Some tasks rely on explicit learning. It is interesting to speculate that some individuals may thrive more on explicit learning than others.

Implicit memory is typically seen when we experience a vague sense of familiarity. Objects, people, or facts identified as familiar are also often preferred, even though we might not know why. Many psychological experiments have studied this remarkable ability. It has been shown that people can learn complex rules by being exposed to sequences that adhere to the rules, without having any explicit notion of the rules or of having learnt them. However, some people may know part of the rules or have feelings of recognition when they are shown the rules.

In a typical experiment, volunteers are shown a sequence of many hundreds of letters and are told that there are various "rules" to which the letter sequence adheres. For example, the sequence:

H D S S O H D F S S A H D

adheres to the rules: H is followed by D; S is always repeated once and the second S is followed by a vowel; vowels are followed by H.

Volunteers are not told about any of these rules but, after being simply exposed to many strings of letters that conform to the rules, people tend to pick up the regularities. This is shown in increasingly faster reaction times, which suggest that after a while it is possible to anticipate the next item in the sequence. When letters are introduced that break the rule, reaction times are slowed at that point.

Although participants in these experiments usually claim not to have a clue and often find the experiment frustrating—it feels as though each answer is a complete guess—their answers actually reveal that they have acquired the rules. Volunteers in these experiments are, needless to say, usually amazed by their own results.

So what is happening in the brain when we learn something at this unconscious, implicit, level? Using *positron emission tomography* (PET; see Appendix), Jonathan Cohen and colleagues at the University of Pittsburgh mapped the brain regions that are responsive to implicit learning of sequences. Volunteers performed the task that we just described. They had no idea of learning anything.

Once the participants were trained, they were scanned. When there was a subtle change in the nature of the sequence, this resulted in blood flow increases in a network of brain regions including the left *premotor area* and *anterior cingulate*, and part of the *basal ganglia* on the right. Blood flow decreases at the rule break were observed in the right *prefrontal cortex*. These changes suggest that these regions are responsive to the rule break, which can occur without awareness. The brain notices things that you do not.

Learning and remembering skills

Procedural learning of a skill, such as riding a bike or throwing a cricket ball, differs from learning facts and remembering events. Amnesic patients who have suffered damage to their *hippocampus* will thereafter be unable to retain memories of new events in their lives. However, they are often able to learn new procedural skills and they retain skills they acquired before their brain damage.

A severely amnesic patient known as Clive, who has been monitored by neuropsychologists for many years, suffered severe damage to his hippocampus

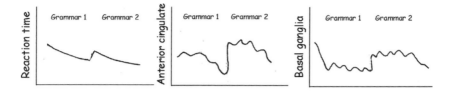

Figure 10.2 Participants were trained to learn a sequence of letters which conformed to various grammar rules. The participants managed to learn the grammar rules implicitly, as shown by the gradual decrease in reaction times for Grammar 1 in the first graph. Occasionally the rules changed (Grammar 2). None of the subjects consciously noticed the rule break, but it resulted in increased reaction times. When the participants were scanned, activity in the *anterior cingulate* and the *basal ganglia* increased at the rule break. Source: adapted from figures 2 and 3 in Berns et al. *Science* 1997; 276(5316): 1272–5. Copyright © 1997 by AAAS. Reprinted by permission of the authors and AAAS.

Figure 10.3 Procedural memory is what is required to learn how to ride a bike. This is distinct from other types of memory, such as semantic and episodic memory.

caused by encephalitis. Before his illness Clive used to conduct a top level choir at a college in Cambridge. Clive's ability to lay down short-term memories has been all but wiped out. He has no memory for events that happened more than five minutes earlier, although he can recognize his wife and knows who he is. He has retained memories from before his encephalitis. He just cannot lay down new memories. His wife describes Clive "as if he is no longer conscious." Clive himself writes a diary, and every entry begins something like, "I am conscious for the very first time," and Clive duly scribbles out the previous entry in which he said something similar. What he seems to be lacking, therefore, is the continuity of consciousness from moment to moment.

Despite having had a detrimental effect on his short-term memory for events, the encephalitis did not seem to affect Clive's memory for motor skills. He is able to play the piano as beautifully as he could before damage to his hippocampus occurred, even though he has no memory of having played the piano before, or of the college in which he worked for so many years. He can conduct a choir just as perfectly as before his illness, although he has no memory of ever having seen the choristers previously or ever having conducted before in his life. Neither has he forgotten his language and he can talk and write in perfectly grammatical sentences. The asymmetry of his memory abilities is astounding.

Amnesic patients are often able to acquire new skills, despite not explicitly remembering being taught the skill. Their memories are implicit or subconscious. This is because in these patients, like in Clive, the *basal ganglia* remain intact. The basal ganglia are still capable of procedural learning and maintaining previously acquired movement skills. Amnesic patients have no trouble walking or talking, motor skills that are acquired by the basal ganglia. People with selective damage to the hippocampus can also learn new skills, such as riding a bicycle or playing the piano, even though they are unable to lay down the explicit memories of being taught such skills.

The opposite pattern is seen in people with Parkinson's disease, whose basal ganglia function abnormally. Such people normally have good memory for episodes and facts, but they appear to be unable to learn new skills. So here we have a *double dissociation* between learning facts and learning motor skills. This has been confirmed by recent functional imaging studies, which have demonstrated activity in the hippocampus but not in the basal ganglia when new facts are learned, and activity in the basal ganglia but not in the hippocampus when new motor skills are learned.

Working memory

A memory system that starts to develop in the first year of life is *working memory*. This is the system that allows us to hold and manipulate information "online." We rely on working memory constantly during our waking lives because it allows us to keep in mind information while doing something else. Without working memory it would be impossible to have a conversation, read this sentence, add up numbers in your head, or dial a phone number. Working memory has been likened to an erasable mental blackboard that allows you to hold information briefly in your mind and manipulate it, be it words, menu prices, or a phone number.

In 1971, Joaquin Fuster at the University of California in Los Angeles, obtained results with monkeys suggesting that a small region in the *prefrontal cortex* plays a role in storing memories for a short time. In one experiment, monkeys were first shown two identical objects—one on the right and the other on the left. On top of one of the objects was a piece of apple, which the monkey could eat. After the monkey had eaten the apple, the two objects were hidden from view for up to 60 seconds before being shown once again to the monkey. The monkey could then reach for the object previously associated with the food by remembering its location.

During these 60 seconds neurons in the prefrontal cortex were highly active. They were not active before, when the objects were presented, or afterwards, when the monkey made a choice. Patricia Goldman-Rakic, at Yale University, expanded this work in the 1980s. Her experiments revealed that groups of prefrontal cells are dedicated to specific memory tasks and that by recording the activity of a particular prefrontal neuron, the next action a monkey was about to perform could be predicted.

The prefrontal cortex continues to develop throughout childhood and into adolescence, as we saw in Chapter 8. So, while infants show a basic capacity for short-term and working memory, this capacity continues to be refined throughout childhood. The development of prefrontal cortex and the progress in performance on memory tests go hand in hand. It is likely that some tasks, which seem negligible to adults, are in fact quite taxing for children.

Doing two things at once

People often have to carry out more than one task at a time and this makes demands on working memory, typically requiring the switching between information appropriate for one or the other task. Even just comparing numbers across two columns that are in a different order requires this sort of memory: you need to keep the place in column one to return to it, after you have dealt with the place of the information in column two. Patients with frontal lobe damage tend to be disproportionately impaired at doing two things simultaneously. This suggests a frontal lobe role in these aspects of working memory.

A recent brain-imaging study by Susan Courtney and colleagues at Johns Hopkins University in Baltimore compared brain activity when participants performed two tasks simultaneously with brain activity when each task was performed alone. This experiment confirmed that the prefrontal cortex plays a crucial role in doing two things at once. Neither of the two tasks, a spatial rotation task and a semantic judgment task, produced significant activation of prefrontal cortex when performed alone; only when they were combined was activation of this area observed. Since the frontal lobes are later maturing structures of the brain (see Chapter 8), it may be possible to adjust task demands during teaching according to the neurological maturity during development. If

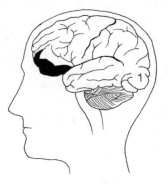

Figure 10.4   Prospective memory, which involves doing one task while keeping in mind the intention to do something else in the future, activates the frontopolar cortex.

little Jack seems extremely forgetful, it may not be that he cannot remember facts or events. It may be that he finds it hard to keep in mind simultaneously the instruction to do several tasks at once.

Memory for the future

Even if we are not actually doing two things at once, we often have to remember to do something in the future while we are in the middle of doing something completely different. You might be in the middle of having a conversation with someone when an internal alarm bell rings: you had previously unconsciously set this clock to remember to make a phone call. So you need to interrupt your conversation for a while but get back to it after the call. Or you might be cooking a meal and all the while you are trying not to forget to put the garbage out in the next 30 minutes or you'll miss the garbage collection. Remembering to do one thing at a future time when you are engaged in some other activity is called *prospective memory*. We use it all the time, and some scientists, including Paul Burgess and Tim Shallice at the University of London, have argued that this ability is unique to humans.

In experiments on prospective memory, Paul Burgess and his colleagues have found that bearing in mind an intention to do something in the future interferes with the task at hand. In one experiment, volunteers were shown two numbers on either side of a screen. Imagine you are taking part as a volunteer in this experiment. You are required to press one of two keys on a computer keyboard—a key on the left (A) if the number on the left is bigger, or a key on the right (L) when the number on the right is bigger. On some trials, you are told to carry on doing this task, but in addition, to look out for whether the two numbers are both even, in which case you have to press a different key altogether (the space bar). Although it is easy to remember this instruction and easy to do the task, people are slower in these types of trials, even when two even numbers never appear.

What is going on in the brain in this kind of task? Damage to the frontal lobes seriously impairs prospective memory performance. Patients with frontal damage simply do not remember to do the second task at the right point in time. Brain-imaging experiments have shown that a specific part of the frontal lobes, called *frontopolar cortex* at the front of the brain, just behind the forehead, is activated when your internal alarm bell is set to remind you to do something while you are absorbed in an ongoing task. This part of the brain seems to be key to remembering to do something in the future.

Memory for events

There is another kind of memory that involves the *frontal cortex* and the hippocampus. This is called *episodic memory*, and it is the type of memory that is lost, amongst other things, in patients with Alzheimer's disease. Clive, who we described earlier, is an extreme case. Episodic memories are memories of events that have occurred with you as main actor or witness in a specific time and place.

The hippocampus starts to mature from late infancy. Although babies and young children are constantly acquiring information and laying down new memories, they seem to do this implicitly, that is, without keeping a record in their mind of when and how they acquired the information. Young children, even when they can speak, cannot tell you much when you ask them about an event. This phenomenon is known as *childhood amnesia*. Three year olds seem unable to remember how they learned about something even when the events took place only moments before. After the age of three, children become better at remembering specific events and episodes, how they occurred, and when they happened.

You might think at first that you would surely remember something where you yourself took part, or were a witness. Memories of events we have witnessed, or participated in, form an important part of our lives and yet, as we all know, such memories are unreliable and can be lost. In old age, people tend to forget that they have just told you that they have been to see the doctor, for instance, and sure enough, they will say it again and again. They cannot remember where they last put their glasses down. We might imagine a record keeper in the mind who continuously keeps track of what you say, do, or observe with interest. This record normally prevents you from repeating yourself, and from forgetting a personally important event but, in old age, it gets sluggish. Of course, memory problems in old age are very varied and not all people suffer to the same extent.

However, it seems that the brain system involved in episodic memory is not only quite slow in developing at the beginning of life, but is also the one that is first to fade.

Episodic memories (e.g., what you had for breakfast this morning) are stored in different brain areas from semantic memories (e.g., who is the current President of the USA or what people typically have for breakfast). People with profound amnesia cannot remember episodes they personally experienced—even what they were doing just a few minutes ago—but, as in the case of Clive, they can retain their semantic knowledge and can still talk. It is possible to some extent to make up for a poor episodic memory by using a fact-type memory instead. So you might rehearse what you had for breakfast like a shopping list, and you can then recite it if asked. Although the different types of memory are distinguishable by the brain, what we actually recall might well be a mixture, drawing on different systems of memory. Our conscious mind is unaware of the intricate workings of the neural systems that sustain these memories.

Disorders of memory in childhood

Developmental disorders often have a genetic origin but other causes exist as well, for instance, damage to the brain at a very young age. Such damage may not even be noticed at the time. One example of this is developmental disorder of memory, which was not recognized until very recently. Faraneh Varga-Khadem at the University of London found that some babies who are born prematurely and, for various reasons, at that time had received an excessive dose of oxygen, sustained damage to the hippocampus. The hippocampus is measurably smaller in these cases. As we have just mentioned, the hippocampus is crucially important to remember what happened when, who did what, and so on.

Varga-Khadem and her colleagues found that the children who had hippocampal damage were not conspicuous in many respects. They did well at school and seemed to perform well on IQ tests. However, when asked what they did the day before, they were unable to answer. Yet they could answer memory questions of the type: "What is the capital of Turkey?" and "What is your address?" This type of semantic memory has a different brain basis, probably in the *entorhinal cortex* and *temporal lobes*, and this was intact.

The hippocampal damage was subtle but it had profound effects on the children as they grew up and tried to adjust. They were unable to remember appointments or assignments, and they did not have a normal continuous memory of what happened to them in the past. They remembered facts, but not when and how they had learned these facts. Yet compensation was possible to some extent. We have already alluded to the fact that you can turn memories that are normally treated as episodes into facts that you acquire like any other knowledge.

So you can recite, when asked, what you had for breakfast, even if you do not recall having had breakfast.

For a teacher it might be important to know that learning facts, such as mathematical equations and historical dates, relies on different brain regions than remembering events that you were personally involved in. Children are not necessarily equally good at all of them, and this may not be just a matter of being less interested in some skills than in others.

Brain basis of teaching

We know a little of what goes on in the brain when we learn, but hardly anything about what goes on in the brain when we teach. We believe that in the future neuroscience will eventually illuminate the nature of teaching. Teaching is one of the most species-specific capacities that we can list for humans, although some rudimentary forms of implicit teaching may exist in other species. At a minimum, teaching may just mean providing people with the right opportunities and encouraging them to take up these opportunities. An analogy may be a mother duck who takes the young ducklings to the water: as soon as she sets in herself, the ducklings follow her. The teaching that a human mother provides goes much further. She has to teach the child all sorts of complex things, such as how to greet strangers, and how to wash their hands. The teaching that a professional teacher provides goes further still. We can learn things within a lifetime that were originally unique inventions and the accumulated work of many generations. Thus writing and number systems, navigational maps, astronomy, law and so on are transmitted through explicit teaching and specialist teachers.

We need to go back here to *theory of mind*, or *mentalizing,* as discussed in Chapter 7. *Mentalizing* has a distinct brain basis and can be considered at least to some extent an innate module. It is one of the cognitive capacities that is abundant in humans and appears to be critical to our social interactions and communications. It also appears to be a prerequisite for purposeful teaching. At the very least, to be effective, the teacher has to estimate the appropriate state of knowledge of the student: the teacher needs to make some assumption about what the student knows already and what he or she needs to be told to advance their understanding further. The teacher also needs to estimate the degree of interest that the student brings to the task, and their receptiveness to teaching.

Successful teaching is based on many of the same component skills as in ordinary two-way communication. You do not wish to bore another person. Neither can you always assume that they know the background to what you are talking about. So you need to judge what they already know about a topic. You want the other person to listen to you carefully and you need to alert them that you have something useful and new to teach them.

You may be very ambitious and as a public speaker you may wish to change the other people's attitudes and beliefs. This needs rhetorical skills, which have been studied in great detail since antiquity. They involve many artful devices, such as exaggeration, repetition, and irony. All this relies on the fine-tuning of your ability to read others' minds. You need to know others' existing attitudes and beliefs. Your success depends on your mastery of persuasive techniques, such as flattery, promised rewards, or threats. The teacher's task may not be too dissimilar. Both tasks rely on our ability to attribute feelings and beliefs to others and to manipulate them so as to produce the desired outcome. Teachers and learners have reciprocal roles and mutually help each other. Studying this by observing two people in two scanners simultaneously presents a methodological challenge. This challenge is currently being tackled.

The ability to learn is vastly more ancient and automatic than the ability to teach. All animals learn, very few teach. It may well turn out that teaching has a long way to go yet to reach its optimum potential. In the future, it should be possible to establish systematic programs of research that reveal, in terms of brain activity, the complex interactions that must arise between factors such as teaching style and learning type.

different ways of learning

Memory without meaning

One of the simplest and most popular methods of learning is by *rote* (i.e., repeating words or other items over and over). You can do this if you are familiar with the sound structure of a language and its grammar, even when you do not know much about the meaning of words you rehearse. Rote learning has been used in educational settings throughout the ages and in many different cultures. Learning sound patterns is a way of storing information and was the main means of transmitting song, poetry, and other literary works before writing existed.

In India, for example, the *Vedas*, the oldest sacred texts of Hinduism composed about 1500 BC, were transmitted orally from one generation to the next over hundreds of years. The priests knew the holy texts by heart and were specially trained to be able to recite them verbatim, even if they did not themselves understand the meaning of the Sanskrit words. Some scholars even believed that it was better not to know the meaning of the text—reciting it was the essential point for religious ceremonies and the meaning might only distract from the proper recitation.

Rote learning seems to undergo changes with age. The older you get the harder rote learning seems to become. On the other hand, older people can often recite poems, songs, and nursery rhymes that they learned as children, even if they have not practiced them at all during their adult life. Striking examples of a distinction between early rote-learned and other skills can be found in cases of brain damage. A woman who learned Welsh as her first language, but then moved to London where she only spoke English, suffered a stroke. As a consequence, she lost the ability to speak English, but was able to recite all the hymns she had once learned in Welsh.

Another woman we know suffered a stroke, which severely affected her memory. She could not remember where she was, what year it was, or anything about her life in the past decade or so. But she was able to recite perfectly her favorite recipe, which she had learned 60 years earlier, and her favorite childhood poem.

How does rote learning work? Does rote learning have its own brain basis? Recently, brain-imaging studies have investigated how rehearsing words affects brain activity. A consistent finding from these studies is that the *premotor cortex* and *inferior frontal cortex* in the left hemisphere are involved in rehearsing items to be recalled. This is true whether the words are rehearsed out loud or silently. Now, these brain areas are known to be involved in speech production. Rehearsal involves the use of articulatory codes (internally or out loud) of the material to be recalled, which might explain why brain areas that control speech production are active.

Meaning and short-term memory

Look at this list of letters and try to learn them by repeating them for one minute, then cover them up, try to remember them and see how far you get:

T T L S H I W W Y A U A T W S H L A D I T S

How many letters did you remember? Now if we tell you that they are the initial letters of the first verse of "Twinkle, Twinkle, Little Star"—how do you do now? Have another look, cover them up and try to remember them. You probably got further this time. Why is this? You are getting extra help because the learning of meaningful material recruits an additional brain area, the left *inferior prefrontal cortex*.

Giving meaning to information makes it much easier to learn. Short-term memory is only good for immediate repetition. It is also quite limited—it can handle only about seven items of information at a time and lasts only 15 to 20 seconds. In contrast, meaningful information is automatically stored and can be remembered for much longer. Some memory "athletes" can train themselves to make even random number strings meaningful and can recall enormously long sequences of numbers.

Rote or not?

The role of rote learning in education has long been controversial. Is it possible that rote learning actually hinders access to meaning? Does the ability to recite a poem detract from the ability to reflect on its content? Does the emphasis on singing a song faultlessly prevent the performer from focusing on its meaning?

These sorts of questions are amenable to being answered by brain science, but relevant studies have yet to be done.

It has been argued that rote learning stifles creativity and reduces individuality. Furthermore, rote learning comes easy to some people, for instance, many people with autism, but is very hard for others, for instance dyslexic people. In makes no sense to force people to rote-learn material that they would prefer to learn in some other way. On the other hand, not giving people a chance to use their ability to learn by rote would be absurd. Rote learning is very effective when learning foreign vocabulary, the periodic table, lines in a play, or a speech. Learning information by rote has never been known to affect the creativity of writers or composers.

Perhaps because of the obvious individual differences that exist, educators have been divided about the use of rote learning. Unlike the teachers of the ancient Vedas, they have also been concerned that rote might bypass meaning. When teaching children to read, for instance, so much emphasis might be put on sounding out words that in the end the meaning of the message gets lost. Interestingly, different areas of the brain are involved when *meaning* is attended to compared with attending to the *sound* of words.

Young children, before they learn to read, find it hard to attend to sound rather than meaning. It seems likely that meaning is dominant for all of us and some effort is required to wrench ourselves away from meaning to attend to purely formal characteristics of language, such as grammar or sound. The exception here might be people with autistic disorders who are typically less captured by the meaning than the form of the message. This was found to be the case by Beate Hermelin and Neil O'Connor at the University of London, in the 1960s and 1970s. So far no one has investigated what different brain patterns are active in people with autism, compared with other people, when they remember words.

Rote learning is one thing, but integrating pieces of information is another. If these pieces are disparate, as may be the case in rote learning, then retrieval is hard. Rote learning is clearly useful for learning new technical terms. But what about recalling the right word at the right time? Effective learning is more than just cramming one's head full of information. We must also develop our ability to retrieve the information that is useful for a specific situation. Information storage is plentiful and cheap, but access and retrieval are often hard. Many educators believe that what learners need are the tools to access the stored information.

Using the mind's eye to learn

Brain science is providing further evidence for methods of learning, which go way beyond simple rote learning. *Visual imagery* involves "seeing with the mind's

SO SARA

Figure 11.1   It is easier to remember disparate pieces of information if you imagine them interacting, the more ridiculous the better.

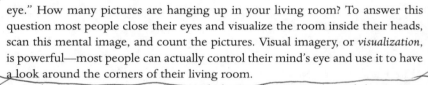

SOSARA

SOSARA

eye." How many pictures are hanging up in your living room? To answer this question most people close their eyes and visualize the room inside their heads, scan this mental image, and count the pictures. Visual imagery, or *visualization*, is powerful—most people can actually control their mind's eye and use it to have a look around the corners of their living room.

In the late 1960s the Canadian psychologist Alan Paivio showed that *concrete* words (such as "forest" and "cup") are more easily learned than *abstract* words (such as "far" and "pleasant"). This was attributed to the fact that concrete words are more imaginable than abstract words. It was suggested that visual imagery could be used to enhance learning. Learning a list of words is indeed easier if you visualize the words. As we shall see, it is even easier if you imagine the objects combined or interacting with each other ("cup in a forest") than if you try to learn them in isolation.

Imagery is frequently used as a tool to aid learning in people whose memory is impaired. Learning techniques have been developed for people with chronic amnesia in which they are taught to link items through "ridiculous-image" stories. For example, if they want to go shopping for milk, a bunch of bananas, and a newspaper, they might imagine a carton of milk rowing a newspaper with two bananas (see Figure 11.1). This seems to help them remember the words.

Employing visual imagery to enhance memory has been put to use for a long time and goes back to the "Art of Memory," which was invented in antiquity, and

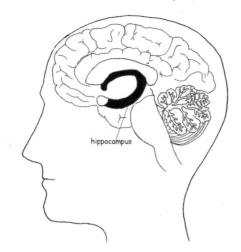

hippocampus

Figure 11.2 Brain regions activated by memory experts include the hippocampus and are involved in memory in everyone.

much practiced in the Middle Ages. In the classical use of the Art of Memory, mental imagery was employed for remembering long and complex speeches. Abstract mental images of a somewhat bizarre (and therefore more memorable) nature were linked to parts of the speech and to parts of the architectural features of the room in which the speech was to be given. When it came to giving the speech, the speaker would scan the room and all its different features—the statues, frescoes, columns, and so on—would trigger all the components of his speech as they were scanned. The room would provide a frame of reference that could be used over and over again for different speeches.

Modern day "memory athletes" use much the same technique. Such people were studied recently in a brain-imaging study by Eleanor Macguire at the University of London. She scanned people who took part in the Memory Olympics. These people, who are renowned for their superior memory skills, were no more intelligent than people who have "normal" memories, nor did they have any obvious differences in the structure of their brains. Instead, they seemed to have trained certain parts of their brain to store and retrieve information. They all made use of imagery, as in the Art of Memory. The brain regions activated included the hippocampus and are involved in memory in everyone. When it came to remembering lists of numbers, faces, and complex snowflake-like shapes, the people with superior memory activated the memory parts of their brains more than people with normal memories. So short-term memory seems to be very much amenable to training.

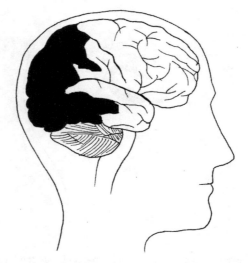

Figure 11.3   Much of the brain's visual system, shown here, is activated by visual imagery.

The mind's eye in the brain

Patients with damage to the back of the brain, where the visual cortex lies, often have visual memory problems and do not benefit from visual imagery when trying to memorize words. This suggests that the visual brain regions (*temporo-occipital cortex*) are necessary to forming visual images. The study of brain-damaged patients has revealed separate verbal and nonverbal systems in the brain. Some patients whose visual brain areas are intact but who have suffered damage to the brain's language areas, have no problems identifying an object from sight but have great difficulty identifying the same object from its name alone. Such patients still have access to their nonverbal (visual imagery) system, but have problems accessing the verbal identity system. In most people these two systems do not work independently, but are continually interacting to enable skills such as object recognition and imagery-based memory.

Brain imaging has provided rich insight into the brain basis of imagery-based learning and memory. Brain-imaging studies by Steve Kosslyn and his team of researchers at Harvard have revealed that at least two-thirds of the same brain areas are activated when you imagine an object compared with when you actually see the same object. So mental images of objects and events can engage much of the same processing that occurs during the corresponding perceptual experience.

But what can account for the finding that the concrete word "cup" is easier to remember than the abstract word "far"? Brain-imaging studies have revealed differences in the neural systems underlying memory for material of different degrees of imaginability. In general, a greater engagement of the brain's visual areas occurs during imagery-based learning of concrete words than learning of abstract words. In addition, a deep structure in the brain called the *parahippocampal gyrus* is involved in laying down and storing memories of imaginable (concrete) words.

A different brain region becomes involved when *retrieving* from memory imaginable, but not nonimaginable, words—this is the *parietal cortex*. The *parietal lobe* is involved in processing spatial relations between objects and in understanding numbers and learning music, and has connections with the rest of the visual cortex. These connections would facilitate its access to visual memory stores. Different brain structures participate in encoding abstract words, which are not easy to imagine. The *temporal lobe* language areas come into play when memorizing abstract words, which makes sense because such words can only be learned using a verbal code—they cannot easily be visualized.

Pairs of words that are related by meaning (such as "tree" and "trunk") are much easier to remember than words that are not related ("apple" and "lamppost"). Brain-imaging studies have shown that when pairs of words that are not related have to be remembered, *prefrontal* brain areas become involved. These prefrontal areas play an important role in decision making and resourcefulness, which may be why they become active when people make an effort to connect semantically unrelated words. Thus extra prefrontal activity is required when people have to search for and establish new meaningful links between unrelated word pairs. This helps when it comes to remembering the word pairs.

Sound plays an important role in recalling a word from its meaning. We are all familiar with the very frustrating *tip of the tongue* phenomenon in which we know the meaning but cannot quite remember the name of something or someone. In this case, we often have a feeling about the sound of the word, how many syllables it has, or what letter it starts with. The *left prefrontal cortex*, which is thought to be involved in retrieving information from memory, is activated when subjects correctly retrieve words. However, when people have a word on the "tip of their tongue," this region is not activated, and many other brain areas become activated instead, perhaps reflecting the hard effort to retrieve the word.

Associating sights and sounds

So far, we have talked about learning and remembering *words*. What about remembering things that do not have names? In Chapter 9, we mentioned the study by Désirée Gonzalo and Ray Dolan from the University of London, where volunteers had their brains scanned after they had learned pairs of quite arbitrary visual symbols and sounds. They had to learn that the color purple always occurred together with a quacking sound, for example. The results showed that, intriguingly, visual brain areas started to respond to a sound when volunteers had learned that a sound is predictive of a specific color. Just as remarkable was the finding that the auditory cortex, which is specialized for processing sound, showed responses to a visual stimulus when it is predictive of a sound.

These findings highlight the possibility that specific brain regions, which are traditionally thought to respond exclusively to information in one sensory modality, can also learn to respond to stimuli in other sensory modalities. And these adaptive responses can be induced very rapidly. The participants in this experiment had been learning the color–sound pairs for just a few minutes before they had their brains scanned. This is an example of *plasticity* in the adult brain. There are many other examples of plasticity in the brain, as described in Chapter 9. The auditory cortex of people who are deaf and can lip-read starts to respond to mouth movements. The visual cortex responds to the feel of Braille in blind people. Such findings highlight the capacity of the brain even in adulthood to modify its function according to use.

Emotional imagery and learning

If you are squeamish you should skip the next sentence. Imagine driving along a road and suddenly noticing a child lying twisted on the side of the road in a pool of blood. Imagining such a scene causes various physiological changes in humans, including changes in heartbeat and breathing rate. In fact imagining an emotionally aversive situation can affect the body almost as much as actually experiencing an emotionally aversive situation. This demonstrates that visual images affect the body. Steve Kosslyn and his colleagues have found that imagining aversive scenes activates certain brain areas more than does imagining neutral stimuli (imagine driving along a road and seeing a grassy strip along the verge dotted with wild flowers). Among the areas activated is the *anterior insula*, which is involved in registering the state of *autonomic* activity (heart rate, respiration rate and so on) in the body and in producing gut feelings. Visualizing aversive events not only affects the body; these imagined events are also processed by the emotional brain.

The finding that people can affect their body's emotional state by forming visual images has implications for learning. It has been claimed that such imagery procedures can affect a host of bodily functions, including the hormonal and immune systems. Imagining your favorite team winning a football match can cause the levels of testosterone in the body to increase. Increased levels of testosterone aids spatial navigation. Thus it might be possible indirectly to improve spatial navigation by using imagery.

Stress is another example of something that might be controllable by visual imagery. Stress is known to affect learning and productivity. Optimal learning

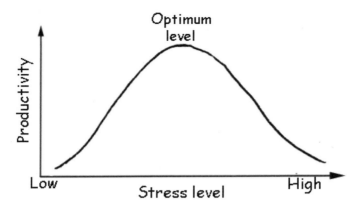

Figure 11.4   A little bit of stress is good for performance. Too little stress results in compla-cency; too much in unfocused anxiety.

occurs under a certain level of stress, but too much stress impairs learning (see Figure 11.4). Emotional imagery could be used to modulate stress levels. By using visual imagery to control stress, people may be able to improve their learning.

However, people differ dramatically in their abilities to use visual imagery. Some people report not being able to form visual images at all. People also differ in their ability on individual aspects of imagery. Some people can easily imagine scanning over their desk and the details of their mother's face, but find it impos-sibly difficult to imagine an object rotating. Try it yourself. Imagine an armchair. Imagine walking around it in a circle. Now imagine standing still and the chair rotating around its axis. Some people can do both, others find one much harder than the other, showing that visual imagery is not necessarily related to mental rotation.

Imitation

Imitation—observing how others do things, and then trying to do the same thing oneself—is a well-established learning strategy. There are examples of animals, including birds, acquiring learned information from one another. It is reported that wild monkeys copy each other's way of walking and climbing trees. There are many reports of chimpanzees in captivity watching people using tools such as hammers and screwdrivers and then copying them later. The word "ape" has even come to mean imitate.

Human babies shortly after birth can imitate some of the communicative gestures of those around them. This was discovered about 30 years ago by the developmental psychologist Andrew Meltzoff at the University of Washington in Seattle. If you know a recently born baby, you can perform a remarkable experiment. Look at the baby, engage his or her interest, and stick out your tongue. Human babies will often copy facial expressions, such as tongue protrusion and mouth opening, when only a few days old. By 10 weeks, they start to mimic the facial expressions showing basic emotions such as happiness (smiling) and anger (frowning).

Unlike this early, automatic, imitation, later appearing imitation is not slavish mirroring, but highly selective. One example of selection is the peer effect. The peer effect in language learning is extremely strong. Children tend to pick up the accent of their peers rather than their parents. Remarkably, children do not imitate the foreign accent of their mother even if she is the main source of speech for them.

Infants are equipped with the hardware to imitate for a reason—imitation is an important learning device and, furthermore, it binds your own identity to that of those around you. We seem to catch the feelings and attitudes of other people around us very easily, without being aware of it at all. This type of contagion might even provide a foundation for developing an understanding of other people. Social psychology studies suggest that there are massive effects of peer groups and role models, the latter being sometimes only seen on television or in movies. Children of all ages—and adults to a certain extent—tend to catch the values, attitudes, and behaviors of their peers, whether in real life, in books, or on TV.

Adults still naturally imitate basic behavior such as gestures and facial expressions, albeit more rarely than infants. The next time you are watching a film in which someone has just had some happy news, you might find that, without any effort on your part, your face has developed a smile. People in conversation often imitate each other's postures and facial expressions without an inkling that they are doing so. This kind of social behavior might have evolved to make people who are interacting feel more aligned with each other.

There is another type of imitation in which we deliberately mimic the attitudes, values, and comportment of people we admire, or when we consciously attempt to copy the exact movement patterns of sport or dance instructors, for example. This ability is obviously important in teaching.

The brain mirrors what it sees

We know more about the brain mechanisms underlying imitation in adults than in children. Brain-imaging studies have revealed that simply observing someone moving activates similar brain areas to those activated by producing movements oneself. The brain's *motor regions* become active by the mere observation of movements even if the observer remains completely still. A brain-imaging study carried out by Jean Decety and colleagues in France showed that activity in the brain's motor regions is further increased if the observer watches someone else's actions with the intention of imitating them later. So, when two people are interacting with each other, the same brain structures are simultaneously activated in both of their brains. When you see someone reaching for a cup of coffee, your brain does not just process the visual percept of hand plus cup—it also reproduces the action. Your brain mimics other people's actions even if you do not.

This is useful because simulating observed actions in the brain might make performing that action easier if and when you come to perform the action yourself. Imagine trying to learn to dance without being able to observe someone dancing first. Learning from observation is usually easier than learning from verbal descriptions, however precise and detailed the descriptions may be. This might be because, by observing an action, your brain has already prepared to copy it.

Mirror neurons

It is not just human brains that are activated in the same way when making and observing actions—we share this phenomenon with monkeys. Giacomo Rizzolatti in Parma, Italy, discovered that neurons in the *premotor cortex* (an area involved in movement control) of a monkey's brain "fire" when the monkey observes a person (or another monkey) grasping an object, say a peanut, even though the monkey makes no movements itself. These cells are called *mirror neurons* because they mirror observed behavior.

Interestingly, these neurons do not respond to the sight of a peanut by itself or a hand alone—it is the sight of a goal-directed action such as a hand grasping a peanut that interests these cells. The monkey that observes the action is not imitating the action, but it might be able to learn something about the goal of the action by *representing* the action in its brain. This is useful because it allows the monkey to understand the meaning of the action and respond quickly to other animals' actions.

What stops us imitating everything we see?

If mirroring observed actions is inherent in our brains, what stops us imitating everything we see? Studies from brain-damaged patients shed light on this puzzle. Patients with damage to the *frontal cortex* often exhibit excessive repetition of other people's actions because these patients are no longer able to inhibit their behavior. They constantly mimic other people's actions even when doing so is entirely

Figure 11.5 Mirror neurons, which are found in the premotor cortex, are activated both when the monkey grasps a peanut itself and when the monkey merely observes a person or another monkey grasping a peanut.

inappropriate. The French neurologist who first wrote about these patients, Jacques Jean Lhermitte, described a man who copied everything the doctor did—drinking, combing his hair, kneeling down and praying. This suggests that the ability to inhibit behavior is controlled by the frontal lobes. Imitation is inherent in the brain and requires *frontal lobe inhibition* to prevent it from occurring.

A principal attribute of the immature nervous system is a lack of inhibitory control because the frontal lobes are undeveloped at birth. The difficulty of inhibiting imitation during childhood is demonstrated by games such as "Simon Says," which are common in many cultures, as is the sometimes unfortunate tendency of children to repeat comments they have heard adults make, however rude and private. It is plausible that this lack of inhibition at the beginning of childhood exists for a reason. If children were able to inhibit their actions, as adults can, they would tend less to imitate, and since imitation is useful for learning, lack of it might not be a good thing. Inhibitory mechanisms in the brain develop throughout childhood and adolescence due to the gradual development of the frontal lobes—as discussed in Chapter 8, the frontal lobes do not fully develop until early adulthood. Not surprisingly, abilities that require inhibition, such as advanced social etiquette and rational decision making, tend to emerge gradually in parallel with the development of the frontal lobes.

Imitation in the classroom

A deeper understanding of imitation, its role in learning, and its brain basis might enable us to understand how it can be exploited for beneficial learning, or controlled in the cases where it might be harmful.

First, an important caveat: as with all neuroscientific studies, it is important to emphasize the difference between the tasks employed to investigate imitation in the brain and the type of imitation relevant to education. In education, imitating attitudes, mentalities, and emotions may be more important than imitating simple movements. However, brain-imaging studies on imitation so far have only involved scanning people's brains while they imitate very simple movements, such as finger tapping and moving a joystick. The results can only be taken so far in terms of their relevance in the classroom.

We are predisposed to imitate those around us. This echoes the belief of many educators that we should not just impart *what* to know, but also demonstrate *how* to know. The teacher's values, beliefs, and attitude to learning could be as important in the learning process as the material being taught. People display their attitudes and beliefs all the time, often without meaning to. It is those attitudes and beliefs that are easily picked up and imitated by learners even when not intending to do so. Of course we do not imitate anything and everything— we are most likely to imitate those we admire. Children and adults imitate their role models, especially leaders of their peer group.

In educational settings it may be useful to remember another type of imitation—*intentional nonimitation*. People often deliberately act differently from someone else, especially young people who are determined to rebel against their elders. Imitation is not enough in education, which requires an understanding and knowledge of the task being learned as much as simply being able to do it. Creativity is required for the flexibility and originality to go beyond imitation. On the other hand, creativity without imitation may generate many novel ideas, but these would often be wasteful because they may not take into account what is already known, tried, and tested. There are clearly some skills and abilities for which imitation is essential. Learning to dance, act, sing, play sport, or speak a new language is almost impossible without a role model to copy. Without imitation humans may never have learned to speak and write, let alone to play squash and dance the tango. But, without creativity, no new dances, sports, songs, or poems would ever have been conceived. Both creativity and imitation are required if one wants to learn well, make good decisions, and be inventive. Educational models tend to combine both creativity and imitation.

Loners and oddballs are just as important as the followers of fashion. Some people may be less inclined to imitate and to learn by imitation. We suspect individual differences in this and many other aspects of learning exist but to what extent? Questions such as these have hardly been touched on by brain scientists. Neuroscientists are understandably more concerned at present with establishing robust facts that are true for the brains of almost all people.

Mental gymnastics

Experimental psychology has long established the value of *mental exercise* for learning movements and physical skills. Imagining making movements without

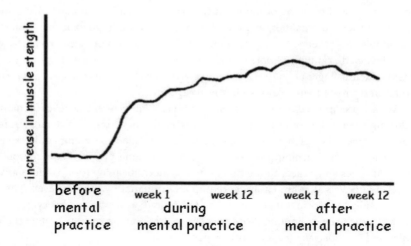

before mental practice   week 1 week 12 during mental practice   week 1 week 12 after mental practice

Figure 11.6 Mental exercise alone increases muscular strength by 13.5 percent. Source: adapted from figure 2 in Ranganathan et al. *Neuropsychologia* 2004; 42(7): 944–56. Copyright © 2004 by Elsevier Science. By permission of the authors and Elsevier Science.

actually moving has detectable consequences. First, mental practice of movement can actually improve muscular strength and movement speed. A recent study showed that people who imagined flexing one of their biceps as hard as possible increased their biceps strength by 13.5 percent in just a few weeks and maintained that increased strength for several months after stopping the mental exercise. Second, prolonged performance of tasks in the imagination can lead to significant physiological changes. Studies have shown that people who mentally simulate leg exercises have increased heart rates and respiration rates, just as they do if they actually perform leg movements.

How might improvement during mental exercise occur? One possibility is that motor imagery is closely related to preparing to move. Preparing to make a movement engages the same processes as those involved in imagining making that movement. Brain-imaging studies of motor imagery by Jean Decety and colleagues in France highlight activity in a subset of brain regions activated while actually making movements. These areas include *supplementary motor cortex, premotor cortex,* and *parietal lobe.*

That similar brain areas are engaged by movement imagery and actually making movements might underlie the phenomenon of motor learning through mental exercise. Regions of the brain necessary for motor learning are activated just by thinking about movement. Mental exercise can be exploited in training of physical skills such as sport, dancing, acting, and possibly even painting and drawing. Training yourself on mental imagery might be useful. Mental

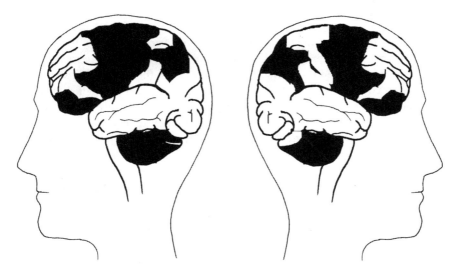

Figure 11.7 Similar brain regions are active when you make a movement (shown on the left) and when you merely imagine making a movement (on the right).

gymnastics in older people may help them maintain muscle strength. Mental exercise is already practiced in many forms of meditation, yoga, and tai chi. Brains are made for moving.

Learning through therapy

Behavioral therapy, which is often successful at treating problems such as phobias and obsessive-compulsive behavior, is derived from learning studies in animals. The assumption on which behavior therapy is based in the treatment of phobias, for instance, is that the phobic person had an initial negative experience with the phobic object, and that the avoidance of that object helps to maintain the phobia. From research on aversive conditioning in animals, it is known that avoiding the aversive object (an object that is perceived as unpleasant or negative) maintains the aversion, while encountering the object and discovering that in reality it is not harmful reduces the aversion. Behavioral therapy often involves the phobic person having to confront the phobic object (say, for example, spiders) in very secure and safe conditions and when fully relaxed, and "relearn" that it is not harmful.

Instead of trying to change someone's behavior, cognitive therapy retrains people in the way they *think* about a particular issue. For example, it is clearly vital to persuade anorexia sufferers to change their behavior, but it is just as important to change their attitudes towards themselves and food. Normally, only this latter, cognitive, change will have long-lasting effects.

Brain-imaging studies carried out by Helen Mayberg and colleagues from Toronto have revealed that physical changes occur in the brain when someone undergoes cognitive therapy. We have known for a long time that different types of drugs can affect brain function—antidepressant drugs were discovered to alleviate depression by affecting the brain's serotonin system over 50 years ago. However, the finding that training a person to think differently can have similar effects on the brain is intriguing.

Parallels might be found between cognitive therapy techniques that teach new ways of thinking in depressive or anorexic people and techniques in teaching mathematics, language, or life skills. Training and teaching presumably have effects on the brain, just as cognitive therapy changes brain function. In the future it might be useful to develop training programs that attempt to retrain the brain to learn, in the same way that cognitive therapy retrains the brain. Lessons from how cognitive therapy is carried out and how it works might be useful for rehabilitation of people who did not have access to good education as children, who are not naturally good learners, or who simply want to improve their learning abilities.

Chapter 12

harnessing the learning powers of the brain

In the future there will be all sorts of new and radically different ways to increase the brain's potential to learn. In this chapter, we discuss various new directions of research on unconventional ways in which the brain learns. In particular, we will look at research on how sleep, hypnosis, emotion, reward and risk taking, and food and vitamins affect the brain processes responsible for learning. Perhaps one day it will be possible to pop a pill to learn!

Sleep and learning

Why are we generally awake during the day and asleep at night? The sleep–wake cycle is an important part of the system of bodily daily patterns, called *circadian rhythms*, from the Latin meaning "daily cycle." As well as sleep, circadian rhythms also regulate alertness, cognitive ability, and movement functioning. Stress and anxiety can disrupt our circadian rhythms, which can have serious consequences for learning. Recent scientific research has confirmed the critical role of sleep in the way that people learn and the level at which they perform. Sleep influences the manner in which we acquire and maintain new skills, how we remember information, and our ability to think creatively.

What is sleep?

Sleep is a state of unconsciousness in which the brain behaves dramatically differently from its waking state. There are two main types of brain state during sleep. In *rapid eye movement (REM)* sleep, the brain is very active—it generates frequent impulses, which resemble brain activity during wakefulness. However, there is a major difference between REM sleep and wakefulness: during REM sleep all the body muscles are paralyzed (except the eye muscles, which move

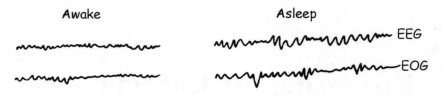

Figure 12.1   Rapid Eye Movement (REM) sleep is characterized by spontaneous brain activity (measured by EEG) and eye movements (measured by electroculogram—EOG).

rapidly, hence the name REM). It is during REM sleep that most dreaming occurs. The other type of sleep is referred to as *slow wave sleep*. During slow wave sleep the impulses generated by the brain are slow and infrequent. It is during deep slow wave sleep that sleepwalking and talking can occur, because, unlike during REM sleep, in slow wave sleep the muscles are not paralyzed.

An experiment performed by Chiara Portas and her colleagues at the University of London used fMRI to investigate what is going on in the sleeping brain. It was a labor of love: all the volunteers in the study had to be kept awake for a night, so that they would be sure to sleep in the brain scanner the next morning. Portas stayed up with each volunteer and conducted the brain scanning the next morning—and unlike her volunteers, she did not get to sleep! Portas wanted to know whether the brain responds to a salient stimulus even during sleep. So while the subjects slept in the scanner, she made sure they were in REM sleep, and then played their own name to them, over and over again.

Remarkably, the same regions of the brain, including the *auditory cortex* (the sound-processing area), responded more to the participant's own name than to any other sound. It is as if the brain, although fast asleep, is still taking in information, especially information that has special importance to the sleeper. The difference is that while sleeping, the participants were completely unaware of their names being played to them. When awake, an extra part of the brain in the frontal lobes was activated when the volunteers heard their own names. This region was not activated during sleep and therefore activation of this area might determine awareness of the salient stimulus.

The body clock

Our circadian rhythms govern many bodily functions including body temperature, blood pressure, and blood hormone levels. The circadian system also regulates our ability to be alert, to think clearly, and to use our movement faculties optimally. Physical ability, as well as mental alertness such as the ability to solve crossword puzzles, varies according to the time of day. The performance of

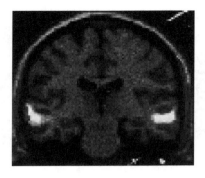

Auditory cortex activation to name when awake

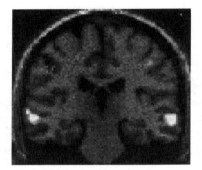

Auditory cortex activation to name when asleep

Figure 12.2   The auditory cortex was activated by the participant's name even when the participant was fast asleep. Source: adapted from figure 4 in Portas et al. *Neuron* 2000; 28(3): 991–9. Copyright © 2000 by Elsevier Science. Reprinted by permission of the authors and Elsevier Science.

runners, for instance, peaks between noon and 9 p.m., and is at its lowest between 3 a.m. and 6 a.m. By organizing training and races according to this circadian rhythm, top athletes can maximize their chances of winning races.

Daylight is an important regulator of our circadian rhythms. The circadian clock resides in a part of the brain called the *suprachiasmatic nucleus* (SCN). The SCN regulates the synthesis of *melatonin* in the pineal gland during the night. Melatonin conveys to the body when it is nighttime—it causes feelings of sleepiness. The production of melatonin at the "wrong" time of day is one of the main reasons that we feel so odd when traveling to different time zones.

How jet lag affects the brain

Recent research has shown that the long-term effects of jet lag are more severe than just feeling tired and spaced out. Kwangwook Cho from Bristol University,

Figure 12.3   Because exposure to light sets the body clock, one idea is to wrap bright lights around the legs during flights to different time zones. This may conceivably combat jet lag, but is rather impractical.

UK, scanned the brains of women who had been working as cabin crew for five years. He compared two groups of flight attendants: one group worked for an airline that gave them a short recovery time (less than five days) between long-haul flights; the other group worked for a different airline that allowed them more than 14 days between long-haul flights. The research showed that the short-recovery group performed worse on spatial memory tasks than the long-recovery group. They also had increased levels of the stress hormone *cortisol*. Furthermore, the volume of parts of the *temporal cortex* and *hippocampus*—brain regions associated with learning and memory—was smaller in the short-recovery group than in the long-recovery group.

Jet lag appears to confuse the circadian clock in the brain (the SCN) which sends out signals—such as cortisol and melatonin—to reset the rest of the body. According to the research, this confusion can have long-term consequences on the brain and on cognitive ability if sufficient time is not allowed to recover after a long-haul flight.

So what can be done to circumvent jet lag? Some people use melatonin pills to help them adjust to new time zones. However, studies of the benefits of this method have been inconclusive, and potential side-effects are not yet known. Because daylight is the crucial factor in melatonin production, manipulating light exposure has been exploited in treatments devised for disturbed sleep patterns. The use of bright light to bring the circadian clock and the environment more in tune has been shown to be useful. Exposure to light causes an increase in total sleep time and quality, and speeds up the shift in circadian melatonin rhythms to

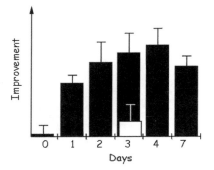

Figure 12.4   Sleep deprivation affects learning. This graph shows the gradual improvement on a task over a few days with normal sleep (black bars). When the participants were sleep deprived on the second night, their performance on the task the following day was dramatically reduced (white bar). Source: adapted from figure 2 in Stickgold et al. *Nature Neuroscience* 2000; 3(12):1237–8. Copyright © 2000 by Nature Publishing Group. By permission of the authors and Nature Publishing Group.

be in line with the new environment. One innovative treatment in development is the use of bright lights that are actually wrapped around a person's legs during a long plane flight. This may be a bit impractical. Instead, one of the most productive things you can do is to spend time in daylight as soon as possible in the new time zone.

Sleep deprivation disrupts learning and decision making

Many studies have shown the detrimental effect of sleep deprivation on learning. When animals or humans learn a particular task—for example, the spatial layout of a new environment or a set of complex rules—and are deprived of sleep the night following the training session, their performance on the task the following day is dramatically reduced (see Figure 12.4). A study on the effects of shiftwork on nuclear power operators signaled potential safety risks due to the increased distraction, sleepiness, irritability, and reduced alertness of the workers during night shifts. The effect of sleep deprivation on performance can be alarming—research in the 1960s showed that after 36 hours of wakefulness, artillery army officers started to make bad decisions and could even start to bomb their own troops.

Studies have demonstrated that, for tasks such as logical reasoning, the brain can overcome the effects of sleep deprivation, but only temporarily. Research on insomnia and sleep deprivation clearly show that after a few nights of no sleep, concentration and learning abilities are severely affected.

A psychological study by Jim Horne and Yvonne Harrison from the University of Loughborough demonstrated that going even one night without sleep

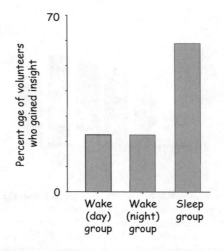

Figure 12.5   Participants were more likely to have sudden insight of a hidden rule after eight hours of sleep than after eight hours of being awake. The same percentage of participants gained insight after eight hours of being awake during the day as those who had been kept awake all night. Source: adapted from figure 2 in Wagner et al. *Nature* 2004, Jan. 22; 427(6972): 352–5. Copyright © 2004 by Nature Publishing Group. By permission of the authors and Nature Publishing Group.

impairs innovative thinking, decision making, and the ability to update plans in the light of new information. In this study, researchers used a realistic game involving decision making. Performance on the game significantly deteriorated after 32–36 hours without sleep. The participants who had gone without sleep showed evidence of more rigid thinking: they tended to repeat the same decision for different tasks instead of coming up with new ideas, and had difficulty in appreciating the implications of a situation that had changed or been updated. In other words, the sleep-deprived volunteers were less creative and less innovative than volunteers who had slept.

Recently, a research group from Germany found that sleep can inspire insight. The volunteers in the study had to work out what the final number would be following a series of numbers. The order of numbers, and hence the identity of the final number, was determined by two simple rules. However, volunteers were not told about the rules. The sequence could be solved either by trial and error or by working out the hidden rules. Volunteers were trained on the task, and split into three groups. One group was retested after eight hours of being awake during the day. The second group was retested after staying awake overnight. The third group was retested after eight hours' sleep. After a night's sleep, almost twice as many volunteers gained sudden insight into the sequence rules than after eight hours of being awake (shown in Figure 12.5). Sleep, then, seems to facilitate insight into a newly acquired task.

The brain tries to compensate for lack of sleep

Brain researchers have discovered that the brain strives to compensate for lack of sleep. One brain-imaging study demonstrated that the brain's temporal lobes were activated by a verbal fluency task, which requires the participant to come up with as many words beginning with a certain letter as possible, after a night of normal sleep but not after sleep deprivation. The brain's *parietal lobes*, however, were only activated in the people who were sleep-deprived. It appears that the parietal areas help out under sleep deprivation conditions as part of a compensatory mechanism.

How much sleep do we need?

In a large survey on sleep carried out in the USA in 2000, over two-thirds of the respondents claimed to have sleep problems a few nights each week. Most adults get less sleep than they need. On average, adults require at least seven and a half hours sleep a night. Children require more. But most adults sleep for fewer than seven hours per night during the week. Some people seem to be able to train themselves to need less sleep, a famous example of such a person being former British Prime Minister Margaret Thatcher, who is said to have needed only four or five hours sleep each night. But sleeping more during the night, as well as increasing energy levels the next day, may improve learning, decision making, and innovation.

Learning while you sleep

Many important things happen to the brain and body during sleep. Some sleep scientists have suggested that during sleep we regenerate energy expended during the day. Research has also demonstrated that cells in the brain and body become detoxified during sleep. Restoration of body tissues and cells can also occur. A fairly old, and previously controversial, idea was that sleep plays an important role in learning. Recently research in animals and humans has provided overwhelming scientific support for this claim. This does not mean that you can put a book under your pillow and absorb the information while you sleep. But during sleep, the brain is still active. This activity has been interpreted as memories being laid down about experiences and information encountered during the day.

Scientists have found that the brain regions involved in learning the day before are reactivated during sleep. In one study, carried out by Pierre Macquet at the University of London, volunteers were trained on a complex sequence task during the day. As they learned, a brain scanner recorded their brain activity. That night, while asleep, the volunteers had their brains scanned again. The

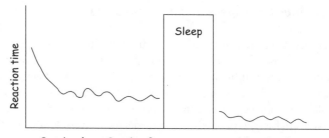

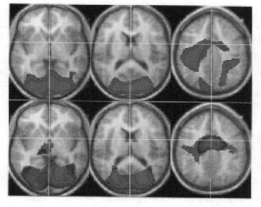

Activations during task during day

Reactivations of same brain regions during sleep the following night

Figure 12.6   After a night's sleep, performance on a task is superior to performance when the task was last practiced the previous day, shown here by the decreased reaction times. This might be because the brain regions used to perform a task are reactivated during sleep, enabling memory consolidation to take place. Slices through the brain are shown, viewed from above. Source: adapted from figures 1 and 2 in Maquet et al. *Nature Neuroscience* 2000; 3(8): 831–6. Copyright © 2000 by Nature Publishing Group. By permission of the authors and Nature Publishing Group.

researchers found that the same brain areas that were activated during the training became activated again during REM sleep. The brain activity recorded during REM sleep presumably reflected reinforcement of the learning that took place during the day. Moreover, participants' performance on the task had improved the following day, after sleep. The brain reactivations observed were indeed beneficial to memory and learning.

An earlier study looked at the manner in which birds learn to sing their distinctive song patterns. In order for a young zebra finch to learn its own song, it has to establish a correspondence between the vocal production (that is, the specific movements it makes with its vocal cords to produce a sound) and the sounds it is hearing (the results of its own vocal production). This correspondence cannot be monitored during the actual singing. Scientists have discovered that the bird song arises from a tightly time-coded sequence of brain activity in the bird's dedicated "song area." The auditory feedback, necessary to correct the bird's own vocal production, is delayed. When does the necessary learning occur? As the finch sleeps, stored brain patterns of the vocal activation and the auditory feedback can be compared and the song can be learned. And this is indeed what happens: the spontaneous brain activity during sleep in the song area matches the activity recorded while the bird is awake and singing.

Napping aids performance

The idea that a person faced with new information should "sleep on it" has indeed some truth behind it. Having a nap immediately after learning a task seems to improve performance on the task. The brain reactivations during sleep may reflect the reinforcement of connections between neurons that are important for the task. In this way, they allow the new skill to be incorporated into long-term memory.

In a series of studies by Robert Stickgold and colleagues at Harvard, a group of students were instructed to perform a complex texture discrimination task four times in one day. This task involved having to detect and report the orientation of a target-array of bars presented briefly against a background of horizontal bars. This is a difficult task and requires a great deal of attention and concentration. All the volunteers who took part in the study practiced the task until they had reached 80 percent accuracy.

The researchers found, as others have before, that with each testing session participants needed more and more time to respond accurately. This deterioration in performance is not caused by general fatigue: performance can be restored if the stimuli are presented on the opposite sides of the computer screen in each session.

The new finding in this study was that performance could also be restored by taking a nap of between 30-60 minutes between sessions. What's more, the longer the nap, the better the subsequent performance. Simply resting without sleep had no effect on performance. The lesson from this research is that it may be a good idea to take a nap after learning.

Planning learning events for maximum effectiveness

The scheduling and pacing of training sessions and school classes could take advantage of these scientific discoveries about sleep. If, for example, one were

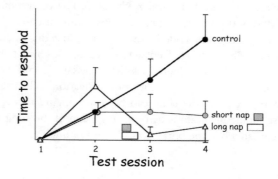

Figure 12.7   Having a nap improves performance. In the control group, who did not nap, the time to respond gradually increases over trials. Naps reduce the time taken to respond, and the longer the nap, the quicker the response. Source: adapted from figure 2 in Mednick et al. *Nature Neuroscience* 2002; 5(7):677–81. Copyright © 2002 by Nature Publishing Group. By permission of the authors and Nature Publishing Group.

planning a two-day workshop with one major topic each day, the research suggests that the effectiveness of the learning would be enhanced if both topics were introduced the first day, then revisited on the second day. Reinforcement of the learning would take place during sleep, and during the second day of the workshop, to enhance learning. Learning sessions could also be scheduled in the evening, permitting the beneficial aspects of sleep to improve the performance of the learned tasks.

Hypnosis and suggestibility

Hypnosis is a fascinating phenomenon that is amenable to being studied by brain science. Hypnosis is after all not something weird or some very different state from either sleep or waking. Most scientists who work with hypnosis these days believe that it is simply a form of focused attention and absorption in thoughts, images, or activity. Entry into this state through a hypnotic induction process can increase an individual's responsiveness to suggestions to a greater or lesser degree. Highly hypnotizable individuals (approximately 15% of the population) are those who respond to the majority of the suggestions given to them following a hypnotic induction. Low hypnotizables (again about 15% of the population), on the other hand, respond to none or very few of the suggestions under these circumstances. Most of us are somewhere between these two extremes of hypnotizability. Suggestions given in hypnosis can produce changes in experience ranging from relaxation, increased concentration, and a sense of well-being, which most people can achieve, to paralyses and hallucinations, which are only seen in highly hypnotizable individuals. Entry into hypnosis is often guided by another person, the hypnotist, but can also be achieved by individuals themselves (self-hypnosis).

In brain-imaging experiments, hypnosis is accompanied by activity in large portions of the *visual cortex* and the *frontal lobes*. The visual activations are hardly surprising because hypnotic induction usually involves a lot of visual imagery— imagining oneself in a place that one finds particularly relaxing and peaceful: the beach or a forest, for example. People who are highly hypnotizable are often people who are very good at forming visual images.

Perhaps one day the practice of hypnosis, and the deep relaxation that it can produce, will be exploited to increase learning and productivity. Of course, this will not work for everyone. And, of course, it could be exploited in negative ways. But just as hypnotizable people can gain a lot in therapy, so they might gain a lot from the use of positive suggestions in education.

The overwhelming importance of emotion

Studies often emphasize performance changes and ignore the subjectively much more striking changes in mood and memory that accompany performance. Brain research has started to investigate the relations between emotions and memory, which most of us, from personal experience, would expect to be intricately linked. Emotions often involve memory and memories often involve emotion. Emotional events are better remembered than neutral events and this is especially true for negative emotional events. Research involving both animals and humans has shown that the *amygdala*, an important part of the brain's emotional system (sometimes called the *limbic system*) is involved with the formation of enhanced long-term memories associated with events that arouse fear or sadness.

In one fMRI study by Steve Kosslyn's group in Harvard, people were scanned while viewing and subsequently remembering emotionally arousing films. The *amygdala* (shown in Figure 7.8) was activated while viewing the emotional films and the level of activity in this brain structure was highly linked to the number of emotional films subsequently recalled. Amygdala activity was not related to the number of neutral films recalled. This suggests that the amygdala is crucial for memory of emotionally salient events, and its activation during emotionally salient events might be why they are better recalled than neutral events. The same group of researchers has shown that the amygdala interacts with the *hippocampus*, a nearby structure that is also part of the limbic system and is crucial for nonemotional memories. It might be the connections between the amygdala and hippocampus that make memories of emotional events so rapidly established and long-lasting.

The amygdala is particularly involved in *fear conditioning*. Fear conditioning occurs when an animal learns to avoid a particular event, such as a sound or place, because of a previous painful or frightening experience of that event. Fear conditioning can occur after just one exposure to the negative event and, as such, is an example of one-trial learning.

Joseph LeDoux at New York University has been studying fear conditioning in rats for the past 25 years. He discovered that the amygdala plays a critical role in fear conditioning. It is the amygdala responding when, for example, you see a car coming towards you and quickly jump out of the way. Often in these situations you become aware of why you moved *after* responding. The brain, via the amygdala, is able to detect and respond to danger extremely quickly and efficiently, interrupting whatever else you are doing or attending to, in order to trigger a rapid bodily reaction. This turns out to be critical for survival—by the time you are aware of the car and have to make a decision about what to do, it may be too late.

The amygdala, responsible for unconscious fear learning, is distinct from brain areas in charge of other more conscious learning, such as remembering people, places, and dates (see Chapter 10). These types of conscious neutral memories are processed in the hippocampus and parts of the *prefrontal cortex*. So unconscious emotional learning, which is automatic and impulsive, and higher cognitive processing, such as understanding why a situation is frightening, occur separately within the brain. There are multiple strong connections between these different brain regions, and these two types of memory together determine what an individual will actually do in a particular situation.

An elegant experiment, conducted by neuroscientist Elizabeth Phelps in New York, showed just how crucial the amygdala is in enhancing our perception of potentially dangerous stimuli. By testing patients with amygdala damage, she found that it was just the left amygdala that mattered in this respect. In her experiment patients with damage in this structure simply watched a series of words coming up in succession. It is well known that when one word appears very quickly after another, people do not notice it. This is called the *attentional blink*—it's as if your attention has blinked and missed something. It seems that each time you see one word your attention needs to recover a bit for a new word to be perceived. Now, this blink is not experienced in the case of an emotionally laden word. If a word in your list is "rape" or "murder" then you see it even if it is presented in quick succession. The emotional significance overrides the need to recover.

In the case of patients with left amygdala damage this does not happen. Here the emotional significance is no longer registered under speeded conditions—they experienced the attentional blink even for very emotive words. When the patients had plenty of time to look at each word, they were able to judge correctly their emotional significance. This example shows that intuitive and conscious "emotional intelligences" are two quite different things, based on different brain systems.

Acting on impulse and resisting temptation

A learner needs to be emotionally competent for optimal learning to occur. This includes being able to restrain oneself and one's impulsive reactions to events; handle new educational settings, new teachers and new topics; and cooperate with teachers and other learners. Brain research might be able to provide insights to educators into how to assist children in becoming emotionally competent. Research on the amygdala and the impulsive aspects of emotional processing suggests that the ability to act and react with emotional intelligence relates to establishing communication between different parts of the brain. This requires interaction between the deeply situated regions that process emotions automatically, unconsciously, and extremely rapidly, and the cortical, highly evolved structures of the brain that deal with more conscious cognitive processes such as planning and decision making.

One of the functions of the amygdala is to interrupt ongoing activity in order to induce quick responses to dangerous situations. Another function is to enhance the perception of potentially dangerous stimuli. This is a special tool that not only helps us survive in extreme conditions, but also sets priorities in the comparative safety of the classroom or the playground. This function of interruption is relevant to the school context because it may be responsible for distractibility. Stress, anxiety, and fear in the classroom can impair the capacity to learn by reducing the ability to pay attention to the task at hand. But fearful stimuli are learned particularly quickly.

In order to learn efficiently at school, children need to learn how to control impulsive behavior and to inhibit emotional reactions to events. Walter Mischel and his colleagues at Columbia University in New York carried out a study that illustrates the importance of delaying "gratification" of a desired object. They tested the ability of four year olds to delay gratification. The child was seated next to a table on which sat one enticing marshmallow. The child was then told that the experimenter had to leave the room for five minutes to go and get something and that they must not eat the marshmallow while they were left alone in the room. The child was also told that as long as they did not eat the marshmallow they would be allowed to eat two marshmallows when the experimenter returned.

This and further studies by the same team had two important findings. First, they found that children were able to wait longer if they could distract them-

Figure 12.8   Children who were able to resist the temptation of eating a marshmallow while the experimenter left the room had better grades at school several years later than children who were unable to resist the temptation.

selves from the marshmallows or if they were encouraged to think about the marshmallow's abstract qualities, such as its shape and size, rather than thinking about the taste. That makes sense. Thinking about how delicious a big pink marshmallow would taste does not help when you are trying to avoid eating it. On the other hand, it is a difficult task—most of the children gave in to the temptation and ate the marshmallow, and even those who resisted often resorted to sitting on their hands or turning away. The brain at this age is still relatively immature, and the all-important *frontal lobes*, which help us to control our impulses and enable us to show restraint, are not fully developed until adulthood.

Second and more controversially, these studies demonstrated that the four year olds who displayed the greatest self-control grew up to be teenagers who did better in school than their impulsive peers. The self-restrained children later scored better on tests of perseverance, concentration, and even on cognitive and logic tests. In addition, the self-restrained children seemed better able to cope with stress and in social situations as adolescents than the children who were less able to resist the temptation of the marshmallow. These studies suggest that being able to control one's impulses at a young age could play into later academic success and social skills. Resisting temptation is always harder than succumbing to it. What factors are responsible for being able to do the hard thing?

We do not yet know. What we do know is that resisting temptation may be difficult because there are large and ancient brain networks dedicated to processing rewarding stimuli, while the brain systems (in the frontal lobes) that enable the inhibition of these networks are comparatively recent.

The feel-good factor

The brain produces several chemicals, called *neurotransmitters*, one of which is called *dopamine*. It is the brain's dopamine system that is involved in risk-taking behavior and reward. The dopamine system in the frontal lobes and the brain's emotional (*limbic*) system, which lies deep in the center of the brain, responds to various intrinsically pleasurable stimuli, including food and certain narcotic drugs. Studies that have used brain imaging to study the brain's response to nicotine and cocaine have shown that the rewarding effects of these drugs are associated with brain responses in the brain's limbic system and the *anterior cingulate cortex*. The pleasurable feelings produced by these brain regions could partly explain why certain drugs are highly addictive. Interestingly, the same brain regions also respond to risk taking in most people.

The effects of risk and reward on the brain have been evaluated in studies on gambling. While gambling, most people rapidly respond to reward and punishment. They take more risks if the potential rewards are high and fewer risks if there is a greater likelihood of losing (a greater risk of "punishment"). Antonio Damasio and colleagues at the University of Iowa have found that people with damage to frontal brain regions (in the *orbitofrontal cortex*) exhibit strange behavior on specially designed gambling tasks. They do not respond to differential levels of reward and punishment. Such people continue taking risks when most people would stop, that is, when it is clear that continuing will almost certainly result in a large loss. Clearly the frontal lobes, which are strongly connected with the limbic system, normally help to curb risk-taking behavior.

A group of researchers including Ray Dolan and Rebecca Elliot at the University of London used fMRI to measure how the brain responds to reward while healthy volunteers performed a gambling task. Correct responses were associated with financial rewards and incorrect responses with financial penalties, and the researchers assessed the relationship between the level of accumulated gain or loss and brain activity. Different areas deep inside the brain responded to financial rewards and to financial penalties. Several deep brain areas became activated to high reward levels that occurred when the participants were already winning. These areas, situated mainly in the *basal ganglia*, might therefore be responsible for producing the feel-good factor that encourages gamblers to keep going when they are on a winning streak. Regions in the brain's dopamine system were also

Figure 12.9 Seeing a pair of attractive eyes looking at you (top left) activates the brain's reward centers more than if the same eyes are looking away. Source: adapted from figure 1 in Kampe et al. *Nature* 2001; 413(6856):589. Copyright © 2001 by Nature Publishing Group. By permission of the authors and Nature Publishing Group.

activated when participants took big gambling risks when they were "losing." So the same brain regions, that rely on dopamine, are activated by rewarding and addictive substances (such as cocaine and nicotine), and by risk taking.

Moderate positive experiences are not only nice to have at the time, they can improve memory too. Researchers presented three groups of volunteers with lists of words to learn. After testing their memory of the words, one group was thanked, one group was praised, and the third group was given a dollar. At an unexpected recall test a week later, the group who were paid a dollar performed better than the other two groups. This suggests that moderate unexpected rewards strengthen memories and that financial rewards can produce significantly better effects than social reinforcement alone. Clearly, the financial rewards were small, showing that a little reward can go a long way.

Social stimuli too are rewarding and important for the brain systems involved in reward evaluation. Even the mere expectation of a potentially rewarding social stimulus is effective. This was demonstrated in a brain-imaging study by Knut Kampe at the University of London. When volunteers were scanned and shown faces of the opposite sex, the reward system in their brains was activated depending on whether the faces looked in their direction or elsewhere. When an attractive person is gazing at you, the brain anticipates the reward of interacting with them. When this person is pointedly gazing away from you—and presumably gazing at someone else—this is disappointing. The reward system of the brain shows strong reactions in this case. Intriguingly, the gaze of people who were rated as unattractive made no difference to this brain system.

Smart drugs and the placebo effect

The delicate balance of chemicals in the brain—the brain's *pharmacology*—can influence learning and memory. Drugs exist that enhance memory directly; other drugs and stimulants such as caffeine, alcohol, nicotine, and glucose, can facilitate or impair learning. Drugs that act on the brain's pharmacology might enable neurons to become more responsive in the learning environment. Research is being carried out into substances called "smart drugs" or "cognitive enhancers," which are said to improve mental abilities such as learning, memory, concentration, and reasoning abilities. The "cognitive-enhancing" drinks and food substitutes currently on the market, which claim to contain smart chemicals that improve mental agility, are dubious to say the least. There is little scientific research that has demonstrated a reliable effect of these products on learning or mental agility.

Even if a positive effect of these drugs on learning can be shown, what would that mean? It is very difficult to disentangle real effects of smart drugs from *placebo* effects. Placebo effects, which are presumably due to the belief that a drug is working, are so strong that it is sometimes hard to show a "real" effect over and above the placebo effect.

Recently, a number of studies have shown the unequivocal effects of placebos on brain and behavior. In one study carried out by Martin Ingvar and Pregdrag Petrovic in Stockholm, volunteers were scanned while they endured various levels of pain. In fact, none of the painful stimuli was very painful, just enough for the volunteers to rate them as "mildly painful." In some conditions, at the same time as receiving the painful stimuli, volunteers received either an injection of a pain-killing drug or a placebo—this was simply saline solution and had absolutely no pain-killing nor any other therapeutic properties whatsoever. The volunteers, however, were not aware that it was saline—they were told that they were being given the pain-killing drug throughout the experiment. In other words, the volunteers thought the saline solution was a painkiller. The results of this study showed the impressive effects of placebos: all participants reported that the stimulus was less painful after both the pain-killing drug and the placebo saline solution.

More amazing still, the brain scans showed that the saline solution had a very similar effect on the brain's pain networks as the real pain-killing drug. Just the belief that a drug will decrease pain affects those parts of the brain that process pain.

To explain the placebo effect the psychologist Nicolas Humphrey at the University of London has suggested that the therapeutic effect may be due to the mobilization of extra energy. It is like using a reserve tank. Clearly, this can only be done for a limited time and may not be without cost to the system. One of the remarkable aspects of enhancement through drugs (real or otherwise) is that the individual seems to benefit from the implicit "permission" to use the extra reserve, signaled by the readiness to take the drug. Without this implicit "permission," the individual finds it harder to muster up the reserves. A possible reason is that normally the organism has many competing demands, and resources need to be fairly evenly distributed. In particular, reserve energy needs to be preserved for unexpected events. By analogy, we can imagine that a reserve tank comes into operation only at the specific request from the driver who first needs to obtain permission from the owner of the car.

Herbal learning

Several experiments that have hinted at positive effects of herbal remedies, such as ginseng, on learning have been carried out on rats. Some of these studies have shown that rats given large doses of ginseng learn the layout of a maze faster than rats that were not. This was due to production of a brain chemical used in memory, called *acetylcholine*. But can we be sure that it is *learning* that is improved? Instead of directly improving learning and memory, ginseng might help rats find their way around the maze for other reasons. It might make them hungrier, which would increase their running speed because they know that finding their way round the maze gets them a food reward. Or ginseng might motivate them in some other way. Herbal remedies and other smart drugs might interact with other medication or even certain types of food or drink. The long-term side effects of taking such herbs are currently unknown.

So we do not currently have sufficient knowledge of the benefits, mechanisms, or side effects of herbal remedies or smart drugs to recommend them as learning aids. However, research on how different drugs and chemicals affect learning is an expanding field. It is quite possible that different types of teaching styles have the same effects as taking a drug, or placebo, in terms of the chemical systems in the brain. Understanding how drugs can improve the brain's capacity for learning might tell us more about how certain teaching styles could improve functioning of the same brain circuits.

If we can extrapolate from the effect of placebos to improve performance, then we can remember pep talks from teachers and other ways of creating enthusiasm in children and adults. Having an increased wish to learn and being receptive to a role model's words can be for good or for ill. We can readily see things that are dangerously close to thought manipulation, as in advertising and politics. Because some of the ways of influencing the mobilization of reserve energy to learn are through persuasion, it may be necessary to add a health warning. "By watching this advert, you may learn things that you did not wish to learn"!

You are what you eat

The brain requires a continual source of oxygen in order to function. Physical activity, such as running, walking briskly, and any other type of aerobic exercise improves oxygen circulation to the brain. But the brain needs more than oxygen. It also requires water and glucose. The brain is more than 80 percent water. Dehydration can seriously impair learning, and simply increasing the amount of water you drink each day can improve concentration and memory—up to a point.

The brain obtains most of its energy from glucose, which is transported in the bloodstream. Not surprisingly, eating regularly is important for brain function—we all know the spaced out feeling and mental lethargy that occurs if we skip meals.

One of the most spectacular demonstrations of the effect of eating on brain function is shown in the rare disorder phenylketonuria. In this condition, which is due to a metabolic disorder, ultimately due to genetic faults, the body is unable to digest food that contains phenylalanine, which is in most things we eat. Because this chemical is not properly digested, complex chemical reactions affect the brain and in particular the frontal lobes. The result is low intellectual functioning, and lack of planning and control of attention and action. A simple blood test at birth can detect the condition and steps for an appropriate (if rather restricted) diet can be taken straight away. In this way, brain development can proceed almost normally. Even when the diet is introduced later in life, an improvement of IQ scores can be obtained. On the negative side, even those cases that are only mildly affected show deficits in intellectual functioning.

Fish and other protein-rich foods contain two amino acids, called tryptophan and L-phenylalanine, which can help to increase energy reserves and stimulate the production of *serotonin* and *noradrenaline* (which play a role in producing feelings of happiness) in the brain. Tryptophan, which alone can improve mood in depressed patients and affects the brain's mood circuitry, is also found in eggs, milk, bananas, dairy food, and sunflower seeds. One of the amino acids in the brain that produces feelings of energy and get-up-and-go is *tyrosine*, which is used in different biochemical processes to produce the brain chemicals dopamine and noradrenaline. This is found in fish, tofu, and vegetables. *Endorphin* is another "happy" chemical that can be ingested in food. The primary endorphin-producers are foods that are rich in animal protein, such as turkey, chicken, lean red meat, eggs, and cheese.

Long chain fatty acids, known as omega-3 and omega-6 fatty acids, are crucial for normal brain development and function. Long chain fatty acids are the building blocks of cell membranes and about 30 percent of the brain is made up of them. Brain synapses require long chain fatty acids to be efficient. These nutrients are also vital to the functioning of the eyes. Long chain fatty acids can only come from the diet, and yet the average Western diet is generally deficient in these oils, which are naturally present in fish such as salmon, herring, and tuna. These fish oils are thought to be extremely beneficial not just for health. They also have a positive effect on mood and cognitive abilities. There are neuroscientists, including Jack Pettigrew from the University of Queensland, Australia, who believe that fish oils have a stabilizing effect on mood and are effective as antidepressants.

Peter Willatts, from Dundee, has shown that young children's visual and cognitive development can be influenced by the fatty acid content of their diet as babies. John Stein from Oxford University, recently campaigned for the benefit of fish oils to brain development. He suggested that children with dyslexia in particular should try eating extra fish oil.

Clearly, there are many substances that are beneficial to mental ability and learning. However these are all naturally present in food and there is no suggestion that any dietary supplement is needed over and above a balanced diet. We cannot be confident that ingesting more than an adequate diet with an adequate supply of minerals and vitamins will be beneficial. Equally it seems obvious that if nutrition is inadequate negative consequences can occur. We can see here a parallel with the debate about a rich and stimulating environment on early brain development (discussed in Chapter 2). We know in both cases that too little is damaging, but we know very little about the effects of too much.

Towards a new science of learning

Throughout this book we have developed a number of themes that we believe will be important to consider in a new science of learning, an interdisciplinary science that is informed by neurophysiology, psychology, and education. Here, we summarize three themes that all underline that learning is not limited to childhood. A new learning science will span much more than the school years. It needs to take into account that learning can be lifelong.

First, we have emphasized in many sections of this book that the brain's connectivity is constantly changing. In fact the brain's baseline state is plasticity. That is, whenever you learn anything new, your brain changes in some way. Contrary to previous assumptions, the brain's plasticity is not limited to childhood.

Second, influencing the brain's plasticity is its disposition to become fine-tuned by experience. This fine-tuning, although it results in a loss of flexibility, is a vital part of development because it confers efficiency and permanency. Although most fine-tuning happens early, during the brain's sensitive periods, certain brain regions, including the frontal lobes, continue to develop throughout adolescence and even into adulthood.

Third, the brain is dramatically reorganized at various points in life. We have discussed three main types of change that the brain undergoes. Most cells grow before birth, but new cells can grow even in the adult brain. This seems to be true in particular of the hippocampus, which is one of the most crucial brain areas for learning and memory.

Another change involves growth and cutting back of synaptic connections. This depends on genetic programs but also on usage. It is likely that there are several waves of this reorganization, during childhood and adolescence.

Finally, during the remarkably long-drawn-out development of the brain the axons of cells are gradually myelinated. This speeds up the transmission speed of signals passing from one neuron to another. All of these changes seem to be dependent at least in part on environmental experience, and this is where learning plays the critical role.

Everyone would agree that education changes minds. Teaching someone to read means that they can take meaning from a page covered in scribbles or from a stone covered in runes. Once you have learned to multiply numbers, your mind treats numbers as multipliable. But education changes your brain and not just your mind. Every time you learn something new, whether it is a new face, a new word, or a new song, something in your brain has changed. Education is to the brain what gardening is to a landscape. Not just education, but culture in a broader sense changes brains. The examples we have considered in any detail are literacy and music, but many more exist.

What happens when the brain develops according to a faulty program, and learning cannot proceed normally? A theme developed in this book is that brains can compensate for, but rarely reverse, faulty programs that stem from birth or before. When considering disorders of development where learning is impaired, we had occasion to consider a breakdown in one or more modules of the mind. In the normal case, modules can hardly be distinguished, because brains develop and operate as an orchestra of many interacting parts. In the abnormal case, different members of the orchestra, by their absence, or their playing out of tune, can become conspicuous. Research on how the brain learns has particular uses in designing remedial education programs for such cases.

Can education make better brains? The answer is emphatically yes. The past knowledge of generations can be transmitted to us so that we can store and access more knowledge, learn and use more skills, and be more aware of what affects our mental life. Education can also ameliorate problems of the growing brain.

How can we use our brain power more effectively? We passionately believe that brain science will eventually give us answers to this important question. At the very least this belief can enhance our desire to learn and to teach.

appendix: tools used to study the brain

We have referred time and time again to real experiments that have been or are being carried out on the brain. Although we have attempted to describe the hard science in friendly terms, it might be useful to have a brief look at the tools that are used in these brain experiments. A century ago, scientists were only really able to study the nonliving human brain—that is, they looked at brains that had been removed postmortem. The scientists living at that time would no doubt be astonished at how quickly technology has progressed in the past 50 years.

We are living in an exciting time to study the brain because there are now many tools that can be used to study the living human brain. Most of these are based on the principle that brain cells transmit information in the form of electrical impulses.

The brain transmits information in the form of electrical pulses

Like all other cells in the body, neurons act like tiny batteries. There is a difference in voltage (nearly one tenth of a volt) between the inside and the outside of the cell, with the inside being more negative. When a neuron is activated it fires an impulse, called an *action potential*. Here, sodium ions rush in through pores in its membrane, briefly reversing the voltage across the membrane.

Electrical impulses can be measured from neurons directly using electrodes. So-called electrophysiological studies are normally carried out in animals and involve recording from single neurons. This is technically very difficult because neurons are extremely small (although they vary in size over different brain regions, some neurons being easier to record from than others). Recordings are made with hair-like needles inserted into the brain while an animal is anesthetized and presented with sensory stimulation, or awake and performing a certain task. This technique gives a direct measure of activity in the neuron. Although we have concentrated on experiments on the human brain in this book, we have occasionally referred to important experiments that have been carried out on animals. This is particularly the case in Chapter 2, where we discussed brain development.

Recording neuronal activity in the human brain is difficult. Very occasionally it has been possible to find out what happens when human brain cells are stimulated electrically. Such studies, although rare, are astounding in the wealth of detail they reveal about memories, emotions, and actions that can be accessed by a mere "touch" of a particular nerve cell, or rather, bundles of hundreds or thousands of nerve cells. The American neurosurgeon Wilder Penfield was the first to demonstrate that it is possible to stimulate bundles of neurons in the brains of patients undergoing brain surgery. The people who volunteered for this research were usually undergoing open skull surgery to cure epilepsy. This is possible because the brain contains no pain receptors, so the patient can be kept awake and conscious during the surgery and feel no pain. Penfield was amazed to discover that stimulating small regions in the temporal cortex caused the patients to recall vivid memories from their childhood. Some surgeons like to keep the patient awake during brain surgery for the prime purpose of discovering whereabouts in the brain they are operating: they know that they should not operate on the brain areas that, when stimulated, affect speech, for example.

There are several noninvasive ways of evaluating brain activity in humans, which measure activity of groups of thousands or millions of neurons that are linked together in particular brain regions. The number of neurons each brain region contains is comparable to the number of people living in a large town!

Measuring electrical activity from the scalp using EEG

The voltage changes inside all active neurons produce tiny electrical fields that radiate through brain tissue, the skull, and the skin, and can be picked up through electrodes stuck on the surface of the scalp—this is called an *electroencephalogram* (*EEG*) recording. EEG measures activity from populations of neurons. It requires many thousands of neurons to be active in order to detect a signal. Typically this is averaged over several seconds, minutes, or even hours. Different "rhythms" have been measured during sleep and awake states, which typically indicate how "awake" someone is at the time. During sleep more or less awake periods can be distinguished using EEG.

Brain scientists often use EEG to record *event-related potentials* (*ERPs*), which are electrical responses that occur at a fixed time relative to a particular stimulus (the "event"). To understand this concept, imagine a simple stimulus such as a single tone. If we recorded the brain activity following the presentation of this tone, we would have recorded an event-related potential. That is to say, we would have a record of the voltage fluctuations induced in the brain by the event (the tone).

Plate A.1   This photograph shows a volunteer wearing an EEG cap. Courtesy of the Institute of Child Health, University College London.

Recording magnetic activity using MEG

An electrical current always generates a magnetic field, which also radiates through the skull and can be measured outside the head by means of sensitive magnetic field detectors. Such magnetic measurements are called *magneto-encephalograms (MEGs)*. In the first MEG experiment in 1975 participants were presented with visual stimuli while scientists measured the magnetic fields on their scalps. The scientists showed that there were magnetic responses at the back of the brain, where the visual cortex lies (see Plate A.2). These days MEG is increasingly used for research investigating the workings of the human brain, since unlike in the case of EEG, no fiddly electrodes are needed to make contact with the skull.

The relationship between neuronal activity and blood flow in the brain

When a population of neurons becomes activated, they require an increased amount of blood flowing to them to replenish their supply of oxygen and glucose,

Plate A.2 This photograph shows a volunteer sitting in an MEG scanner and about to have her brain scanned. The two scientists on either side of the MEG scanner are preparing the volunteer for the scan, which is completely noninvasive, and lasts up to two hours. Courtesy of the Brain Research Unit, Low Temperature Laboratory, Helsinki University of Technology, Finland.

which they depend on for energy. This regular supply of energy is crucial for normal brain function—in fact the brain uses one fifth of all the energy used by the body. The tight coupling between neuronal activity and the associated glucose and oxygen metabolism and therefore blood flow is the principle underlying two of the most widely used brain imaging techniques—PET and fMRI.

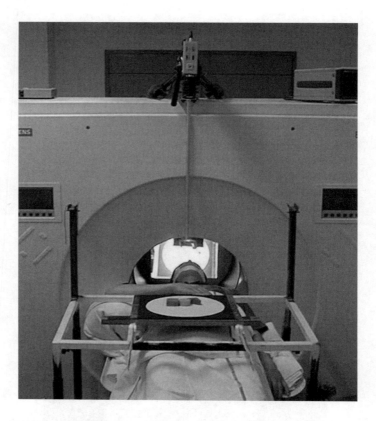

Plate A.3   This photograph shows a volunteer undergoing a PET scan. In this example, the volunteer is performing an experiment in which he moves different colored wooden blocks. Courtesy of Thierry Chaminade, CERMEP, Lyon, France.

Measuring blood flow in the brain using PET

Positron emission tomography (PET) measures the volume and location of blood flow in the brain. This is usually achieved by injecting minute amounts of radioactively labeled chemical (called a "tracer") into the person's bloodstream, which carries the tracer all round the body. The tracer can be followed as it flows in the blood around the brain and emits *positrons*. A special radiation detector camera (see Plate A.3) surrounds the person's head and measures whereabouts in the person's brain the positrons emitted from the tracer—and therefore the blood—are located.

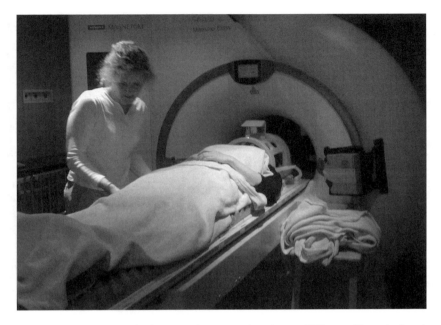

Plate A.4   This photograph shows a volunteer undergoing an fMRI scan. The volunteer is lying inside the scanner while a radiographer sets up the scanner position and makes sure the volunteer is comfortable. Courtesy of the Wellcome Department of Imaging Neuroscience, University College London.

Next, in a process called "computed tomography," high-powered computers use the PET data to produce a multicolored three-dimensional image that displays in which regions of the brain the blood flow increased most. Although PET studies have provided incredibly important information, the method requires tiny amounts of radioactive substances. More and more, PET is being replaced by other brain-imaging techniques that do not involve injections of radioactive substances, in particular, functional magnetic resonance imaging (fMRI).

Using magnets to scan the brain

Magnetic resonance imaging (MRI) uses a very large magnetic field to produce high-quality three-dimensional images of brain structures without injecting radioactive tracers. A large cylindrical magnet creates a magnetic field around the person's head, and a magnetic pulse is sent through the magnetic field (see Plate

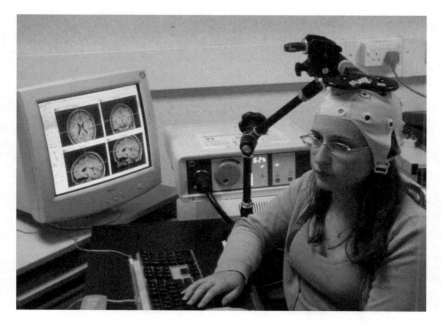

Plate A.5   This photograph shows a volunteer being stimulated over the top of her brain with TMS. Courtesy of Vincent Walsh at the Institute of Cognitive Neuroscience, University College London.

A.4). Different structures in the brain (so-called white matter and gray matter, blood vessels, fluid and bone, for example) have different magnetic properties and therefore they appear different in the MRI image. Sensors inside the scanner record the signals from the different brain structures and a computer uses the information to construct an image. Using MRI, scientists can image both surface and deep brain structures in great anatomical detail. This looks just like an x-ray photograph.

In the past 15 years, techniques have been developed that enable scientists to use MRI to image the brain at work. This is known as *functional MRI* or *fMRI*. When neurons become active they require a supply of oxygen to be carried to them in the blood. It is this oxygen carried in the blood that the fMRI scanner detects because oxygen has magnetic properties. In the same way that PET measures the amount of blood flowing to particular regions in the brain, fMRI measures the amount of oxygenated blood that is sent to particular regions in the brain. This information is used to make "films" of changes in brain activity as volunteers see or hear certain stimuli and do other things, like answer questions or press buttons.

Magnetically stimulating the brain

Transcranial magnetic stimulation (TMS) is the technique that involves using a magnetic coil held above the scalp to stimulate, with suitably weak pulses, groups of neurons in a circumscribed region of the brain and to create temporary disruptions of function. TMS can be used to investigate the functioning of the human brain because it allows us to find out what happens to behavior when a particular part of the brain is stimulated, and therefore temporarily disrupted. This technique allows researchers to draw conclusions about whether a region is actually necessary to perform a task. If the person can still perform the task despite disruption to a certain brain region, then the region is clearly not essential for performance.

Studying the damaged brain

For centuries, the workings of the brain have been studied by investigating the behavior of patients with damage (a "lesion") to a certain part of their brain. This gives us insight into which behavioral functions that area normally controls.

Particularly interesting to scientists is evidence of two patients who are the mirror image of one another. Imagine that one patient has a lesion in one region of her brain (called X) and shows an impairment on one skill (let's call it A). That suggests that brain region X is involved in skill A. But we cannot really say more than that. To make the claim that brain region X specifically processes skill A, we need to find a second patient who has a lesion to a different brain region (Y) and shows an impairment on a different skill (B), but no impairment on skill A. The existence of two such patients is called a *double dissociation*. It demonstrates that brain region X specifically processes skill A (and not B), and brain region Y specifically processes skill B (not A). Knowledge gained from brain-damaged patients in this way is complemented by knowledge gained from TMS studies in healthy people.

There are many other methods of investigating the workings of brain cells, brain chemicals and the general functioning of the brain. Studies come from animals as well as humans because our brains, at least for most basic functions, are very much alike.

suggested further reading

Baron-Cohen, Simon (2004) *The Essential Difference: Men, Women and the Extreme Male Brain*. London: Penguin.

Blair, James (2005) *The Psychopath: Emotion and the Brain*. Oxford: Blackwell.

Bloom, Paul (2000) *How Children Learn the Meaning of Words*. Cambridge, MA: MIT Press.

Bruer, John (1999) *The Myth of The First Three Years: A New Understanding of Early Brain Development and Lifelong Learning*. New York: Free Press.

Butterworth, Brian (1999) *The Mathematical Brain*. London: Macmillan.

Damasio, Antonio (1994) *Descartes' Error: Emotion, Reason, and the Human Brain*. New York: G. P. Putnam's Sons.

Dehaene, Stanislas (1998) *The Number Sense: How the Mind Creates Mathematics*. London: Penguin.

Frith, Uta (2003) *Autism: Explaining the Enigma*, 2nd edn. Oxford: Blackwell.

Gellatly, Angus, Zarate, Oscar, and Appignanesi, Richard (1999) *Introducing Mind and Brain*. Cambridge, UK: Icon Books.

Gazzaniga, Michael S. (1998) *Cognitive Neuroscience: The Biology of the Mind*. New York: W W Norton.

Gelman, Rochel and Gallistel, C. R. (1978) *The Child's Understanding of Number*. Cambridge, MA: Harvard University Press.

Gopnik, Alison, Meltzoff, Andrew, and Kuhl, Patricia (2000) *How Babies Think*. London: Weidenfeld & Nicolson.

Hermelin, Beate (2001) *Bright Splinters of the Mind: A Personal Story of Research with Autistic Savants*. London: Jessica Kingsley.

Johnson, Mark H. (1997) *Developmental Cognitive Neuroscience*. Oxford: Blackwell.

Karmiloff, Kyra and Karmiloff-Smith, Annette (1998) *Everything Your Baby Would Ask if Only He or She Could Talk*. London: Cassell/Ward Lock.

LeDoux, Joseph (1996) *The Emotional Brain*. New York: Simon & Schuster.

McManus, Chris (2002) *Right Hand, Left Hand: The Origins of Asymmetry in Brains, Bodies, Atoms, and Cultures*. Cambridge, MA: Harvard University Press.

Nunes, Terezinha and Bryant, Peter (1997) *Learning and Teaching Mathematics: An International Perspective*. Hove: Psychology Press.

Pinker, Steven (1994) *The Language Instinct*. New York: Morrow.

Rakic, Pasko (1995). Corticogenesis in human and nonhuman primates. In M. S. Gazzaniga (ed.), *The Cognitive Neurosciences* (pp. 127–45). Cambridge, MA: MIT Press.

Sainsbury, Clare (2000) *Martian in the Playground: Understanding the Schoolchild with Asperger's Syndrome.* Bristol, UK: Lucky Duck Publishing.

Scientific American (2003) Special issue: Better brains. September.

Shaywitz, Sally (2003) *Overcoming Dyslexia: A New and Complete Science-Based Program for Overcoming Reading Problems at Any Level.* New York: Knopf.

Slater, Alan and Muir, Darwin (1999) *Developmental Psychology.* Oxford: Blackwell.

Snowling, Margaret J. *Dyslexia.* Oxford: Blackwell.

Vygotsky, L. S. (1986). *Thought and Language,* trans. A. Kozulin. Cambridge, MA: MIT Press.

Walsh, Vincent and Pascual-Leone, Alvaro (2003) *Transcranial Magnetic Stimulation: A Neurochronometrics of Mind.* Cambridge, MA: MIT Press.

glossary

Acetylcholine   Neurotransmitter in the central nervous system; important in the stimulation of muscle tissue.

Action potential   An electrical signal that travels from the cell body of a neuron along its axon to a synapse in order to transmit information to other neurons.

ADHD   Attention deficit hyperactivity disorder. A developmental disorder characterized by inappropriate impulsivity, attention problems, and in some cases, hyperactivity.

Amnesia   Memory loss, which can be more or less severe.

Amygdala   Almond-shaped region in the center of the brain, part of the limbic system and involved in the speedy and automatic processing of emotions, in particular fear and distress.

Angular gyrus   Region at the border of the temporal and parietal lobes.

Anterior   At the front of the brain.

Anterior cingulate cortex   A long stretch of the frontal cortex with many functions including monitoring behavior and emotions and paying attention.

Anterior insula   Front part of insular cortex, which is involved in sensory perception and gut feelings.

Acquired dyslexia   Loss of ability to read and/or write after lesion to left hemisphere language areas.

Asperger syndrome   The mild end of the autism spectrum. Named after Hans Asperger, who wrote a landmark paper in 1944, one year after Leo Kanner first identified and described autism.

Attentional blink   Failure to notice a second stimulus for a short time after a first stimulus is presented.

Auditory cortex   Part of the temporal cortex that processes sound.

Autism   Developmental disorder characterized by severe social communication difficulties, language impairment, and an obsessive desire for sameness.

Autonomic nervous system (ANS)   Part of the nervous system that controls organs and muscles within the body, such as heartbeat and breathing. We are unaware of the workings of this system because it functions in an involuntary, reflexive manner. It is responsible for quick action in emergencies—fight, flight, or freeze.

Axon   The long stem extending from the body of a neuron. Axons are used to communicate over a distance by means of action potentials.

Basal ganglia   A network of structures deep in the center of the brain, and involved in movement coordination and learning.

Bilateral   Both sides (of the brain).

Biological   Explanations in terms of anatomy and physiology.

Brain cell   See **Neuron**.

Brain imaging   Techniques used to measure activity in the living brain, including EEG, MEG, fMRI, and PET. See **Appendix.**

Brain mapping   Mapping behaviors and sensory processing to different brain regions, usually using brain imaging.

Brain region   This term is generally used to refer to a part of the brain, comprising millions of neurons, which is specialized for a particular process (or processes).

Broca's area   A region of the left frontal lobe that is dedicated to the production of language. Named after French neurologist Paul Broca.

Central nervous system (CNS)   The brain and the spinal cord.

Cerebellum   From the Latin, meaning "little brain." The cerebellum is at the back of the brain and is involved in movement coordination, learning, and balance.

Cerebral cortex   Outermost layer of brain tissue, particularly evolved in the human brain.

Childhood amnesia   Inability to remember personally experienced events before age three or so.

Circadian rhythms   The body clock, which determines wakefulness and sleepiness. From Latin meaning "daily cycle."

Cognitive   Explanations in terms of psychological constructs.

Cognitive behavior therapy   A therapy based on altering person's mental attitudes, beneficial for many emotional problems including depression, panic disorder, and obsessive-compulsive disorder.

Comorbidity   Coincidence of several conditions. From Latin *morbus* meaning "illness."

Conditional learning   A particular action is associated with a particular response.

Conditioned response   An acquired behavior that is under the control of a previously associated stimulus, for example a salivary response to the bell alone when the bell has been conditional on the presentation of food in Pavlov's dogs.

Corpus callosum   The mass of fibers connecting the two hemispheres of the brain together.

Cortex   Literally "rind" or outer layer. See **Cerebral cortex**.

Cortisol   A stress hormone.

Critical period   The period during which certain kinds of environmental stimulation are necessary for the brain's sensory and motor systems to develop normally. Recently, most scientists have abandoned the term, because the term *sensitive period* is more fitting.

Dendrite   Slender forms projecting from the cell body of a neuron. Dendrites often have many synapses which receive information from other neurons.

Dendritic spines   Tiny protuberances on the dendrites of the neuron, where synapses are often found.

Developmental disorder   Disease usually caused by a genetic fault. Onset of symptoms can occur at any age.

Dopamine   Brain chemical produced primarily in the basal ganglia.

Dyscalculia   Developmental disorder characterized by a difficulty in the acquisition of arithmetic skills.

Dyslexia   Developmental disorder characterized by a difficulty in learning to read.

Dyspraxia   Developmental disorder affecting motor coordination.

EEG   Electroencephalography. A brain-imaging technique used for measuring electrical activity arising from neurons through the scalp. See Appendix.

Electrophysiology   The study of brain function by recording electrical impulses generated by neurons.

Empathizing   Putting oneself in the emotional shoes of others.

Endorphin   A chemical naturally released in the brain to reduce pain, and which in large amounts can make you feel relaxed and/or energetic.

Entorhinal cortex   An important memory center in the brain. It provides input to the hippocampus, another memory center.

Episodic memory   Memory of events or episodes.

Event-related potentials (ERPs)   Electrical responses generated by the brain that occur at a fixed time relative to a particular stimulus and can be recorded using EEG.

Executive functions   High-level processes of the frontal lobes, such as the ability to inhibit inappropriate behavior, plan, select actions, hold information in mind, and do two things at once.

Fine-tuning   The process by which certain skills are improved and others are lost, often as a consequence of what environmental stimuli an animal or human is exposed to.

fMRI   Functional magnetic resonance imaging. A brain imaging technique used for measuring blood oxygen levels in the living brain. See Appendix.

Frontal cortex   See **Frontal lobe**.

Frontal lobe   The large region at the front of the brain, just behind the forehead. This region is responsible for high-level cognitive processes including planning, integrating information, controlling emotions, and decision making. The human frontal lobe is much bigger than the same region in any other species.

Frontopolar cortex   A region at the front of the frontal lobe above the eyes, involved in remembering to do something in the future.

Functional anatomy   See **Brain mapping**.

Functional imaging   See **Brain imaging**.

Genetic   Passed from one generation to the next via gene or genes.

Glia   Support cells for neurons.

Gray matter   Masses of cells bodies in the brain that appear gray under the microscope and as viewed by MRI.

Hardwired   Genetically programmed to develop.

Hebbian learning   If two neurons that have synaptic connections between them are excited at the same time, the connection between them will be strengthened. This means that in future it will be easier for the first neuron to fire the second. This mechanism is the basis of learning in the brain.

Hemisphere   Left or right half of brain.

Heritable   Inherited from one's parents through a gene or genes.

Hippocampus   A seahorse-shaped structure deep in the brain's temporal lobe and part of the limbic system, involved in storage and retrieval of memories and spatial navigation.

Hothousing   Teaching young infants academic skills such as language, logic, and mathematics, using flashcards, videos, and other audiovisual materials.

Imitation   Observing how others do things, and then trying to do the same thing oneself.

Implicit learning   Learning or memory without awareness.

Inferior   Lower side (of the brain).

Inhibition   As in frontal inhibition; stopping or preventing a behavior.

Innate   From birth. See also **Genetic**.

Interdisciplinary   Combining different fields of study.

Intraparietal sulcus   A deep fold running down the parietal lobe, involved in attention, comparative judgments, and many other functions.

Lateralized   Either left or right; on one side more than on the other, asymmetrical.

Limbic system   A group of brain structures that are involved in various emotions such as aggression, fear, pleasure, and also in the formation of memory. The limbic system consists of several structures including hippocampus, amygdala, cingulate gyrus, and hypothalamus.

Lobe   Large portion of cortex. The brain has four lobes: occipital, temporal, parietal, and frontal.

LTP   Long-term potentiation. An enduring (lasting over one hour) increase in the efficiency of a synapse caused by incoming neuronal activity. If two connected neurons are stimulated at the same time, the amount of signal passing from one neuron to the other increases. This is believed to be due to Hebbian learning.

Medial   At or near the middle of the brain, where the two hemispheres meet.

MEG   Magnetoencephalography. A brain-imaging technique used for measuring magnetic activity arising from neurons through the scalp. See Appendix.

Melatonin   Hormone that helps regulate sleep–wake cycles and circadian rhythms.

Mental   Anything to do with the mind as we talk about it in everyday language.

Mental exercise   Imagining making movements or practicing some physical skill.

Mentalizing   Automatic ability to attribute mental states, such as desires, beliefs, or feelings to others and oneself. In this way we explain and predict behavior. See also **Theory of mind**.

Midtemporal area   Part of the temporal cortex.

Mind   Thoughts and feelings in the head, whether or not we are aware of them consciously. Unlike in everyday language, where mind is often seen as opposed to the brain, most neuroscientists consider the mind a product of the brain. **Mind-brain** is an expression that emphasizes this close relationship.

Mind-blindness   A theory of the social impairments in autism based on an inability to mentalize, that is, to be automatically aware that other people have different thoughts from one's own.

Mirror neurons   Cells in the premotor cortex of the monkey brain that fire when the monkey makes a grasping action as well as when the monkey merely observes another monkey, or a human, making a similar action.

Module   A discrete component of a system; modules of the mind can be separated out only with great ingeniousness and are currently a matter of controversy.

Motor cortex   Brain regions involved in preparing and executing movements.

MRI   Magnetic resonance imaging. A brain-imaging technique used for viewing the structure of the living brain. See Appendix.

Myelin   The white sheath of fat and protein that covers each axon and speeds up transmission of electrical impulses down neurons. The addition of myelin to axons is an important, and long-term, process in brain development.

Nature and nurture   Two factors that are both important in development: genetic make-up and environmental experience.

Nerve cell   See **Neuron**.

Neuroanatomy   The structure of the brain.

Neurobiology   The study of the structure and function of the brain.

Neurogenesis   Generation of new brain cells.

Neurology   The clinical diagnosis and treatment of patients with neural disease or lesions.

Neuropsychology   The diagnosis, study, and treatment of people who have sustained brain damage.

Neuron   Brain cell; the human brain contains 100 billion neurons.

Neuroscience   The study of the structure and function of the brain, mind, and behavior.

Neurotransmitter   A chemical released at a synapse to allow information to be transmitted from one neuron to another.

Noradrenaline or **norepinephrine**   A chemical that is important for the control of attention and impulsivity. It also acts as a hormone when released by the adrenal glands, particularly in response to stress.

Occipital cortex   See **Visual cortex**.

Occipital lobe   Large region of cortex at the back of the brain, where visual attributes including color, form, and motion, are processed.

Orbitofrontal cortex   Part of the frontal cortex, above the eye on both sides of the brain, involved in processing and controlling emotion.

Parahippocampal gyrus   Part of the underside of the temporal cortex, an area known to be important for the recognition of complex stimuli.

Parietal cortex   See **Parietal lobe**.

Parietal lobe   A large region of cortex at the top and back of the brain on both sides, where spatial processing and mathematics occurs.

Parietotemporal cortex   A brain region encompassing the bottom of the parietal cortex and the top of the temporal cortex.

PET   Positron emission tomography. A brain-imaging technique that measures blood flow in the brain. See Appendix.

Phoneme   A small part of speech that corresponds to a grapheme or letter.

Phonology   The processing of language sounds.

Placebo   A dummy drug that has no chemical agents, often a sugar pill.

Planum temporale   Region in the temporal cortex. The left planum temporale, which is usually larger than the right, is dedicated to decoding speech and writing.

Plasticity   The brain's capacity to adapt continually to changing circumstances.

Posterior   At the back.

Prefrontal cortex   Anterior part of the frontal cortex, particularly evolved in apes and humans, involved in planning and selection of behavior and memory.

Premotor cortex   Part of the frontal cortex, on both sides of the brain, involved in planning and making movements.

Procedural memory   Memory for motor skills like tying shoelaces, playing the piano, and walking.

Prospective memory   Remembering to do something after a delay.

Psychology   Study of the brain, mind, and behavior.

Psychopathy   Developmental disorder characterized by lack of empathy for others and lack of remorse.

Recognition memory   The ability to recognize objects and faces.

Representation   A concept, image, or memory in the mind; a pattern of neural activity in the brain that relates to a concept, image, or memory.

Rote learning   Rehearsal by repeating items to be remembered without meaning.

Semantic memory   Memory for names, numbers, dates, and facts.

Sensitive period   The period during which the brain is particularly likely to be affected by experience. After a sensitive period, if the brain has not been exposed to certain environmental stimuli, it is unlikely that it will develop certain sensory or motor functions normally without special remedial input.

Sensorimotor cortex   A strip of cortex running from one ear to another over the top of the brain, which is involved in controlling movements and processing inputs from the skin.

Sensory homunculus   Map of the sensorimotor cortex that shows the different areas that are important for sensation in different parts of our body. This map is organized like the body and hence looks like a little man or homunculus.

Serotonin   A neurotransmitter that plays an important role in depression and anxiety disorders.

Social brain   The network of brain areas that are involved in understanding others and in social communication.

Somatosensory cortex   Brain regions involved in processing touch and texture.

Spatial representation   Brain-based knowledge and memory of positions in space.

Split-brain patient   A person whose right and left hemispheres are no longer connected together because of damage to their corpus callosum, usually caused by surgery to treat intractable epilepsy. In these few cases, the two sides of the brain work independently of each other.

Start-up mechanism   A mechanism that the brain is equipped with and that enables fast track learning of a particular skill.

Stem cells   The cells that divide to form all new cells in the brain.

Subcortical   Relating to the brain structures that are below the cerebral cortex. These include the amygdala, hippocampus, and superior colluclus. These are part of a pathway in the brain that allows us to make movements quickly and automatically on the basis of what we see. These abilities are shared with many other animals.

Superior colliculus   Subcortical structure involved in fast sensory processing, especially visual processing.

Superior frontal sulcus   The upper part of the frontal cortex.

Superior temporal sulcus   A deep fold running down the temporal lobe, involved in perceiving other people's movements and actions and faces.

Supplementary motor cortex   Area just in front of motor cortex in the middle of the brain associated with preparation and imagination of movement.

Suprachiasmatic nucleus (SCN)   Deep brain structure that regulates the synthesis of melatonin during the night, thereby contributing to circadian rhythms.

Synapse   Connection or specialized junctions that allow information to be passed between neurons.

Synaptic density   The number of synapses per unit volume of brain tissue. Synaptic density increases dramatically in early childhood.

Synaptic pruning   The process by which infrequently used synapses are eliminated. The first and major wave of synaptic pruning follows synaptogenesis in early infancy.

Synaptogenesis or **synaptic proliferation**   The process by which the brain forms new synapses. A first wave of synaptogenesis occurs in early childhood.

Synesthesia   The mixing of different sensory inputs. People with this condition often perceive color when they hear words.

Temporal cortex   See **Temporal lobe**.

Temporal lobe   The region of cortex on both sides of the brain, where visual recognition and language comprehension occurs.

Temporal pole   A small region at the front of the temporal lobes, adjacent to the amygdala.

Temporo-occipital cortex   The brain region encompassing the back of the temporal cortex and the front of the occipital cortex.

Theory of mind   The implicit and sometimes explicit understanding that other people have mental states, such as beliefs, desires, and intentions, which may differ from one's own.

TMS   Transcranial magnetic stimulation. Stimulation of brain regions through the outside of the skull by magnetic pulses. This results in temporary disruption of the affected region, and can therefore tell us something about the role of the brain region that is stimulated during a particular task. See Appendix.

Tyrosine   A building block protein for several important brain chemicals (including dopamine), which work to regulate mood.

V4   Region of the visual cortex that processes color.

V5   Region of the visual cortex that processes motion.

Visual cortex or **occipital cortex**   Brain regions involved in processing visual attributes, including form, color, and motion.

Visual imagery or **visualization**   Seeing with the mind's eye.

Wernicke's area   Region at the base of the left temporal lobe involved in understanding words. Named after German neurologist and psychiatrist Carl Wernicke.

White matter   Masses of axons, which appear white under the microscope or as viewed using MRI due to their myelin sheaths.

Word form area   Region of the inferior temporal lobe on the left, also called occipital temporal lobe; important for skilled reading as it is involved in instantly recognizing and retrieving the name of words.

Working memory   System that allows us to hold and manipulate information "online" and to do two tasks at once.

illustration sources and credits

The authors and publishers gratefully acknowledge the following for permission to reproduce copyright material:

Figure 2.5: adapted from Huttenlocher, P. R., Dabholkar, A. S., Regional differences in synaptogenesis in human cerebral cortex. *Journal of Comparative Neurology* 1997; 387(2): 167–78. Copyright © 1997 by John Wiley. Reprinted by permission of John Wiley & Sons, Inc.
Figure 2.10: adapted from Grossman, A. W., Churchill, J. D., Bates, K. E., Kleim, J. A., Greenough, W. T., A brain adaptation view of plasticity: is synaptic plasticity an overly limited concept? *Progress in Brain Research* 81 2002; 138: 91–108. Copyright © 2002 by Elsevier Science. Reprinted by permission of the authors and Elsevier Science.
Figure 3.1: adapted from figure 2C in Dehaene-Lambertz, G, Dehaene, S., Hertz-Pannier, L., Functional neuroimaging of speech perception in infants. *Science* 2002; 298: 2013–5. Copyright © 2002 by AAAS. Adapted by permission of the authors and AAAS.
Figure 3.2: adapted from figure 1B from Burnham, D., Kitamura, C., Vollmer-Conna, U., What's new pussycat? On talking to babies and animals. *Science* 2002; 296: 1435. Copyright © 2002 by AAAS. Reprinted by permission of the authors and AAAS.
Figure 3.3: adapted from figure 2 in Neville, Helen J. and Bruer, John T. (2001), Language processing: How experience affects brain organization, Chapter 7 in: *Critical Thinking About Critical Periods*, edited by Donald B. Bailey, Jr., John T. Bruer, Frank J. Symons, & Jeff W. Lichtman. Baltimore: Paul H. Brookes Pub Co. Copyright © 2001 by Paul H. Brookes Pub Co. Reprinted by permission of the authors and Brookes Publishing.
Figures 6.1 and 6.3: adapted from figures 1 and 4 from Stewart, L., Henson, H., Kampe, K., Walsh, V., Turner, R., Frith, U., Brain changes after learning to read

2004 by Elsevier Science. Reprinted by permission of the authors and Elsevier Science.

Figure 12.2: adapted from figure 4 in Portas, C. M., Krakow, K., Allen, P., Josephs, O., Armony, J. L., Frith, C. D., Auditory processing across the sleep-wake cycle: simultaneous EEG and fMRI monitoring in humans. *Neuron* 2000; 28(3): 991–9. Copyright © 2000 by Elsevier Science. Reprinted by permission of the authors and Elsevier Science.

Figure 12.4: adapted from figure 2 in Stickgold, R., James, L., Hobson, J. A., Visual discrimination learning requires sleep after training. *Nature Neuroscience* 2000; 3(12): 1237–8. Copyright © 2000 by Nature Publishing Group. Reprinted by permission of the authors and Nature Publishing Group.

Figure 12.5: adapted from figure 2 in Wagner, U., Gais, S., Haider, H., Verleger, R., Born, J., Sleep inspires insight. *Nature* 2004, Jan. 22; 427(6972): 352–5. Copyright © 2004 by Nature Publishing Group. Reprinted by permission of the authors and Nature Publishing Group.

Figure 12.6: adapted from figures 1 and 2 in Maquet, P., Laureys, S., Peigneux, P., Fuchs, S., Petiau, C., Phillips, C., Aerts, J., Del Fiore, G., Degueldre, C., Meulemans, T., Luxen, A., Franck, G., Van Der Linden, M., Smith, C., Cleeremans, A., Experience-dependent changes in cerebral activation during human REM sleep. *Nature Neuroscience* 2000; 3(8): 831–6. Copyright © 2000 by Nature Publishing Group. Reprinted by permission of the authors and Nature Publishing Group.

Figure 12.7: adapted from figure 2 in Mednick, S. C., Nakayama, K., Cantero, J. L., Atienza, M., Levin, A. A., Pathak, N., Stickgold, R., The restorative effect of naps on perceptual deterioration. *Nature Neuroscience* 2002; 5(7): 677–81. Copyright © 2002 by Nature Publishing Group. Reprinted by permission of the authors and Nature Publishing Group.

Figure 12.9: adapted from figure 1 in Kampe, K. K., Frith, C. D., Dolan, R. J., Frith, U., Reward value of attractiveness and gaze. *Nature* 2001; 413(6856): 589. Copyright © 2001 by Nature Publishing Group. Reprinted by permission of the authors and Nature Publishing Group.

Plate A.1: Courtesy of the Institute of Child Health, University College London.

Plate A.2: Courtesy of the Brain Research Unit, Low Temperature Laboratory, Helsinki University of Technology, Finland.

Plate A.3: Courtesy of Thierry Chaminade, CERMEP, Lyon, France.

Plate A.4: Courtesy of the Wellcome Department of Imaging Neuroscience, University College London.

Plate A.5: Courtesy of Vincent Walsh at the Institute of Cognitive Neuroscience, University College London.

The publishers apologize for any errors or omissions in the above list and would be grateful to be notified of any corrections that should be incorporated in the next edition or reprint of this book.

index